E. Janes

Human Psychology

E. Janes

Human Psychology

ISBN/EAN: 9783337370367

Printed in Europe, USA, Canada, Australia, Japan

Cover: Foto ©Thomas Meinert / pixelio.de

More available books at **www.hansebooks.com**

HUMAN PSYCHOLOGY.

AN INTRODUCTION TO PHILOSOPHY.

BEING A BRIEF TREATISE

ON

INTELLECT, FEELING AND WILL.

By E. JANES, A. M.

REVISED EDITION.

W. B. HARDY, OAKLAND, CAL.

BAKER AND TAYLOR,
9 Bond St., New York.
1885.

PREFACE.

My purpose in preparing this book has been to furnish something which might be adapted to the use of college classes, and at the same time useful to thoughtful readers in general, who may desire to review the elements of Psychology and Metaphysics, or bring down their acquaintance with these subjects to a more recent period. I was led to see the need of such a work by actual experience in teaching. The existing text-books were unsatisfactory to me for various reasons.

Some are too large for use as text-books, others so small as to give no adequate idea of the extent of the subject. Some are too abstruse and difficult in style and matter, others display no familiarity with the recent, especially the German, literature of the subject. Some are too one-sided, either as giving only the peculiar views of the writers, or as neglecting important parts of the subject. Some are ill-proportioned, some are ill-arranged, some are unsound in doctrine.

In the preparation of the present work, a serious attempt has been made to keep in mind and avoid these defects. I have had the advantage of testing large parts of it by actual experiment with young students of the subject, whose suggestions, generally unconscious, have been valuable to me at many points.

The first part, "The Intellect," has been already before the public nearly a year, and the very favorable opinions which have reached me, from the best sources, encourage me to hope that I have not wholly failed in my purpose, and that the completed work may also receive the approbation of those best qualified to judge. Attention is requested to the following features of the book:—

1. It is small, as all text-books should be; but this brevity is attained, not by leaving out important parts of the subject, or by omitting adequate reference to its literature; but by condensation of style and carefully studied arrangement and proportion of treatment. Yet clearness has been aimed at, equally with condensation; obscurity, prolixity, and abstrusity are alike

out of place in an elementary treatise. Moreover, in treating those parts of the subject which require illustration by examples, but a few of these have been given in each case, selected from the best. A vast mass of such material has been accumulated in the easily accessible and popular works of Carpenter, Maudsley, Ribot, Sully, Taine, etc., not to speak of more special treatises. A text-book should not be burdened with many of these. The teacher can read to the class his own selection of them, and will find new material constantly in current literature.

Thus the book is small enough to be read through by a college class in one term, and yet, I believe, large enough to contain a fair introduction to the study of philosophy, and give the attentive student some idea of the literature of the subject.

2. The arrangement is progressive, beginning with the Senses, advancing to Perception and Consciousness, and thus gradually approaching the metaphysical questions involved in Psychology. The Nature of the Soul and the Mind of the Lower Animals are postponed until the phenomena of Intellect have been studied. How much metaphysics ought to be introduced into an elementary treatise, is one of the most puzzling questions that an author has to deal with. In my view, it is chiefly as an introduction to Philosophy that Human Psychology is an important study. It is the best stepping-stone to Philosophy because it is not merely the science of nerve currents and of the association of ideas, but the science of Mind and its necessary relations. My plan, therefore, has been to join the two in a progressive arrangement, with a little Logic added.

3. Quotations are freely made from the highest authorities of different schools, but none are treated as infallible. The "*Dictate*" from the lectures of Lotze, published after his death and containing his maturest opinions, have been found very valuable. Drbal's "*empirische Psychologie*" has been of great service, though not often quoted. The works of Hamilton, Porter, Spencer, and Bain have, of course, been constantly in my hand.

4. The Historical Sketch, though very brief, is intended to show the

great fact, that Philosophy is continuous and progressive, and familiarize the student with a few of the greatest names in its literature. A full account of the opinions of great Philosophers would be often too abstruse and always too prolix for such a work, but much is gained if interest in them can be excited, and the way pointed out for further study of them.

5. Far more space than is usual has been given, in proportion, to Feeling and its derivatives, and the Will has been discussed somewhat in detail. In both these departments it is hoped that greater clearness and better arrangement have been attained than in previous text-books.

Due credit has been given for whatever has been borrowed, I believe, except in the case of the Idea of the Comic, which was suggested to me by a friend whose name I am not at liberty to mention. The Theory of Beauty is, so far as I am aware, entirely original; but I well know that unconscious plagiarism is easy and common.

If this book shall be of service in making the study of Philosophy easier and more attractive, I shall feel amply repaid for all my labor.

CONTENTS.

INTRODUCTION.

Philosophy, its Nature, Necessity, and Value 5
Philosophy, Definitions and Divisions of.......... 9
Psychology Defined and the Term Defended.................... 11

INTELLECT.

PRESENTATIVE POWER.

Classification of the Mental Powers............. 13
Sensation, Definitions of................................... 15
Sensation in the Lower Animals and in Man.................... 17
Sensations Classified...................... 20
Perception Defined................... 22

THE SENSES.

Sense of Smell.. 25
Sense of Taste.. 27
Sense of Hearing.. 30
Sense of Sight, the Eye Described... 33
Perceptions of Sight and Color................. 37
Perceptions of Form and Direction............................ 39
Perceptions of Distance and Solidity...... 43
Binocular Vision, the Pseudoscope... 47
Sense of Touch.. 49
Muscular Sensation.. 52

TOPICS CONNECTED WITH SENSATION.

Localization of Sensations....................................... 55
Illusions and Hallucinations................... 58
Feeling in Sensation.. 59
Attention... 64
Qualities of Matter in Perception........................... . 67
Sir W. Hamilton on the Qualities of Matter.................... 71
Substance and Attribute... 73
Consciousness, in Man and the Lower Animals................ 74
Authority of Consciousness, etc................................ 80
Uses of the Term Consciousness................................ 83

NECESSARY ELEMENTS IN PERCEPTION.

SPACE, Two Great Theories of.................................. 85
Spencer, Kant, Herbart, Lotze, Hamilton, etc.................... 88
TIME, Different Views Concerning............................... 92
Schopenhauer's Parallelisms..................................... 96
CAUSATION, Necessity of the Idea Defended...................... 97
Theories of Hume, Brown, and Mill.............................. 101
Monadology and Pre-existent Harmony of Leibnitz................ 107
Teleology and Teleophobia...................................... 110
IDENTITY and Similarity, Lotze, Spencer, etc.................... 112
REMARKS on "Intuitive Ideas," etc.............................. 117
Spencer's "Psychogenetical Hypothesis"........................ 119
Enumeration of "Necessary Elements"........................... 121
"Regulative Faculty".. 122
Criteria of First Principles................................... 123
PERCEPTION, Completed Doctrine of.............................. 125
Perception, Theories of.. 126

HISTORICAL SKETCH.

Plato, Aristotle, and the Schoolmen............................ 129
Descartes, Leibnitz, Herbart, Lotze, etc....................... 131
Locke, Berkeley, Hume, Brown, Mill, etc........................ 136
Bain, Spencer, Fiske, etc...................................... 142
Reid, Hamilton, Porter... 144

REPRESENTATIVE POWER.

MEMORY, Divisions of, True Nature of........................... 147
Diseases of, Mystery of.. 151
ASSOCIATION of Ideas... 154
Dreams, Cause, and Nature of................................... 159
Somnambulism, Hypnotism, etc................................... 161
IMAGINATION, Varieties and Nature of........................... 163

REASONING POWER.

Definitions of Reason and Reasoning............................ 171
Judgment, the Power of Discrimination.......................... 172
THE CONCEPT, A Mental Product.................................. 174
REASONING, Deduction, the Syllogism............................ 180
Induction.. 185
Uniformity of Nature... 187

CONCLUDING TOPICS.

THE LOWER ANIMALS, Intelligence of............................. 191
Their Mental Life, Associative and Instinctive................. 193
Beast Minds and the Human Mind................................. 197
NATURE OF THE MIND... 198
"Series of Sensations" Theory.................................. 199
Lotze on Materialism... 201
"Thought-Stuff" Theory, Brain and Mind......................... 203
Comparison with the Lower Animals.............................. 205
Metempsychosis, Location of the Soul, etc...................... 206

FEELING.

PRELIMINARIES.

Definitions, Feeling, Pleasure, Pain	208
Nomenclature, Feeling, and the Feelings	209
Classification of the Feelings	210
Feeling and Sensation	212
Feeling and Intellect	213

PLEASURE AND PAIN.

Physiology of Pain and Pleasure	214
Philosophical Formula of Pleasure and Pain	216
Feelings of the Different Senses	219
Digression on Feeling in Music	221

ÆSTHETICS.

Beauty not Mere Pleasure of the Senses	224
Beauty Intellectual, the True Theory	225
Confirmations of Our Theory of Beauty	227
Beauty not Wholly in Expression	230

EMOTION.

Emotion and Reflex Movements	232
Expression of Emotion, Spencer and Darwin	233
Curious Experiments and Theories	234
FEAR, Defined and Described	236
ANGER or Defensive Emotion	237
GRIEF AND JOY, Expectation, Wonder, etc.	238
LAUGHTER, Herbert Spencer's Explanation	240
THE COMIC, as a Mental Feeling	240

APPETITE.

Natural and Artificial Appetites	244

DESIRE.

The Term Desire Defined and Limited	246
Desire of Property and Power	247
Desire of Knowledge	248

THE AFFECTIONS.

NATURAL Affections, Love, Sympathy, and Self-Love	250
LOVE, Altruism, Benevolence, etc.	251
Sympathy, Physical and Mental	253
Self-Love and Selfishness	255
MORAL Affections	257

WILL.

DEFINITIONS AND DISTINCTIONS.

Will and Spontaneity	260
Volition, Different Meanings of	261
Executive Volition	263
Generic and Specific Volitions	265
MOTIVES, Objective and Subjective	268
Motive as Cause	270
Motive as End, Strength of Motives	272
Conflict of Motives	273
DESIRE, as Related to Will	274

FREEDOM OF THE WILL.

Freedom and Causation	278
Freedom and the Soul	285
Freedom and God's Foreknowledge	288
DIRECT ARGUMENTS for Freedom	288
Testimony of Consciousness	290
Uniformity of Human Action	291
Power of Rational Conduct	293
LIMITATIONS of Freedom	294

INTRODUCTION.

PHILOSOPHY is the science of first principles, that is, the principles which underlie all science and all knowledge. Though often derided by those who say, "Let us study phenomena, and leave abstractions to take care of themselves," philosophy is yet justified even by these ungrateful children, for they, too, are constrained, even unconsciously, to resort to metaphysical principles, and have each a philosophy of his own.

"The adepts in any of the special sciences never come to a full understanding of their own subjects of inquiry without encroaching on metaphysical ground, and even our physicists find themselves studying and teaching metaphysics unawares." (Bowen.) "We are compelled in every explanation of natural phenomena to leave the sphere of sense, and pass to things which are not objects of sense, and are defined by abstract conceptions." (Helmholtz.)

Indeed, the most characteristic conceptions of modern physical science, evolution, development, morphology, conservation of energy, correlation of forces, pangenesis—all are philosophical ideas, not subject to observation. "When the doctrine of morphology was first explained to Schiller, he exclaimed, 'This is not an observation, but an idea.'" "The fundamental ideas of modern science are as transcendental as any of the axioms of ancient philosophy." (Lewes.) "The highest generalizations of physical research bring us face to face with certain conceptions which are purely ideal and rational, that is, metaphysical ideas. Such are the ideas of substance, cause, force, life, order, proportion, law, purpose, unity, identity."

Philosophy, then, is a necessity of the human mind; even those who assail it do so with its own weapons. "Aristotle long ago remarked that we are compelled to philosophize in order to prove that philosophy itself is illusory and vain." (Bowen.) Many modern scientific writers "are endeavoring to substitute for philosophy proper a species of speculative physical science, in which, however, careful analysis will always detect an unsuspected residuum of purely metaphysical principles." (Cocker.)

Philosophy may therefore be said to be a defence of fundamental truth. Errors in science, in ethics, in theology, in government, in legislation, are usually founded on abstract principles, assumed, perhaps unconsciously, without proof, or without the application of the criteria of truth. To detect and expose such errors requires us to recur to first principles, and establish them on firm and reasonable bases, to define those fundamental truths without which science and reasoning are alike impossible. The science of geometry depends on the abstract conception of space, arithmetic on number, law on right, ethics on duty, physics on cause, esthetics (the science of criticism) on beauty.

In English the word philosophy is often used in connection with the names of the sciences, as philosophy of geometry, philosophy of physics, of law, of education, of art, etc. This does not imply that each of these subjects is a branch of philosophy, nor that each has within itself a different kind of philosophy, but denotes the abstract principles, the metaphysical ideas of each science or subject, as philosophically determined.

Philosophy may thus be defended as a delightful pursuit and exercise of the mind. As Molière's M. Jourdain was delighted to find that he had been talking prose all his life, so it is very pleasant for an acute mind to find that the questions and difficulties which naturally arise within itself have been experienced, discussed, and answered by other such minds in all the ages. To many minds the pursuit of knowledge is the highest of all pleasures; much more, then, is there attractiveness in the highest kind of knowledge, in pure science, where ultimate truth is sometimes difficult and disputed, but, when found and proved, embraces all being in its scope, and brings together all the sciences in a fascinating unity.

Philosophy, besides being necessary and valuable for its own sake, is useful:—

1. For training the mind to a philosophical temper, a candid love of truth, a calm confidence in itself. "There is a philosophic spirit which is far more valuable than any limited acquirements of philosophy; . . . a spirit which is quick to pursue whatever is within the reach of human intellect, but which is not less quick to discern the bounds that limit every human inquiry; . . . which knows how to distinguish what is just in itself from what is merely accredited by illustrious names; . . . adopting a truth which no one has sanctioned, and rejecting an error, of which all approve, with the same calmness as if no judgment were opposed to its own; . . . yet applauding gladly whatever is worthy of applause in a rival system, and venerating the very genius which it demonstrates to have erred." (Dr. T. Brown.)

2. For counteracting some injurious tendencies of the current devotion to physical studies. "The utility of metaphysics rises in proportion to the progress of the natural sciences, and to the greater attention which they engross." (Sir W. Hamilton.) The natural tendency of exclusive attention to any one class of studies is toward a narrow-minded dogmatism. In these times physical studies need no recommendation; they are forced upon the attention of every person who thinks or studies at all. There is no danger that physics will be neglected for philosophy, but quite the opposite. A symmetrical culture demands that some attention be paid to the first principles of knowledge, the nature of reasoning, the limitations of the mind, the existence of the soul and God.

3. For developing intellectual power. "The intellect" says Aristotle, "is perfected not by knowledge but by activity." Says Malebranche, "If I held truth captive in my hand I should open my hand and let it fly, in order that I might again pursue and capture it." "Energy," says Hamilton, "is the means by which our faculties are developed. All profitable study is a silent disputation, an intellectual gymnastic. . . . It is this condition, imposed upon the student, of doing everything himself, that renders the study of the mental sciences the most improving exercise of intellect." But it is not only the power of abstract thought which is developed and strengthened by the study of philosophy; clearness and accuracy of thought and of language are cultivated by these studies as by no others; and only those accustomed to philosophical discussions can appreciate the great scarcity of these all-important qualities in the world of thought and literature.

The term metaphysics is often used as the equivalent of philosophy; indeed, some writers formally define the one term by the other. The best and most recent usage, however, tends to restrict the term metaphysics to a more narrow province.

Philosophy is, in this usage, a more general term, covering all study of abstract principles. The term science was formerly much used in the same signification, and the science of any thing was said to be the knowledge of its principles and causes. But science is now generally used to denote the knowledge of phenomena, experimentally ascertained. Thus we have the "sciences" of botany, of mineralogy, consisting almost entirely of classification and description; and even the "science of psychology" is sometimes understood to mean the mere description and classification of the phenomena of the senses and the intellect. The term empirical psychology is also used for this, the concrete, and rational psychology for the abstract or metaphysical part, of this science.

According to Lotze, the problem of philosophy is to bring the separate departments of thought into unity and connection, and especially to investigate those ideas which are principles of judgment in life and in the various sciences. And the term philosophy means either the investigation which has this end in view, or the systematic presentation of the results so obtained. (Dictate, Logik, etc., §88.)

Lotze also says that metaphysics has for its aim to reconcile all the contradictions into which we are led by unscientific thought and by the separate pursuit of the different sciences. He divides metaphysics into three parts, (1) ontology, which asks, what are being, existence, action, etc.; (2) cosmology, which asks, what are space, time, motion, etc.; (3) rational psychology, which treats of the connection between the objective world and the spiritual world, or the problem of knowledge. (Dictate, Metaphysik, §§1, 6.)

Logic, which discusses the principles of reasoning, ethics, which discusses the principles of obligation, and theology proper, which discusses the being and attributes of God, are often called departments of philosophy.

There is a tendency in some quarters to use the term Philosophy in a restricted sense, nearly equivalent to Ontology. By these writers Philosophy is defined as the "Science of the Absolute," the "Science of Being," the "Investigation of those principles on which all knowledge and all Being ultimately rest." We approve rather of the following definitions.

Plato calls Philosophy a "Sentinel on the boundaries of the sciences, fixing and preserving their limits, uniting and demonstrating, and in all morally purifying." Aristotle defined it as "A knowledge of things by their causes," and again, "The science of Truth, derived from principles." Among the most recent writers, Ulrici says that Philosophy is "The science of sciences;" Calderwood, "A rational explanation of things existing and of things occurring;" Ferrier, "The attainment of truth by the way of the reason;" and Lotze considers it as a reconciling power among the sciences, furnishing those general conceptions which are indispensable for them all.

Definitions.

A few necessary definitions will be given here, but we prefer, in general, to explain terms when they occur.

PSYCHOLOGY is the Science of Mind. Obviously, then, the extent of the meaning of the term Psychology will depend on that given to the term Mind. Those who hold the mind to be nothing more than a function of the brain, or a series of sensations, will define Psychology as the science of the action of the brain and nervous system, or of sensations, with their combinations and derivations. But those who hold, as we do, that mind is a spiritual agency, and that the human mind contains a higher principle than that of the lower animals, find in psychology a higher department, concerned with the various metaphysical questions which are inseparable from the study of this higher power of thought.

This last department may be called Rational Psychology, and the former Empirical Psychology. But we believe that these two departments cannot profitably be entirely separated.

HUMAN Psychology is the science of the mind of man. Yet though our present subject is the human mind, frequent comparisons will be made with the mind of the brutes, and explanations and arguments drawn from thence will by no means be excluded.

COMPARATIVE Psychology is a description of the mental phenomena of the lower animals, so called because it necessarily involves comparison of those animals with each other and with man. It has not, as yet, however, proved a very fruitful science, since the nature and limits of instinct, association, and reason in them are doubly in dispute, first in themselves, and again as involved in the great debates concerning human intelligence.

PSYCHOLOGY is the best term to designate the science of mind, for the following reasons.

1. It has long been in use in other languages. In Latin it can be traced as far back as 1594. In German and French it is said to have been in use over two centuries.

2. It covers the exact field intended, excluding neither the metaphysical conditions of cognition, nor comparisons with the lower animals, nor descriptions of the senses and feelings.

3. It corresponds with many other names of sciences, Theology, Physiology, Philology, Archæology, Anthropology, etc., and, like them, forms an adjective in -cal, an adverb in -cally.

SCIENCE is accurate knowledge, systematically arranged. The term Science is used by many as including physical and natural science only. Such a restriction of its meaning is entirely unwarranted. Any branch of knowledge becomes a science when its principles are to some extent agreed upon, and a body of facts can be shown to be reduced to order and consistency by those principles. Logic, Ethics, Theology and Psychology are as truly sciences as Geology or Chemistry.

MIND is that which knows, feels, and wills. The reality and nature of the agent of these peculiar phenomena can better be discussed after we have studied the phenomena, and are therefore reserved until then. This three-fold power of the mind, to know, to feel and to will, is usually called by three distinct names, Intellect, Feeling and Will. It is not meant by this that the mind is divided into three departments, whose activities are separately carried on. In fact, every act of the mind involves all these great divisions of the mental powers. For example, the mind, acting as Intellect, knows some external object; the mind, acting as Feeling, at the same time experiences pain, pleasure, disgust, or interest, excited by some relation of the object; while the mind, acting as Will, chooses to what part of the object, or which one of several objects, the attention shall be directed.

And it is a mistake to suppose that philosophers have generally committed the error of dividing the mind into separate organs or parts. Scarcely a work on the subject can be found which does not contain a caution on this point. But for the purposes of discussion, it is necessary to adopt some division of the powers of the mind, and some system of names for them.

We accordingly adopt the ordinary classification and nomenclature, because they are well known and are sufficiently convenient, not because we think them entirely free from objections and difficulties.

INTELLECT, FEELING and WILL are therefore the titles of the main divisions of the present work. The first of these will be further subdivided into three "faculties" or "powers," called, respectively, the Presentative or Cognitive, Representative or Reproductive, and Reasoning Powers. These terms will be discussed each in its proper place.

THE INTELLECT.

PART I.

PRESENTATIVE POWER.

As a preparation for the discussion of the first great division of the powers of the mind, the Intellect, we need to make a further subdivision of this intellectual activity into various departments or modes. The terms which we shall use in this connection are, Presentative Power, Representative Power and Reasoning Power. Here again we adopt the usual division, not because we consider it entirely unobjectionable, but because it is well known, convenient, and more useful than others which have been proposed in its place.

Prof. A. Bain, for example, endeavors to reach a division from the opposite side, beginning with the principles of knowledge, which are, he says, Identity with its correlative Difference, and Similarity with its correlative Dissimilarity. But he is forced, after all, to add a third thing, Retentiveness or memory, which is by no means a principle parallel with the other two, but a "faculty" taken from the old division, which even he cannot, thus, wholly escape. Moreover, his arrangement leads him into numerous repetitions, several cross-divisions and some contradictions. We judge it to be far better to adhere to the old method, classifying the powers of the mind, rather than the results of their action, or the ultimate elements of knowledge. But these mental powers are not to be viewed as parts of the intellect, each of which may act alone, but inseparable forms of mental activity, discussed separately for the sake of conveniece. For example, in Perception the Intellect may be said to exert all its powers. Sensation must furnish the materials, but the very method of sensation, as we shall see, is discrimination, distinguishing between diffcrent states of the sense-organs, and discrimination is usually classed as a function of the Judgment, under the Reasoning Power. Perception, again, is inseparable from consciousness, and the method of this may be said to be discrimination, distinguishing between external objects and the Ego. Moreover, perception is to such an extent cultivated by experience, that practically, as we shall see, we never perceive without former perceptions being supplied by the memory, while the imagination very often comes in to construct the object in full which is really perceived only in part. Thus we shall be forced, on any system, to repeat ourselves occasionally, and to discuss separately things which never actually occur in separation.

Under the head of Presentative Power we shall discuss Sensation in general, and as distinguished from Perception; the Senses, in some detail; several connected topics, such as Localization, Attention, the Qualities of Matter, Consciousness, etc.; the necessary or a priori elements involved in Perception, such as Space, Time, Causation, Identity, etc.; giving then a historical sketch of the doctrine of perception, with such other biographical and critical matter as may seem necessary.

SENSATION.

Sensation is feeling occasioned by some state of the body, or by some impression upon the organs of sense by an external object. Thus it is a narrower term than Feeling. For example, grief, fear, joy, and anger, are feelings, but not sensations; the feeling of heat or cold, the pain of a wound, are sensations, and yet may be called feelings; but we also speak of sensations of light, color, sound, taste, etc., which can only with doubtful propriety be called feeling. And when sensation carries with it the knowledge of an external object, that knowledge is called perception. For example, if I smell an apple, I merely, in the first place, experience a sensation of smell; but when I recognise this as the odor of an apple, by recalling my previous experiences of the same kind, or, especially, when I know it as an external object, and as an apple, by combining this sensation with others, as of touch, taste, or sight, this is called Perception, the nature of which will be discussed hereafter.

The method of sensation is discrimination. No sensation can occur unless there be discrimination between like and unlike, or between the same and different. If the same impression be continually made upon a sense-organ, there will be no sensation. If all objects were of the same color, we should have no sensation of color. The roar of the cotton mill is not heard by the weavers; the smell of the tannery does not offend the tanner. In such cases constant indiscriminative use probably produces a modification of the sensory apparatus, so that its receptive power is dulled. On the other hand, constant discriminative use cultivates the organs, so that a smaller stimulus suffices to occasion a sensation. A watch-maker or engraver has far more delicate sight and touch than other men. Blind persons have hearing and touch wonderfully developed.

Different nerves respond to different stimuli; the nerve of the ear is not affected by light, nor that of the eye by sound, nor can either organ, by any mistake, bring into consciousness an impression appropriate to another, nor any hint of the process of sensation. A pain in the finger does not appear in consciousness as a decay of tissue, nor as an engorgement of the capillary vessels, nor as molecular vibration, nor as nerve vibration, but as a pain. An impulse of sound-waves upon the ear does not reach the mind as a picture of a bell, nor as a vibration of the air, nor as a process in the ear, or nerve, or brain, but as a sound. The result of the process of sensation is not an idea, nor an image, but a sensation.

How the mind distinguishes these various impressions on the sense-organs and interprets them, is unknown. "Search as we will," says Lotze, the nature of waves of light, we never discover any reason why they are seen as light, not heard as sound, and just as little why they are perceived as red, blue, or green."

And a knowledge, however intimate, of the organs of sense, the brain, the nervous system, and their operations, can throw no light on sensation considered as a mental process. How it is that impulses or motions of the nervous system, occasioned by external objects, are taken up by the mind and transformed into knowledge, is utterly inexplicable. Philosophers of all schools declare the problem insoluble. Even materialists admit that if we could trace all the movements of every molecule of the brain, we could still no more understand how a nerve-impulse occasions a state of consciousness than "the appearance of the Djinn when Aladdin rubbed his lamp." (Huxley.) "A unit of feeling," says Herbert Spencer, "has nothing in common with a unit of motion." And Lotze says, "However we combine the motions of the nerve-atoms, it never becomes self-evident that the last will no longer be motion, but must necessarily pass over into sensation. Hence all efforts to demonstrate how it happens that physical motion passes over into sensation, are completely useless." (Dictate, Psychologie, 3.)

The term Sensation is used by some writers to denote an impression on the sense-organs which does not reach consciousness. But this use of the word is confusing and misleading, and is not sanctioned by the best authorities, as may be easily shown by quotations from writers of widely different schools.

"The sensation arises when the nervous process is transmitted through the nerves to the conscious center, often spoken of as the sensorium, the exact seat of which is still a matter of some debate." (Sully, Illusions, Chapter 3.)

"Where action is perfectly automatic, feeling does not exist. . As the psychical changes become too complicated to be perfectly automatic, they become incipiently sensational." (Herbert Spencer, Psychology, I. 478.)

"Sensation is the feeling which is the result of a single impression on any part of the sensitive organism." (Calderwood, in the additions to Fleming's Vocabulary of Philosophy.)

"Some physiologists, it is true, have spoken of sensation without consciousness; but it seems very desirable, for the sake of clearness and accuracy, to limit the application of the word to the mental change." (Carpenter, Mental Physiology, 148.)

• The term "mental change," used here by Carpenter, means the same as "psychical change," used by Spencer, and does not imply that sensation is a function of the immaterial "soul," or mind alone, but rather includes the sensorium, or conscious center. It is not easy to decide at what exact point the activity of the brain ceases, and that of the soul begins to be exclusive, especially in view of some facts concerning the mind of the lower animals. Hence we use the word Mind, to denote the whole power of sensation and perception, reserving the relation of soul and body until we have studied the phenomena called mental or "psychical."

Sensation in the Lower Animals.

In discussing the intelligence of the lower animals, it is not easy to decide at what precise point, as we descend the scale of being, the term Sensation ceases to be appropriate. In the higher of those animls, such as the horse or dog, we must suppose that sensations are very similar to our own, and that some kind of dim consciousness exists.

But in the lowest animals such a suppostion would plainly be extravagant. The oyster, for example, has from forty to two hundred pigment spots, called ocelli, and when a shadow falls on any of these ocelli, it closes its shell. Such an action can not be regarded as implying knowledge, or consciousness, or true sensation. All the facts concerning these ocelli compel us, rather, to conclude "that they are the medium of an automatic impulse." In certain annelida, according to Dr. Carpenter, such eyes are found in the tail, which seem to direct the movements of that part alone. These automatic actions of the lowest animals seem to correspond to those movements which, in the higher animals and in man, are called Reflex actions, such as coughing and sneezing, in which a slight irritation of the mucous membrane is followed by convulsive, involuntary motions. Probably breathing, the sucking of new-born infants, and the motions of the viscera, belong to the same class.

Evolutionist writers regard such impressions as the rudiments of true sensation. Herbert Spencer says, "As soon as the organism, feebly sensitive to a jar or vibration propagated through its medium, contracts itself so as to be in less danger from the adjacent source of disturbance, we perceive a nascent form of the life classed as psychical. (Psychology, I. 392.)

He also describes "nascent mind" in the lowest animals, as a "confused sentiency, formed of recurrent phases of feeling."

The evolution of higher forms of mind is briefly described by Mr. Spencer as follows; "At a stage above this mind is probably present, under the form of a few sensations, which, like those yielded by our own viscera, are simple, vague, and incoherent. And from this upwards the mental evolution exhibits a differentiation of these simple feelings into the more numerous kinds which the special senses yield." "The skin, being the part immediately subject to the various kinds of external stimuli, necessarily becomes the part in which psychical changes are originated. . . This sensitiveness, which forms the basis of psychical life, is in the beginning diffused uniformly over the whole surface. . . Continued differentiation and integration, concentrating the actions out of which psychical life is evolved, first on the surface of the organism, and afterwards on certain regions of that surface, afterwards on those most specialized parts of it constituting the organs of the higher senses, and finally in minute parts of these parts, necessarily render the psychical life more and more distinct from the physical life, by bringing its changes more and more into serial order." (Psychology, I. 189, 400, 402.)

Many of the lowest animals have no general nervous centers, but only local ganglia, with slight and indirect connections. The star-fish, for example, has a rudimentary eye, a spot sensitive to light, at the tip of each ray, by which the motions of the rays are chiefly guided. The annelida which have eyes in their tails have been referred to above. Sensation, in such animals, must be different in kind, not simply in degree, from sensation in man, or even in the horse or dog. In such an animal, true, conscious, sensation cannot occur. For such sensation is the act of an individual, a unit.

In man the brain is undoubtedly the organ of consciousness and individuality, and also of the power of combining sensations into knowledge, called Perception.

THE INTELLECT.

CLASSIFICATION OF SENSATIONS.

Acts of Sensation, or Sensations, are sometimes divided into two kinds, called Subjective and Objective. The former are caused by some affection of the sense-organ itself, or by some condition of the mind. Thus, a dose of quinine may cause a ringing in the ears, a defect in the eye may cause spots to appear on the page or landscape, a blow on the head makes one see stars, fear may cause one to see a ghost.

The term Objective, though seldom required, may be used, by way of distinction, for all sensations not subjective.

Other and more useful divisions are the following;—

Sensations may be distinguished according to their nature in three different ways.

1. According to their peculiar nature with reference to the object which occasions them; as, sensations of light, sound, smell, pain, heat, etc. This peculiarity is usually called quality.

2. According to the strength of the occasioning impulse; as faint, moderate, intense. It is quite probable that the intensity of the sensation and the intensity of the exciting impulse do not vary in the same ratio. According to Weber, if the intensity of the sensation increases in an arithmetical ratio, that of the impulse must increase in a geometrical ratio. For example, a sound, to be twice as loud in sensation, must be occasioned by four times as violent an impulse.

3. According to the peculiar nature of the sensation as agreeable, disagreeable, or indifferent. This peculiarity is called by the Germans tone. Bain calls it quality.

Sensations may be again distinguished according to their content, or significance, into internal and external, or bodily and mental.

1. Internal sensations, or feelings, relate to the condition and needs of the body, and may be divided into local and

general. Local internal sensations involve only one or a few nerves, and are such as hunger, thirst, pain from a slight injury, tickling, sneezing, nausea, pricking caused by impeded circulation (foot-asleep), tingling caused by striking the nerve in the elbow (crazy-bone), etc. General internal sensations involve entire provinces of the nervous system, and are such as fatigue, exhilaration, shuddering, the depresssion of dyspepsia, spasm, cramp, the shock of a severe injury, etc.

2. External sensations relate to impressions received from the outside world, and may be sub-divided into general and special. Special external sensations are those which involve special external organs, provided with short nerves called sensorial nerves, all situated within the skull. They are sight, hearing, smell, and taste. General external sensations are those which depend upon nerves pervading the whole body, even the special sense-organs themselves. They are touch, heat and cold, motion or position of the muscles, pressure and resistance.

It will be seen that the old division of five senses is very defective. If we are to speak at all of the five senses, however, we may divide them into two classes, direct and indirect; those which receive impressions by direct contact with the external object, touch, taste, and smell; and those which receive impressions through a medium, hearing and sight.

The internal sensations are not of importance to our present purpose, and are sufficiently explained by physiology. We need only attend to those which, when interpreted and combined by the mind, convey to us impressions from the outside world.

Before we discuss the different senses in detail we need to define and explain the term perception, so that we can speak intelligently of the perceptions of each sense under the appropriate head.

Sensation and Perception Distinguished.

Perception differs from Sensation in that it is a higher activity, is more intellectual in its nature, makes use of the results afforded by the latter, and always involves a recognition of the external world. Indeed, Perception is sometimes defined as knowledge of the external world.

Writers of various schools agree, in general, in this definition. Lotze calls Perception "The power of the soul to localize its Sensations." Maudsley says it "groups or organizes several sensations into one idea." Bain calls it "Object consciousness," and "Object experience." Sir W. Hamilton defines it as the knowledge which the mind has of its body as extended, that is, as really existing, and also as affected in certain ways.

It must be remembered that perception is knowledge of objects, not of abstractions. Thus, we do not perceive Space, or Time, or distance, or color, or resistance; but we perceive objects as extended, successive, distant, colored, resisting, etc., or, in other words, under space-relations, and time-relations, under contrasts of color, distance, form, weight, etc., as will be fully described hereafter. And the expression, "perception of distance and solidity," found on a subsequent page, is employed as being the usual, well-known phrase, not as being perfectly accurate.

It should be noticed that sensationalist writers neglect perception, often not treating it separately, but including all that is meant by it under sensation and the association of sensations. This is unphilosophical and misleading, but is favorable to their theories of the mind, to which we shall return.

The term Perception was formerly used in a far wider sense, including the whole intellect, and is still used figuratively to denote the apprehension of abstract truth. In Philosophy it was restricted by Reid to apprehension through sense alone, and is now generally used in this sense. Hence the term sense-perception, used by some, does not seem necessary, since all perception is understood to be sense-perception.

We are obliged in English to use the verb "to perceive" in a somewhat figurative meaning, because the verb "to sense" is not in good usage. Thus we say, "I perceived a smell of musk," where we ought to be able to say, "I sensed a smell of musk," or might correctly say, "I perceived musk by the smell." The verb "to sense," or some exact equivalent, is a term needed in English philosophy, in which confusion has sometimes arisen for the want of it.

The product of perception is called a percept. A sensation of light may be produced by pressing on the eyeball or by an electric current, but this is not perception, nor its product a percept. When, however, a distant light excites a sensation of light through the eye, the mind perceives the light, through the sensation of light, and forms a percept of a light. Then, if other percepts be combined with this one, until the mind perceives, for example, a red lantern of globular form, this process is still called perception, but the completed result of the combination is called an object, or mental object. If the eye be color-blind, the knowledge derived from these sensations may be defective; if the mind be inattentive, or under the influence of association, or prejudice, or excitement, the data of the senses may be misinterpreted, and false results be reached. A large dose of the drug santonine makes all objects appear yellow.

Original or natural perception is the use of a single sense, without aid from experience or the assistance of the other senses. Cultivated or acquired perception is perception as corrected by experience and by the combination of different sensations. This is really a process of association. Thus, we have no natural perception of distance; but by walking or reaching out we establish connections between sensations, by which we ever after seem to perceive distance. Compound perceptions are those which are occasioned by a number of impulses of the same kind; as color from many rays of light, form from many impressions of direction, a musical note from many vibrations of the atmosphere.

The complete presentation of an object is almost always effected through many impressions of one sense or more than one. A star or a distant lamp is seen as a single point of light, and but one sensation is involved, unless it twinkles or changes its place so that we follow its motion with the eye. Ordinary objects, however, occasion more than one kind of sensations, or else a definite series of sensations of the same sense. These sensations, being of common origin, have coherence among themselves in memory, so that if one, or some of them be experienced again or recalled in any way, the others are suggested, and the object, with all its sensible qualities, is perceived or remembered. For example; an orange occasions sensations of smell, color, form, touch, taste, and pressure. After these are firmly agglutinated by habit, any one of them, when repeated, may call up all the rest, and we may perceive the orange with all these qualities, or remember it as having them all, and not merely color, or odor, or form, alone.

The senses of sight and touch are by far the richest in this kind of associations, and especially in connection with each other. This is very important, as we shall see, for the knowledge of form, distance, and solidity, the acquired perceptions of sight. It was upon this that Berkeley founded his theory of vision.

The subject of association in general falls under the representative power, and the acquired perceptions of each sense are more naturally placed each under its own sense.

The universal or necessary elements involved in sensation

THE SPECIAL SENSES.

Before we can intelligently discuss the universal or necessary elements involved in perception, whether called a priori concepts, intuitive ideas, or by any other name, it will be necessary to examine the special senses and the perceptions belonging to them. But the detailed description of the organs of sense, the nerves and the brain, belongs to the science of physiology, and the explanation of the action of light, sound, heat, etc., on the organs, belongs to optics, acoustics, and other branches of physics. We shall therefore describe somewhat briefly the so-called "impercipient senses," which are less important for psychology, but dwell at more length on the Sense of Sight, which is extremely important for the study of Perception.

We begin with the simplest and least complicated, and the one having, in itself considered, the least intellectual content.

SENSE OF SMELL.

The sense of smell is attached to a portion of the mucous membrane which lines the nostrils and nasal passages, called the pituitary membrane. Here is spread out a network of fine branching nerves which have the power of responding to certain chemical properties of some bodies. The excitation of the nerve is probably effected through the oxidation, that is, decomposition, of the molecules of the object, which must be presented in the form of a gas or fine powder, and carried by a current of air in respiration. Solid bodies in a state of fine powder are usually, however, so irritating as to cause sneezing and interfere with the normal action of the sensorial nerve. Gases may also be irritating in the same way, as ammonia. Some refer this irritation to the sense of touch, (Bain), but it is more probably to be referred to an over-stimulation of those particular nerves which are adapted to transmit impulses due to chemical qualities.

A gas or vapor may be exceedingly diffuse and yet produce a strong odor. A very small amount of matter from a volatile substance may give rise to sensation. It is said that a grain of musk will emit a strong odor for years without any perceptible diminution in weight. According to the experiments of Fick a two-millionth of a milligram is sufficient to excite a sensation of smell.

Sensations of smell require a longer time than any other for discriminative attention. When we wish to distinguish a faint odor or a new one, we "take a good sniff." Yet the organ soon becomes wearied and ceases to respond, if the same stimulus is long continued. A constant odor is not perceived. The tanner does not smell his tannery. Students in a close lecture room do not perceive the foulness of the air; but if one goes out for a moment into fresh air 'and then returns, he finds it overpowering. This shows also the necessity of contrast, and goes to establish what we have said of discrimination as the basis of all sensation. Smells can only be described by reference to our previous experience. The terms, pungent, nauseating, sweet, acrid, ethereal, fragrant, applied to smells, have no meaning except through experience. The same is plainly true of those which consist in comparisons, as, like a rose, like musk, etc.

In general, substances which are useful for food and drink have agreeable smells, while those which are injurious have disagreeable ones. Hence this sense is far more acute in the lower animals than in man. The dog, however, though his smell seems miraculously acute, does not seem to distinguish smells, or even tastes, as disagreeable and agreeable.

Some smells cause faintness in sensitive persons, and the sweetest perfume becomes sickening if too often repeated. "*Non bene olet qui semper bene olet.*" (Martial.)

The perceptions of this sense are entirely acquired. The mind knows sensations of smell only as in the nose, and receives through them no knowledge whatever of the external world. Possibly from a number and variety of simple smells constantly changing, we might conclude, even if we had no other sense, that they had an external cause; but that would be inference, not perception. We refer smells to objects because we are familiar with objects through the other senses. Smell itself can never inform us of the existence of anything but our own organism, as affected in some unknown way.

SENSE OF TASTE.

The sense of taste is attached to the upper surface of the tongue, the palate, and perhaps part of the pharynx. As these parts, especially the tip of the tongue, are capable of delicate sensations of touch also, it is almost impossible to separate these from sensations of taste. This probably can be done only in one case, that of a strong odor admitted to the mouth, which gives a sensation of taste in the back part of the mouth, where the current of air converges, with no sensation of touch.

The mucous membrane of these parts is studded with little papillæ, thick-set at the tip of the tongue, which are supplied with nerves having the capacity of being excited by certain chemical qualities of some bodies, when these are in a liquid state or dissolved in a liquid. No solid body can be tasted unless it is soluble in the saliva, and no substance can be tasted unless it is capable of passing through the mucous membrane of the papillæ. The researches of Graham on dialysis, taken in connection with his remarkable investigations on that condition of bodies called the colloid state, are of interest here. They go to show that nearly all bodies that can be tasted belong to the crystalloid class, not the colloid class. Now bodies of the colloid class do not penetrate one another freely, and animal membranes belong to this class. Hence starch, gum, albumen, gelatine, etc., have no real taste of their own, while crystalloid bodies, or those flavored with a crystalloid principle, are capable of exciting strong taste-sensations. (Bain, The Senses and the Intellect, 141.)

The excitation of the nerves of taste is probably effected through oxydation, that is, decomposition of molecules of the body tasted.

The number of adjectives that can be applied to tastes is larger than in the case of smells; tastes are more describable. Yet usually these descriptions amount to little more than comparison with sensations previously experienced.

The amount of matter required to occasion a sensation of taste is in some cases very small, yet far less small than occasions a sensation of smell. Valentin says that a fiftieth of a milligram of quinine is the least that can be tasted. The intensity of the taste depends not only on the nature of the object tasted, but also in part on the amount of matter brought in contact with the organ, and, partly, on contrast; and a sufficient time must be allowed for solution of a solid body in the saliva, in order that the sensation may accumulate its force.

It is held by some authorities that there are three kinds of papillæ, the real organs of taste, one for bitters, one for salts and one for acids. In general, those substances which are useful have pleasant tastes, while those which are injurious are disagreeable. The perceptions of taste, like those of smell, are all acquired. Sensations of taste tell us only of an excitation of the organ, nothing of the external world. Neither sense gives any information concerning the chemical properties of bodies. After those properties have been learned by us in other ways and associated with certain tastes and smells, the taste or smell will recall that knowledge. It does not originate any such knowledge. "Sensations of taste and chemical properties are heterogeneous in nature." (Lotze.)

The impossibility of separating sensations of taste entirely from those of touch, and the extreme delicacy of the sense of touch in the tip of the tongue, with the great mobility of the tongue, give an obstinate impression that we know the external world through taste. But a little reflection upon these facts will enable us to separate them in thought, and compel us to admit that taste is as entirely subjective as smell.

In the case of these two senses, smell and taste, the object in perception is not, strictly speaking, the same as that which excites the nerves by a peculiar impulse. What we actually smell and taste is small particles of the object, detached or volatilized, or dissolved in the saliva. What we perceive, by the aid of association and combination with the other senses, is, not these particles, but the object from which they come. We know nothing about the detached particles until science reveals them to us. When we smell an orange we have a sensation of a peculiar smell, occasioned by certain volatile particles of matter; but, aided by previous experience or by the other senses, we know this smell to be the perfume of an orange; and this is acquired perception. What we perceive is the orange. The formation of these acquired perceptions is vastly assisted by the inseparable connection between taste and touch.

These two senses, taste and smell, are the least intellectual of all the external senses. Taste is usually considered the least intellectual of all, that is, when taken by itself. "We are inclined to think that what are called the ignoble senses are wholly impercipient and would never, by the mere succession of feelings, waken into consciousness the distinction between subject and object, or reveal their own organic seat." (Martineau.)

SENSE OF HEARING.

The organ of hearing is the external ear, with the exceedingly complex apparatus connected with it, the description of which belongs to physiology.

Sound is due to waves of alternate condensation and rarefaction in the atmosphere, caused by the vibration of sonorous bodies, the further discussion of which belongs to physics. The waves of air affect the auditory nerve by causing compression of its filaments, after being transmitted through the internal parts of the organ.

The most important distinctions in sensations of sound are intensity, pitch, and quality, or timbre. Sounds differ in intensity or loudness according to the amplitude of the vibrations of the sounding body, and consequent amplitude of the atmospheric waves. They differ in pitch according to the rapidity of those vibrations, rapid vibration being known in sensation as a high sound, and slow vibration as a low sound. Sounds are inaudible if their pitch is either too high or too low, and the range of audibility is said to be about ten octaves, or from twenty vibrations in a second to 38,000. The squeal of a bat is audible to some persons and not to others. The lowest notes of a pipe-organ are heard by some persons as separate beats or pulses of sound, not as musical notes, showing that noise is audible at a lower pitch than musical sounds.

Noise and music differ as follows; a musical sound is caused by regular and continuous vibrations, and is comparatively rich in overtones; a noise is due to irregular and discontinuous vibrations, comparatively without overtones. Hence the human voice is between the two, and easily passes into music. When the articulation is a little drawled we call it sing-song; when the sounds are dwelt upon and prolonged with regularity, it is called singing, or music.

The differences of quality between different musical instruments or different voices are due chiefly to the varying richness of the overtones, and Helmholtz has shown that the vowel-sounds of language differ in the same way, in their overtones. Pure tones, without overtones, can hardly be produced, and are of insipid quality. Hence every single musical tone is in reality a complex harmony, and its richness depends upon the degree of its complexity. (On the overtones, etc., see Tyndall, On Sound.)

How different sounds affect the auditory nerves in different ways is unknown. Some conjecture that there is a different filament corresponding to each audible pitch, and thus the ear is a kind of key-board, and each of the overtones is separately heard and combined with the others in a kind of harmony. Others think that sounds differ in pitch because the elements of sensation differ in length. (Taine.) But this is only a restatement of the problem.

Sensations of sound do not, in primary, natural sensation, give any knowledge of anything outside the organ. It is only by combination with other senses, by cultivation, and by association, that sounds come to suggest to us the object by which they are caused, with its various relations. If a sound is familiar, we can tell something of its distance by its loudness or faintness. If it is entirely unknown, we cannot judge of it at all.

The directions of sounds can be perceived to some extent through variations of intensity in the two ears, especially on revolving the head; if it is loudest when the ear is turned in a certain direction, we judge its source to be in that direction. In a dense fog the sound of the steam-whistle or fog-horn seems to come from the point whence we are expecting it to come, whatever that may be. But if on going in a certain direction, the sound increases in loudness, we judge its source to lie in that direction. The judgment of direction is at best, however, easily mistaken. This is the reason why ventriloquists so easily deceive us by directing our attention and expectation in certain directions. It also explains why so many accidents occur in crowded channels in foggy weather, in spite of the greatest caution.

The discriminating power is capable of great cultivation, both with reference to musical sounds and articulate language, and even noises. The mind receives a vast number and variety of sensations through the ear.

The sounds of articulate language are only arbitrary symbols, whose meaning is laboriously learned by the mind. If the attention is directed strongly on the sounds, as in listening to a foreigner or a person with an unfamiliar brogue, we often miss the meaning and have to ask for a repetition. When we pay strict attention to the meaning we scarcely notice the individual sensations of sound.

Sensations of sound may be excited abnormally; certain drugs cause roarings in the ears; we seem to hear sounds in dreams.

It is affirmed by some that the mind perceives the external world directly through the sense of hearing. The following considerations will probably suffice to prove the negative.

(1) The organ of sense does not in hearing, as in touch, come into direct contact with the object, but a medium, the air, must intervene and convey the vibration to the organ, a kind of instrument for adapting these vibrations to the sensory nerves. Yet there is no apparatus, as in sight and touch, for following the outline of an object and thus gaining perception of form and solidity. (2) Moreover, if there were such an apparatus, its action would plainly not give pure perceptions through sound, but acquired perceptions through the muscular sense of the movements and the different

positions of the organ, cultivated by memory, experience, and association. Indeed we can to a certain extent, as has been said, vary the sensations of sound by moving the head and body and thus judge of the source of sound. But this is not an original or natural, but an acquired perception.

"That knowledge of this kind is founded on experience only is obvious from the fact that when the usual or the assumed conditions or occasions of our knowledge are changed, we make mistakes in respect to the place, direction, and distance of a sound, and that mistakes in respect to these lead to error in regard to the object which occasions it. . . . The humming of a mosquito may be mistaken for a distant cry of alarm or the sound of a trumpet. In such cases the sound must first be removed by our mistaken judgment to a greater distance, in order that it may be ascribed to a false occasion." (Porter, Human Intellect, 160.) "The knowledge of distance and direction of sounds is in reality an association between sounds and movements or muscular ideas." (Bain, The Senses and the Intellect, 362.)

(3) Again, the sense of hearing cannot convey to us any knowledge of the external world under those modes which are called primary qualities of matter, and are held to be inseparable from the very being of matter,—extension, weight, etc. It is true that in order to produce a sound a body must have extension, hardness, weight, all the necessary qualities of matter; but when we say that a sound which we have heard must have proceeded from a body having these qualities, that is inference, not direct perception.

SENSE OF SIGHT.

The eye is a *camera obscura*, provided with six muscles, by which it is rotated in all directions. It is furnished with a movable curtain in front, the eyelid, to exclude the light and ward off danger. It has an adjustable aperture for the admission of light, the pupil, and a double-convex lens, of adjustable convexity. It is provided with a receiving curtain, the retina, on which an inverted image of the object is depicted, and which is a very complex structure, containing the terminations of a vast number of nerve-fibres, which convey impressions to the brain.

The retina of the human eye has a small depressed spot which is more thickly set with nerve-terminations than the rest of the surface. Distinct vision of very small objects requires a discriminative power which is confined to this spot, but the retina is capable of receiving impressions of light, color, and direction, throughout a considerable segment of a sphere. Sixty degrees from the sensitive spot discriminative power is said to be one hundred and fifty times less than in that spot; that is, a body, in order to make a distinct impression on that part of the retina must be one hundred and fifty times larger than to affect the sensitive spot. Yet a fainter light can be detected by the outside portions of the retina than by the central portion. Fixed stars which cannot be seen directly in front can sometimes be seen by turning the head a little to one side.

The sensitive spot of the retina, being necessary for minute and accurate vision, is evidently of vast importance for the intellectual culture and progress of the human race. (Le Conte, Sight.) Nearly all the rotation of the eyeballs, so conspicuous in man, is for the purpose of bringing this sensitive spot into range with some definite object, for accurate and careful vision.

In most of the lower animals this spot is wanting. We may hence suppose that they receive equally clear impressions on a far larger part of the retina than men, that they use far less rotation of the eyeball, and that they are capable of far less discrimination of minute objects. All of these are confirmed by observation. A cat can catch sight of a rat with extreme quickness, and follow its motions with wonderful closeness, since no motion of the eyeball need intervene to direct her movements, at least for moderate distances. But undoubtedly she could not see to split one of the hairs on the mouse's back, as many a man could do. A skittish horse seems to see objects in all directions, which his rider does not see, but as the horse does not see them clearly enough to recognize them, he is afraid of them. Such an animal always goes more steadily in a dark night.

There is a limit to minuteness of vision, depending on the fineness of the structure of the retina. According to Weber and Volkmann two bright lines must be separated by from one six-thousandth to one twelve-thousandth of an inch, in order to produce a double sensation. That is, if nearer together than this, they will be seen as one line.

The organ of sight, like that of hearing, cannot come into contact directly with an object, but requires an intervening medium to convey the particular vibrations which occasion the sensation. This medium is a supposed elastic, imponderable fluid, the ether, whose vibrations are far more rapid, and are propagated at a far higher rate of speed than any others known to us, and striking upon the terminations of nerve-fibres at the back of the eye, occasion sensations of sight.

Difference in color is due to difference in length of the light-waves, since all travel at the same speed. The vibrations which occasion the sensation of red color are the shortest and most-rapid. How different rates of vibration occasion different sensations of color cannot be said to be well understood. The best conjecture is that there is a different kind of nerve-terminations for each of the primary colors, scattered all over the retina, by combination of which all sensations of color are formed. But microscopic examination discloses only two kinds of minute bodies making up the sensitive coat of the retina, while the primary colors are ordinarily supposed to be three in number. Recent investigations, however, tend to show that there are four primary colors, in two couples, each of two complementary colors. Each of the colors of a pair is supposed to cause an opposite action in the same sensitive body of the retina, thus reducing the kinds of sensitive bodies required to two, which corresponds with the theory given above, which is known as the view of Hering.

According to Le Conte, the phenomena of color-blindness confirm this view. A person who is genuinely color-blind (not merely indiscriminative) is deficient in the red-green couple, while the yellow-blue couple is unimpaired. (Sight, 62.) The phenomena of subjective complementary colors also favor this view. If you look intently at a surface of bright red, then at a white surface, the latter seems to have a greenish tint.

Other colors pair themselves also, in such a way as to favor the theory of two contrary pairs of colors, and two kinds of sensitive bodies in the retina. Possibly also what are called negative images may help support this view. If you look out of a window, in the sunlight, and then shut your eyes, you seem to see the window still, with light and shade reversed; the sash appears brilliant, and the panes of glass appear dark. White and black may be opposites in their retinal effect, in the same way as red and green. The details of these inquiries belong to optics and physiology; we are concerned with them now only in their relation to the mind.

This theory only shows, however, how the ether-vibrations may excite corresponding vibrations in the brain, and does not at all touch the mystery of how the sensation is produced; indeed the process in the brain is probably still more complicated, for the ether-waves do not seem to cause nerve-vibrations directly, but to cause a chemical change in the retinal coating, which excites in turn the sensory nerve to its own peculiar form of action. It is quite possible, however, that the action in the nerve itself is a chemical action or change.

The only sensations directly occasioned by the action of light on the retina are those of light and color, including the so-called colors of white and black. It is evident that this class of sensations can be occasioned by objects having no apparent size. A fixed star has no disc; and a light may be seen as red, white, or green, and yet be so distant as to be a mere point in the field of view. In such a case there is a sensation of direction involved, which is entirely separate from the sensation of light or color, and which is different for each part of the field of vision, because rays of light from each part fall on a particular part of the retina. There is also an automatic tendency of the eye to revolve, in such a case, until the sensitive spot is brought into line with the object, and it is from this, as we shall see, that our knowledge of direction, and hence of form, is chiefly derived.

Such a sensation does not give any knowledge of the external world; it might be merely a subjective sensation. We know that subjective sensations of light can be occasioned by pressure on the eyeball, by a blow on the head, or by a current of electricity, and that these have direction. When you shut your eyes and press a finger on the side of one eyeball, the resulting sensation of light appears to affect the opposite side of the retina, and a constant relation may be traced between the directions of the two.

Now suppose the object to be a colored surface, and we have a plurality of indications of direction at the same time. If the object fills the whole field of vision, we have all the possible points of direction at once, and this gives us a perception of color without limits; for in such a case a limit of direction could only be found by turning the head or rotating the eyeball, which is not the present supposition. It is a matter of dispute whether in such a case there would be any perception of colored extension external to us.

We hold that there is no such perception until voluntary motion of the receiving organ is added to mere receptive sensation, and that this is proved by the experience of persons born with cataract of both eyes and afterward cured. Such persons, those of them at least whose blindness had been most complete, on looking out of a window, for instance, for the first time, could see nothing but blotches of color, which seemed to be in contact with their eyes. The point, however, is not one of importance, for the following reason. Even though we do have a perception of something outside of us, it is not knowledge of a definite thing, not any true knowledge of the external world as it really is, for its real existence is definitely extended in space of three dimensions.

But suppose the field of vision to be divided between two colors. There would then be discriminative sensations of color, and the points of direction would give us a knowledge of whether each was on the right or left, above or below. But still the sensations arising would be mere "blotches of color in contact with the eye." Indeed, this is exactly the experience of the blind-born persons referred to; they did not perceive the boundary lines between the colors, as extended and external, any more than the blotches of color themselves; we have seen that sensations of direction may be subjective, as well as those of light.

Take now the case of a colored surface of definite extent; the directions of the angles or of many points in the boundary line, give us the perception of form or of extended figure. But this perception is obtained through the muscular sensation of the rotation of the eyeball. By this voluntary motion of the organ, making the circuit of the object, especially going around it in reverse order, and leaping, or rather measuring, across from one point to another, we gain a definite knowledge of an extended reality outside of us, real as meeting our voluntary activity, and remaining while we study it. The fact also that impressions on the retina are not strictly instantaneous, but have a duration of about one-eighth of a second, is of assistance in enabling us to perceive the whole of a line, or more than one angle, at a time; since the impression of one part remains until the other is reached. (Bain, The Senses and the Intellect, 236.)

Without this muscular feeling of voluntary activity, in the rotation of the eyes, or something equivalent, such as movements of the head and body, we cannot obtain through vision any true knowledge of the external world. This point is sometimes disputed; but, even if we yield it, and admit that the external world would be perceived in motionless vision, the fact remains, that it is not the external world in its full reality, but only colored surface, which is perceived, or existence in space of two dimensions, not of three. The following considerations, however, are probably sufficient to establish our view, that form is not perceived through simple sensations of light and color.

1. What is difference of direction? When the extreme points of an object send to the eye rays of light which differ in direction by a certain amount, what relation does that express? Merely that the eye would have to be rotated through that number of degrees to bring both successively to the same spot of the retina. There is a natural tendency to direct the sensitive spot of the retina to the first point, and then to the one which is to be compared with it, of course by rotating the eyeball. This rotation, even when not actually performed, seems to be the measure of difference of direction, and so of size, and hence of figure.

2. Although the outside of the retina is very sensitive to light, so that we can see a faint star best by turning the head to one side, yet the accurate discrimination of form is confined to a small area, and is vastly more perfect in the sensitive spot; so that for clear, distinct vision the sensitive spot must be turned successively toward all the parts of an object, or else the object must be small enough for its image to fall entirely within that spot.

3. In the case of small objects, all the rays of which fall upon the sensitive spot at once, we may often by close attention, detect a motion of the eye around or across the object, where it has been unsuspected before. It is quite probable that when we see a small object for the first time, as in learning the alphabet, we study it, feel around it with the eye, a process which is unnecessary afterwards, when it has become thoroughly known.

"Our notions of form are manifestly obtained by working on the large scale, or by the survey of objects of such magnitude as to demand the sweep of the eye in order to comprehend them. We lay the foundations of our knowledge of visible outline in circumstances where the eye must be active and must mix its own activity with the retinal feelings. The visual idea of a circle is first gained by moving the eye around some circular object of considerable size. Having done this we transfer the fact of motion to similar circles. So that when we look at a little round body we are already pre-occupied with the double nature of visible form, and are not in a position to say how we should regard it if that were our first experience of a circle." (Bain, The Senses etc., 373.) Children learning their letters are always taught with large letters. In rapid reading it is certain that we do not wait for a complete impression or image of each letter.

4. Nearly all modern authority is on this side of the ques-

tion. We have already quoted Professor Bain. Many writers deny that we perceive the external world at all through the senses, but declare that our knowledge of it is entirely a matter of inference. (Dr. T. Brown.) Others hold that it is only through the sensation of resistance to muscular exertion that we gain this knowledge. (Pres. Mark Hopkins.) But we hold that when a visible surface has an outline which we follow by muscular movements of the eye, and then follow in reverse order, while the object remains the same, it quite as really resists our activity, and is quite as really demonstrated to be real being thereby, as though we took it in our hands and found all its angles and edges with our fingers. Of course, however, vision gives us in this way but two dimensions of space, not solid matter in its full reality.

The following observations upon persons cured of congenital cataract of both eyes, are of general interest and not without bearing upon this question also, as showing that these patients can at first distinguish nothing but color and direction. In the celebrated case, among the earliest recorded, of a boy twelve years of age, couched by Cheselden, the patient, being taken to a window and told to look out, saw nothing but great blotches of color, which seemed to be in contact with his eyes. This apparent contact with the eyes, common in such cases, is probably due to the habit of perceiving by touch, that is, bodily contact, necessarily formed by blind persons. (Taine, On Intelligence, 306.)

Caspar Hausar, who was kept prisoner in a dark room until his seventeenth year, afterwards said that when he was liberated, on looking out of a window "it seemed to him as if there were a shutter quite close to his eyes, covered with confused colors of all kinds, in which he could recognize or distinguish nothing singly." (Taine, op. cit. 308.)

Wardrop's patient, a lady of forty-five, recognized the direction of a passing carriage, and asked what that large dark object was. Cheselden's patient was unable for some time to distinguish the cat from the dog, until one day taking her up he felt her all over, saying, "so puss, I shall know you another time." Home's second patient, being shown a square card could not at first distinguish it from a circle; but after studying it for some time, not being allowed to touch it, said he had found a corner, and then readily found the other corners. In a case witnessed by Dr. Carpenter, the patient, a boy of nine years, could recognize the direction of a lighted candle at once.

It should be noticed that most sufferers from cataract are not entirely deprived of sensations of light, but can distinguish day from night, or even a window from a blank wall. The eye is perfect but the light cannot reach it, except very faintly. This limited sensitivity to light strongly resembles that of the lowest animals which have any such capacity. We have seen that the oyster shuts its shell when a shadow falls upon its ocelli. "The Hydra habitually shuns the light,— chooses the dark side of the vessel in which it is placed." "The rudimentary eye, consisting, as in a Planaria, of some pigment grains, may be considered as simply a part of the surface more irritable by light than the rest. Some idea of the impression it is fitted to receive may be formed by turning our closed eyes toward the light, and passing the hand backwards and forwards before them." (Herbert Spencer, Psychology, I, 310, 314.)

Why are not objects seen inverted, since the image on the retina is inverted? The inversion of the image is a consequence of the mechanical structure of the eye. The light from the upper part of the object must fall on the lower part of the retina, because the center about which the eyeball revolves lies between the pupil and the retina. As the object goes up the image goes down The rays of light necessarily cross each other in the eye. "It is therefore a prejudice to hold that vision by an inverted image is a mystery, while erect vision would be natural. Like every geometrical property of space, this is entirely lost in the transfer to consciousness." (Lotze, Dictate, Psychologie, §36.)

The perception of direction is an interpretation of signs by the mind; direction is a relation, not a concrete thing like light, or like a stick which can be touched, and it is a combination of directions which gives us perception of form. To see the upper part of an object the eye has to be turned upward, which gives us an impression of height, or of being above, although the image of this part of the object goes to the lower part of the retina. The mind does not see the image on the retina, it sees the distant object by means of it, and by means of the muscular sensations of moving the eyeball from one position to another, which sensations are just as real as the image on the retina. The image on the retina is only known through the sciences of physiology and optics, not at all by sensation.

The rays of light coming from various directions excite sensations which are interpreted as above or below according as we would have to move the eye up or down to direct the axis of the eye upon the object, to "bring it to bear" upon the object. An absolute standard of direction is afforded us by the action of gravity; the direction in which things fall is called "down," and the opposite is called "up."

We have said that there is some dispute as to whether vision alone can give the perception of an external world as extended in two dimensions. As to the third dimension, involved in distance and solidity, there is practically no dispute. These are acquired perceptions, in which, however, the principle of binocular vision is of great importance, but much is also due to associations of the sense of touch, and accumulated experience.

The eye as an optical instrument is capable of being adjusted, to a certain extent, for various distances. For very near objects a change in the shape of the lens, which becomes more convex to the extent of one forty-eighth of an inch, enables us to see minute objects more clearly, producing a somewhat microscopic effect. This change produces a feeling of strain and fatigue, and is usually said to be voluntary. For objects somewhat further away there is a rotation of the eyes, converging their axes, thus increasing the visual angle, and giving us clearness and distance at once, enabling us to judge of the distance of objects whose size is known, or of the size of those whose distance is known. The full explanation of these mechanical adjustments belongs to the science of optics.

The perception of distance is entirely acquired. "The very meaning of distance is such as cannot be taken in by mere sight. The possibility of a certain amount of locomotion is implied in the very idea of distance. Distance cannot be perceived by the eye, because the idea of distance by its very nature implies feelings and measurements out of the eye and located in the other active organs, the locomotive and other moving members." (Bain, The Senses and the Intellect, 366.)

A multitude of observations confirm this theory of the perception of distance. An infant reaches out its hands, evidently for objects at some distance, and only slowly learns what is and what is not within its reach. In the case of couching for cataract witnessed by Dr. Carpenter, already mentioned, the patient, several days after the operation, being told to take hold of a watch, groped for it like an infant. Wardrop's patient, after three months, recognized a grass-plot by its greenness, but could not judge of its distance, and put out her foot to see if it was close by. Yet this patient was forty-five years of age, and had never been quite blind.

In all such recorded cases the judgment of distance has been slowly acquired, and the same process may be observed in children. When we look at an object and then reach out to it or walk to it, the real distance, as thus experimentally learned, becomes associated in the mind with the proper convergence of the axes of the eyes, with distinctness or vagueness of outline, with brightness or dimness of color, and other signs of distance. A vast number of such experiences, continued through years, cultivate the judgment of distance and make one skillful at estimating it.

But the errors into which we fall show that the whole is an acquired art. A landsman at sea cannot judge of distance because he is accustomed to rely on intervening objects. The stranger in Colorado judges mountains at a great distance to be hills near by, owing to the unaccustomed clearness of the atmosphere. The moon appears larger and nearer in the horizon than when in the zenith. Etc.

Some of the lower animals have a certain amount of instinctive judgment of distance which appears to be automatic. A chicken, for example, will dart at and pick up food when hardly out of his shell. But it should be noticed, what is generally overlooked, that this action of the chicken is not like what we call judgment of distance in a grown-up person.

The chicken's object is very near, and the only adjustment necessary to enable him to strike it is a convergence of the axes of the eyes. It is more like threading a needle than judging of a mountain. And this is about all the knowledge of distance which a chicken ever acquires. Even when mature, objects a quarter of a mile away are for him nonexistent. The intellectual judgment and comparison of distance is a different thing from the automatic convergence of the eyes at an object a few inches away, and even though the latter existed in human infants it would not prove the existence of the former.

So far as distance, as an abstraction, comes under the idea of space, it will be discussed hereafter.

The perception of solidity is similar to that of distance, only the assisting sensations are those of touch. The signs of solidity, namely, shadow, foreshortening, and perspective, are a kind of language, which we learn and interpret. A sphere appears, to vision alone, just like a circle, but after handling and seeing spheres we come to join the shading with spherical solidity, and imagine that we see the latter directly.

The perception of solidity is also greatly assisted by what is called binocular vision. Since the two eyes are placed some three inches apart, each one receives, if the object is not too distant, an image of a slightly different portion of the object, and thus the combination of the two images gives aid to the perception of solidity. The stereoscope is an instrument devised by Wheatstone to take advantage of this principle. It is held by the best authorities, however, that the mode in which it operates is that one eye receives the principal impression and the other supplies those additional particular sensations which it has received more than or apart from the first. (Le Conte, Sight.) It is well known that nearly every person has one eye very much stronger than the other, and habitually uses that one, by itself, far more than he is aware of.

The theory that the perception of solidity is entirely intellectual is confirmed, as in the case of distance, by numerous observations and experiments. Cheselden's patient, "for some time after distinct vision had been attained, saw everything flat, as in a picture." (Carpenter, Mental Physiology, 188.) Wardrop's patient could distinguish an orange on the mantlepiece, but could form no notion of what it was. "It has long been known," says Carpenter, (op. cit. 195.) "that when a seal is looked at through a microscope, it will appear sometimes projecting like a cameo, sometimes excavated as an intaglio," a phenomenon which does not occur with the binocular microscope.

Wheatstone has devised an instrument called the pseudoscope, which effects a "conversion of relief," making, for example, the outside of a basin look like the inside. "But this 'conversion of relief,' is generally resisted, for a time at least, by the preconception of the actual form which is based on actual experience; and it only takes place immediately, in cases in which the converted form is as familiar to the mind as the actual form." Thus, looking at the inside of a mask with a pseudoscope, it at once appears to be the outside of a mask, especially if colored like the outside; but looking at the outside of a mask a lengthened gaze is required to make it look like the inside. "In the case of the living human face, however, it seems that no protraction of the pseudoscopic gaze is sufficient to bring about a 'conversion of relief,'" the associations of so familiar an object being too strong to be overcome by optical expedients. (Carpenter, op. cit. 191.)

"The whole technical power of painting," says Ruskin, "depends on our recovery of what may be called the innocence of the eye; that is to say, of a sort of childish perception of these flat stains of color merely as such, without consciousness of what they signify, as a blind man would see them if suddenly gifted with sight." (Elements of Drawing, Quoted in Porter, 155.)

This theory of the indirect perception of distance and solidity is a striking instance of progress in psychology. It was demonstrated by Berkeley in 1709 from theoretical considerations. The defective state of the sciences at that time, especially ignorance concerning the muscular sensations, made his argument less satisfactory and checked its reception. (Bain, Mental Science, 189.) In some points, too, his form of the theory has been abandoned; for example, he held that we have no knowledge of extension through the eye; that the eye gives color only; that there is no necessary connection between visible and tangible extension. None of these points are now held to be a part of the true theory.

This theory, although so contrary to all our natural unreflecting beliefs concerning vision, has made its way, in spite of all difficulties, because, like the undulatory theory of light, it explains every new case which arises and is confirmed by all new discoveries in the sciences of optics, physiology, and psychology, until it is now accepted by almost every person whose opinion is of any value. Some able men have recently opposed it, as Bailey and Abbot, but they have opposed the theory as Berkeley held it, not as improved by more recent writers in the light of modern science.

A question arises in connection with binocular vision,—why do we not see double, since we use two eyes, which may, to a certain extent, act separately? The following considerations will probably remove the difficulty.

1. Form and distance being given by muscular sensations of the eyes, the same set of those sensations in either eye produces the same image, that is, locates the object in the same apparent place, and the two images correspond or are superimposed. If the adjustment of these muscles be altered, by pressing a little on the side of one eye with the finger, or by a voluntary effort, we do see double. (Drbal, Empirische Psychologie, 138. Le Conte, Sight.)

2. We do not, as above said, have two entirely distinct images which are confounded or mixed or superimposed, but one principal image, supplemented in some particulars by another. If the two images were superimposed they would not correspond exactly, since they are not taken from the same point of view. The effect of binocular vision depends on this very fact, that the images are not exactly alike; that is,

our vision of solid objects is not absolutely single, but is, to a certain extent, and in a certain sense, double, but is interpreted by the mind as single. (Bain, Mental Science, 192.)

3. The perception of distance and solidity is, as has been said, an intellectual phenomenon, an interpretation of signs. Hence the mind incorporates with the sensations involved, all the knowledge which it has previously gained in any way, and each perception of this kind is really the result of a long course of training. Hence, even if we do see double at first, the eyes and the mind may be adjusted to see single. This is proved by cases in which persons have been rendered cross-eyed by injury to the head. In such cases, if the divergence is not too great, the eyes are brought into harmony again by one or two years' practice, new associations of the muscular sensations of sight being established in that time.

"It is no more necessary that the two eyes should give two separate and complete pictures to the mind, than that the two hands embracing the same ball should suggest two balls; or that the thumb and finger grasping a pen should suggest two pens." (Bain, The Senses and the Intellect, 302.)

SENSE OF TOUCH.

In one meaning of the term Sense of Touch, this sense is attached to the whole surface of the body, even to the special organs of sense. It has in fact been called "the general sense," and some writers have even attempted to show that the other senses are all developments and refinements of the sense of touch. (Herbert Spencer, Psychology, I, 400.) In the tips of the fingers and tongue the sense of touch has a remarkable development, and the nerves of touch are there so specially sensitive as to constitute them, it might almost be said, a special organ of sense.

In other words the entire skin is capable of receiving impressions of pressure, pain, and temperature, but the tips of the fingers and tongue are usually employed in voluntary seeking for information of the external world.

Some sensations which are probably occasioned through the same nerves with those of touch are not of importance for this part of psychology, and are better classed under organic sensations; they are sensations of heat and cold, pain and pleasure, tickling, etc.

Experiments have been made by Weber to determine the comparative discriminative power of touch in different parts of the body. The blunted points of a pair of compasses are placed at different distances apart on different parts of the body; when they are too close together they are perceived as one, not as two. The smallest distance at which they can be distinguished as two varies from one thirty-sixth of an inch at the tip of the tongue, to about one tenth at the tips of the fingers, about one fifth on the lips, and three inches on the back. It is probable that in order to produce a double sensation the points must be in areas supplied by different and distinct nerve-branches, and separated by at least one such area. Thus each such area would correspond to a separate organ of sense, supplied by a special nerve, branching to every part of the area; for there is no part of the skin where a pin-point can be set down without causing pain.

Under the perception of points should be classed perceptions of roughness or smoothness. The face of a brush, for example, gives a plurality of points, and we can judge to some extent whether they are scattered or close.

Light pressure is usually classed under touch, but when pressure is heavier the muscular feeling of resistance becomes involved, and the two cannot be distinguished. By supporting the hand, as on a table, muscular sensation can be eliminated as far as possible, and it is then found that the tips of the fingers can distinguish between twenty ounces and nineteen and a half ounces.

By moving the hand along the surface or edge of an object, we get a perception of continuance of the sensation, combined with the muscular feeling of motion. This kind of perception is greatly assisted by the fact that we have two hands and several fingers, giving an effect somewhat like that of two eyes in binocular vision.

In this way we gain a knowledge of solidity, of the external world as having three dimensions, assisting the sense of sight and furnishing associations which go to form the acquired perceptions of sight. The similarity of compound touch to binocular vision is curiously illustrated by an experiment resembling that in which the eyes are made to see double by a slight pressure on one of them. If a boy's marble be pressed by the forefinger and at the same time by the second finger, so crossed over as to bring the inside edges of both fingers against the marble, it will seem to be two separate marbles.

When our own body is the object of touch, the double sensations, active and passive, especially when combined with vision, give perceptions of the parts of the body as in a peculiarly close relation with the perceiving subject. In this way, and not by direct consciousness, we get a knowledge of the body as extended and having solidity, and come even to regard it as a part of the external world, distinct from the subject or *ego*.

The sense of touch is capable of very wonderful cultivation, especially where exclusive attention is directed to it, as in the case of blind persons. "There is nothing essential to the highest intellectual processes of science and thought, that may not be attained in the absence of sight." (Bain.)

MUSCULAR SENSATION.

The muscles are all supplied with nerves of sensation as well as motion, and these convey a variety of sensations, some of which are organic, as fatigue, strain, pain, pleasure of motion, passive feeling of support, cramp, etc., and are not of psychological importance.

The intellectual or discriminative sensations of muscle are of two kinds, that of resistance and that of motion or changed place. Those of the first kind are always combined with sensations of touch, since pressure cannot be brought to bear upon the muscles without first affecting the skin. In the case of resistance, as in supporting a weight in the unsupported hand, it is said that an ordinary person can distinguish between thirty-nine and forty ounces. (Bain.) But the muscles soon become tired and then lose their discriminative sensitiveness, which is absorbed in the sensation of strain and painful fatigue.

The sensation of resistance, as when we grasp anything firmly in the hand, gives vividness to our knowledge of external reality in connection with touch. Indeed, it is held by some that here alone do we get a knowledge of the external world as extended and really existing. (Hopkins, Outline Study of Man.)

We have already stated our own view, that we know real being external to us whenever we exercise toward it a voluntary activity of the apparatus of perception, which we cannot do in taste, smell, hearing, or simple vision, but can do in compound vision, and still more perfectly in touch. Muscular sensations of motion and resistance imply, we hold, more than being and space, namely causation, a subject which will arise for discussion later on. Even Bain says, " the sense of resistance is primarily the feeling of expended energy." (The

Senses and the Intellect, 178.) "There is no feeling of our nature of more importance to us than that of resistance. Everything we touch, at the same time resists, and everything we hear, see, taste, or smell, suggests something that resists. It is through the medium of resistance that every act by which we subject to our use the objects and laws of nature is performed." (James Mill.)

In moving a limb, as in the sweep of the arm through space, we have a series of sensations corresponding to the motion, but we need the help of sight, in general, to make the muscular combinations accurate. Extend the arms, then shut the eyes, and try to bring the two forefingers together; they will not, usually, meet exactly. Yet habitual actions can be performed with surprising accuracy even in the dark; fix your eye on the door knob in a familiar room, then let some one extinguish the light, and try to walk to the door and touch the knob. Very often the knob is touched with perfect correctness. In throwing a missile the co-ordination of motions, guided by sight, but trained by previous experience, is wonderfully accurate.

A curious combination of tactual and muscular sensations occurs when we take a stick in the hand and "feel for" something with it, especially if sensations of sight be somehow eliminated. Besides the sensation of resistance directly given by the stick in the hand, we have the muscular sensations of movement, and also the resistance which the stick meets with at its other end and which is transmitted to the hand; we thus seem to feel the object directly.

Similarly in using tools, we seem to feel the tool, often, as a continuation of our muscular and sensitive system. The carpenter can tell by the feeling whether his plane is cutting well or ill, though the real variations of muscular sensation must be almost infinitesimal. Lotze has elaborated this subject, attributing to this peculiar "projection of sensations" all skill in the use of instruments and hence all industrial progress. (Microkosmus II, 195. Drbal.)

A similar class of sensations is not uncommon. Thus, if a fly walks on the ends of our hair, when it is short, we seem to feel him at that place, not in the skin, where the nerves affected really are. Or, if something strikes one of our teeth, we seem to feel the blow in the enamel or bone, which has no nerves, not in the gum, where the nerves really are. A cat's whiskers seem to be capable of similar discrimination. The antennæ of insects probably act in the same way. But this so-called "projection of sensation" seems to be an acquired perception, similar to the localization of sensation, which we shall soon refer to. It is probable that all precise localization is acquired, and if so, it cannot be much more difficult to localize a sensation in the hair, or the teeth, or the nails, or a stick held in the hand, than in the foot or the hand.

Muscular sensations have a tendency to become joined together automatically in rythmical series, and the series goes on without any intervention of the will, when once begun. One learning to play the piano strikes each key by a separate volition, with full attention; but a skillful player, playing a familiar piece can do it without attention, and even talk about something else all the while. So in learning to walk, the child has to give full attention to each step, and then often fails to get just the right muscular adjustment. Later in life the movements of walking may even go on automatically when the man, overcome with fatigue, has fallen asleep.

TOPICS CONNECTED WITH SENSATION AND PERCEPTION.

I. LOCALIZATION.

Many of our sensations are instantly referred by us to the part of the body in which the originating impulse was received. This is called localization of sensations. It does not always occur. When the attention is directed to the interpretation of the sensation, the localizing reference is absent. When we look at an object, we do not think of the eye, we are not conscious of the eye at all. But if the light becomes so strong as to cause pain, the attention is drawn to the organ, and we perceive the eye as affected by the light. So in hearing, we do not think of the ear unless the sound is so loud or so harsh as to be very disagreeable, in which case we at once perceive the ear as affected. Sensations of touch, pressure, temperature, and resistance, seem always to be accompanied by the localizing sensation.

Dr. Carpenter says it is doubtful whether the localization is "primary or secondary; a congenital intuition or an acquired instinct." (Mental Physiology, 149.) The weight of authority is in favor of calling it an entirely acquired perception. On this theory the child has to learn to know its own body and limbs, and to recognize the places of its various sensations, and does this by the combined sensations of touch and sight, and especially that peculiar double sensation described above, in which the organism is both active and passive at the same time. In this way, it is said, we learn to know the body as in one sense belonging to the external world, and yet in most intimate connection with the soul. The following considerations are relied upon to establish this view.

1. Even adult persons often find the localizing power defi-

cient. One cannot always tell which of his teeth is aching, until, by applying the tongue, he "finds out" which one it is; that is, acquires the localizing perception.

2. Frequent mistakes are made in localizing sensations. We refer sensations to insensible parts, the hair, the teeth, even a stick, as described above. After the amputation of a limb the patient continues to have sensations of pain, tickling, pricking, etc., which he refers to the part which has been amputated. In many cases these disappear after a few years, when new associations have been established. Organic feelings are often misleading as to the real seat of disease or injury. Disease of the heart causes pains in the arms. Acid in the stomach causes a pain over the eyes. The first warning of hip-disease is sometimes a pain in the knee.

3. Observations on infants are held to confirm this view. It is a long time before they can indicate the seat of a pain. In the pain of colic they draw up the feet in a peculiar manner, it is true, but this may be a spasm caused by the great intensity of the pain, not a sign of its location.

On the other side the following considerations may be mentioned.

1. Many of those who hold localization to be entirely acquired are idealists, and hold that all sensations are subjective, and that the mind projects its own sensations into space, which is also its own creation. They are thus obliged to account for the localization of sensations in the same way. This meets to a great extent the argument from authority.

2. After amputation of a limb the patient has sensations apparently in the severed limb, in many cases through the rest of his life, though prolonged for many years. This is held to indicate an inherent, specific, capability in the nerve, as in the sensory nerve, to occasion only one sensation, no matter what the stimulus may be. Such a capability would give dim

and vague experiences at the beginning of life, when all the powers are undeveloped and uncertain, but would develop with the gradual perfection of the organism.

3. Localization certainly becomes automatic, and probably is so from the first, so far as it exists. According to Dr. Carpenter, also, it is a reflex activity.

4. The muscular sense seems to be in a certain way a localizing sense in itself, and is possibly the basis on which complete localization is built up. It seems impossible to believe that the muscular sensations by which, for example, we know the movement and position of the arm, give us no knowledge in themselves, but only through association.

The true state of the case seems to us well expressed by President Porter. "All sensations are attended with a more or less distinct and definite relation of place in the sensorium. This relation of place is at first very indefinitely apprehended; indeed, it may not be attended to at all; but there must be furnished, in the original experiences of the soul, the means of discerning such a relation, provided the attention is directed to the sensation." (Human Intellect, 130.) We conclude, then, that localization is a power which can be largely improved and developed by experience and association, but becomes or is automatic, and is founded in original endowment, the structure of the nervous system.

Some writers describe a kind of extension of localization, under the name of projection of sensations, affirming that when we look at an object we are only referring our subjective sensations to a certain point in space, and thus we construct the external world out of our inner consciousness. (Drbal, empirische Psychologie, 155.) This is true only in hallucinations and dreams. M. Taine, indeed, plainly asserts that all our knowledge is hallucination. But the difference between our ordinary life and a dream is plain to right-thinking men, and is only lost sight of by those who have already adopted the presupposition of idealism. The only phenomena which can properly be called projection of sensations have been described above under the sense of touch.

II. Illusions and Hallucinations.

Illusions are errors in the perception of real objects. The senses themselves, in their normal action, do not mistake, but the errors of illusion arise from a wrong interpretation by the mind, when some unaccustomed circumstance, altering the significance of the usual signs, has been overlooked. When a man seems ten feet high in a fog, it is because the dimness of outline due to the fog is associated in our minds with distance, and we judge him to be farther away than he really is.

When we direct our eyes upon a spot in the window, objects beyond seem double, but when we direct our attention to distant objects, the spot on the window seems double; effects easily explained by the principle of binocular vision. When a voice, re-echoed from a building or a cliff, seems to proceed from thence, though the speaker is in the opposite direction, it is plain that the sound-waves, as they really reach us, are rightly judged to proceed from the direction of the echo. When we see the two rails of a railway track apparently coming together in the distance, it is because the real object of vision is the distance between the rails, and this object necessarily subtends a smaller angle as the distance increases. When a stick, obliquely inserted in the water, appears bent, it is because the mind assumes the refraction of light to be unchanged in the new conditions. When the full moon looks larger near the horizon than in the zenith, it is because the number of intervening objects makes us judge it more remote than when no objects are between, and hence larger. When a stump seen in the twilight, seems to be a robber with a gun, it is because the excited imagination is prepared to construct such an object, and the slight resemblances reported by vision are misinterpreted.

Hallucinations are subjective sensations, caused by abnormal action of the brain or mind. A blow on the head makes one see stars. Pressure on the eyeball causes a flash of light to appear. Electric currents stimulate several of the senses so as to cause false perceptions. Dreams will be spoken of under the head of Imagination. Visions, ghosts, and phantasms are not very uncommon. The case of Brutus is celebrated. Martin Luther is said to have seen the devil frequently. Pascal, having nearly fallen into the river, with nerves weakened by asceticism, saw a fiery gulf beside him, and could not get rid of it. Benvenuto Cellini, in a dark prison, thought himself visited by the holy virgin Mary.

Perhaps the most remarkable case is that of Nicolai, a bookseller of Berlin, who was visited by many of these dream-people. The so-called dreams of opium, haschish, and other drugs, seem to the victim as real as actual events. The delusions of insane persons are fundamentally of the same character, and by constant repetition and brooding upon them become "fixed ideas," which dominate the patient's mental life, and impel to all sorts of extraordinary actions. It is well known that nervous children sometimes take images in the mind for perceptions. (Dr. Clark, Visions.)

III. Feeling in Sensation.

A curious question has been raised how far sensation is accompanied by feeling. This question is somewhat complicated by the various meanings in which the words feeling, and to feel, are used in English, viz:—

1. Feeling is used of the sense of touch; we feel of a thing, and say it feels soft, smooth, hard; or we feel it to be soft, rough, sticky, etc.

2. Feeling is used for the emotions, including pleasure, pain, disgust, interest, gratitude, and all the sentiments, or finer feelings.

3. For all the sensations and emotions together. "All sensations are feelings, but all feelings are not sensations. Sensations are those feelings which arise immediately and solely from a state of the bodily organism." (Fleming, Vocabulary of Philosophy.)

4. Professor Bain uses feeling to include most of those sensations which we have called organic and muscular, and also the emotions proper. Thus he says, "Feeling includes all our pleasures and pains, and certain modes of excitement, or of consciousness simply, that are neutral or indifferent as regards pleasure and pain. The pleasures of warmth, food, music; the pains of fatigue, poverty, remorse; the excitement of hurry and surprise; the supporting of a light weight, the touch of a table, the sound of a dog barking in the distance, are feelings. The two leading divisions of the feelings are commonly given as sensations and emotions." (Mental Science, 2.)

Evidently he does not here intend to include the discriminative feelings of the special senses. But the distinction is not an easy one to carry out. It obliges him to treat of feelings twice, in two connections, first among the sensations, and then after the intellect, as emotions. And he is not thoroughly consistent in applying the term. Thus, he speaks of muscular feelings, organic feelings, feelings of respiration, of heat and cold, hunger, nausea, and disgust, and yet calls many of them sensations.

5. To feel is used in the meaning of to believe. We say, "I feel it to be true," "I cannot help believing it, because I feel it is so." This is a popular, colloquial use.

Some authorities teach that every sensation is accompanied by feelings of pleasure or pain, or rather an agreeable or disagreeable feeling. (German lust and unlust.) According to Lotze, sensation and feeling, though different in nature are always conjoined, yet not derived from one another. The relation between simultaneous impressions or states acts as an impulse upon the soul, and arouses a new activity, the soul responding in the shape of feeling. (Dictate, Psychologie §46.) Drbal, following Herbart, says that all feelings, including emotions, arise from the conflict and hindrance, or co-incidence and mutual strengthening (förderung) of ideas, but that weak or momentary relations of ideas do not produce feeling, and are not further noticed by us. (empirische Psychologie, 200.)

President Porter introduces the element of feeling into his very definition of sensation, which he calls "the subjective experience which the soul, as animating an extended sensorium, has of its own states as pleasurable or painful." (The Human Intellect, 128.) He does not account for this combination, nor explain the origin of feeling in connection with sensation, nor do we understand that he makes any use of it. Writers of the sensational or of the Herbartian school can make great use of the principle, because they derive all the emotions from these simple feelings.

Lotze divides feelings into sensuous, esthetic, and moral. The first are such as the feelings of harmony or discord of sounds and colors, agreeable and disagreeable sensations of smell, taste, touch, the last rising at one extreme into pain; these are personal, as depending on each one's physical organism. The second are the pleasures and pains (rather displeasures) of taste, aroused by beauty and ugliness, etc., in which the personal element is wanting, and which are universal in their application, since all men may derive pleasure from the same picture or statue. The third is moral approbation or disapprobation. Professor Bain, as we have seen, gives a similar extent to the term feeling.

But President Porter compares the pain of a cut or blow with the pain of the death of a friend, and says, "the one is experienced by the soul as connected with an organism, while the other is felt in the soul without reference to the sensorium at all.' We should prefer to say that the pain of a cut belongs to the body alone, as an organic sensation, while the pain caused by the death of a friend belongs to the mind, and cannot be derived from, related to, or classified with the other in any way. But, however stated, this correct doctrine removes the need of any mention of pleasure and pain as universal elements of sensation. It may be true that if we could abstract our attention sufficiently from the mental content of our sensations, we should find that they are all, or were originally, accompanied with feeling. The child learning to read may do so with pleasure or with pain and disgust. But the skillful reader has none of either feeling in consciousness; his attention is entirely absorbed by the meaning of what he reads, and the higher feelings which it arouses in him. When we hear a piece of news or read it in the newspaper, the articulate sounds of the voice or the black characters on a white ground, are neither agreeable nor disagreeable in the sensations which they directly occasion, but only in the intellectual content of their meaning.

Sir W. Hamilton elaborated a theory that feeling and knowledge are in inverse ratio in every act of perception, or, as he phrased it, the more intense the sensation proper or subjective consciousness, the more indistinct the perception proper or objective consciousness. But he himself was obliged to restrict this by saying "above a certain limit," for it is obvious, as we have seen, that some sensations have no content of feeling, and some never appear in consciousness at all, but excite automatic actions, if any, and hence have no mental content. It is disputed, however, whether these last are properly called sensations.

One of Hamilton's illustrations is that of a dog, to which, though his "sense of smell is so acute, all odors seem in themselves indifferent." It might be difficult to prove that odors are indifferent to a dog, though it is quite possible that he abstracts his attention from the feeling and gives it entirely to discrimination, as we ourselves often do. Another illustration is the human skin in the sensation of touch. The tips of the fingers are more discriminative, but less sensitive to pain than the arm or the back. But the explanation seems to be that the skin is thicker at the tips of the fingers; a pin or a sliver there, if it really reaches the nerves, causes sharper pain than elsewhere; and the heel, where the skin is thickest of all, has almost no discriminative sensibility. Yet there is a good deal of truth in Hamilton's comparison, which we think, however, can all be covered by the following statements better than by laying down a universal dogma.

1. The sensations may be arranged in a series, from those which have no mental content but are wholly feeling, to those which have no content of feeling but are all mental. A toothache is all pain; a glance at the sun is nearly all pain; a sweet taste is part pleasure and part discrimination; a pleasant musical air has more complicated and difficult discrimination; in reading a book the mental process is complicated and difficult, gathering up the arbitrary symbols and interpreting them into sounds, combining these into words and interpreting out of them the author's meaning, with all the subsidiary trains of thought and association going on at the same time; sensuous feeling is usually entirely absent, unless, indeed, feeling be expressly defined so as to include all sensation.

2. The attention may be directed to either element, when they are combined, to the exclusion of the other. In comparing two samples of cloth to see if they are of exactly the same color we have sensation about as pure as it can be found, yet

discrimination is intense; we know nothing of the colors as agreeable or the contrary, for the moment, but only know them as alike or different.

Mr. Herbert Spencer, criticising this doctrine of Hamilton's says, "It would seem not so much that sensation and perception vary inversely, as that they exclude each other with degrees of stringency which vary inversely." (Psychology II, 248.)

IV. ATTENTION.

Attention is a necessary condition of perception, and consists in the narrowing or concentration of the activity of the mind upon one or a few sensations to the exclusion of others. It may be either voluntary or spontaneous. When a number of different sensations are occasioned by different objects at the same time, they may only cause confusion, and no one of them may originate a perception. If one of them or one set of them is much stronger than the others, so as to overbear them, it will force the recognition and attention of the mind, and occasion a perception. Or if one of them calls up a more exciting image than the others, owing to previous associations or familiar knowledge, the voluntary attention of the mind is instantly directed to this one. Thus, if I am intently reading a book, the clock may strike in the same room, but the well-accustomed sound cannot force its way among the set of sensations which I am receiving from the printed page. But the sound of a distant fire-bell, or the gnawing of a rat close by, is a more exciting set of sensations, and I stop reading and give my attention to the new sound.

The will often determines a change in the flow of the nerve-currents, and a particular organ with its set of nerves is rendered more active; this is called innervation. We often suspend the action of one organ to render another more acute, shut the eyes or hold them fixed, in order to catch a faint sound. We do not hear what a friend is saying to us while we are watching an exciting scene in a play, or scrutinizing a distant object with a glass; when we are through we ask him to repeat, innervate the ear, that is, give him our attention, and hear him then distinctly.

If any sensation is extremely intense this attracts the attention, and the mind knows nothing through the sensation. If you look at the sun you cannot see anything, but the intensity of sensation is painful and injurious. With a bit of smoked glass to render sensation less intense you can see an eclipse at its very beginning. An intense pain overpowers all the faculties; while your tooth is being pulled you can neither perceive nor reason. But, on the other hand, soldiers in battle often receive severe flesh wounds without knowing it, so intense is their excitement. That attention is necessary to perception is also shown by every-day occurrences, such as when one goes around looking for a thing which is in his hand, or for glasses which are on his forehead.

In spontaneous attention it is only the direction of the attention which is automatic, the continuance of it is voluntary.

"In attention we submit to an impression, we keep the mind steady in order to receive the stamp." (Coleridge.) "Attention is concentrated observation." (Calderwood.) "The greater or less energy in the operation of knowing is called attention, which is another term for tension or effort." (Porter.) "The content of our mind at each moment can be only very limited, and we can entertain simultaneously only a very small number of ideas." (Drbal.)

No power of the mind is more susceptible of cultivation than attention. Young children cannot fix their minds on one thing more than a few minutes. To teach scholars how to study, to train the power of attention, is perhaps the most difficult office of the teacher.

It is a curious question how many objects can be attended to by the mind at the same time. Dugald Stewart propounded a theory that the number is only one, and that in comparing two objects the mind goes with almost infinite rapidity from one to the other. This theory is disproved by the commonest experience. The most important part of all our knowledge is the knowledge of relations, which presupposes at least two objects in the mind at once.

Yet it is probable that the most complete, intense attention can be given to only one set of sensations at the same time. The truth seems to be that the mind can distribute its activity among several objects to some extent, but cannot perceive them all with the same vividness. Mr. Herbert Spencer says; "Consciousness cannot be in two equally distinct states at the same time." (Psychology, II, 250.) But he also says;—"I find that there may sometimes be detected as many as five simultaneous series of nervous changes, which in various degrees rise into consciousness so far that we cannot call any of them absolutely unconscious. When walking there is the locomotive series; there may be a tactual series; and there is the visual series; all of which are subordinate to the dominant consciousness formed by some train of reflection." (Ib. I, 398.)

A still more curious subject connected with attention is the influence of excited attention and expectation in producing illusions and hallucinations, and even bodily disorders. Sir Walter Scott, soon after the death of Lord Byron, having been engaged in reading an account of the departed poet, on going into another room, saw an exact representation of Lord Byron before him. Sensible that it was an illusion he examined the object, and found it to be a screen covered with coats, shawls, etc. (Carpenter, Mental Physiology, 207.)

During the burning of the Crystal Palace in London, many

spectators saw the chimpanzee, which was known to have escaped from his cage, writhing around one of the iron ribs of the building in the midst of the flames. But the object turned out to be a tattered piece of blind, tossed about in the wind. (Id. ib. 208) Hypochondriacs come to have the very disease they fancy. The victims of witchcraft pine away and die, because they believe they are bewitched, and so brood over their fate with intense attention. Many wonderful cures have been wrought by the king's touch, by holy water, by mesmeric passes, all due to expectant attention.

Baron Reichenbach discovered a new force which he called odyle, and performed many wonderful experiments to prove it, all with excitable and nervous persons. But Mr. Braid performed the same experiments without any odyle, through expectant attention alone. His patients, being taken into a dark room and told that there was a magnet in a certain corner, used to see the magnetic force issuing from it in the form of flames of fire, although there was really no magnet there. Mr. Home, the "medium" was proved to have floated out of one window and in at another by the testimony of two witnesses; but another witness who was present saw nothing of the kind. (See the works of Carpenter, Maudsley, Abercrombie, Tuke, Brodie, Sully.) The ventriloquist and the conjuror deceive us by directing our attention where they wish, quite as much as by their dexterity.

V. Qualities of Matter.

The question naturally arises in connection with perception, how it is that matter can affect our sense-organs. The power of occasioning sensation in any particular way has usually been called a quality, and the description and classification of the qualities of matter has been a topic of some importance. It is obvious that in order to occasion sensation the qualities of matter must exist, or its powers must be exerted, in certain relations and under certain conditions. Qualities are called by such names as color, weight, hardness, size, smell, etc. But in order to have color a body must be in the light; and in order that it should have color for us, we must have eyes, must look at the body, and must give our attention to what we look at. In order to have smell a body must be volatile, to have taste it must be soluble, and that it may have these qualities for us, it must come into proper relation with our nerves of sensation.

It is commonly said, and is an obvious thought, that the qualities of matter are entirely in our minds, not in the objects which we perceive; that there is no color, no sound, unless an eye or an ear be present to see and to hear. There is a sense in which this is true. Sweetness does not exist in sugar as sweetness, but as a peculiar combination of atoms of oxygen, hydrogen, and carbon, probably held in combination by their coincident or rythmical vibrations, and ready to change their combination under certain influences, in such a way as to affect the organ of taste. So color does not exist in the object as color, but as a power of checking some of the light-vibrations, and reflecting others unchanged, probably because some of the vibrations of light are in accord or in rhythm with its own atomic vibrations and some are not.

There is then really some power in the object of impressing or influencing objects around it by its activities, and hence of affecting our sense-organs, which are a set of instruments, varying in delicacy and nature from a pair of scales for measuring gravity, to a photographic plate for recording the vibrations of light. The popular mode of speech is justifiable and proper. The roar of the ocean and the colors of the flowers are real things, motions or actions of matter, not indeed sensations; but then they could never be sensations, in any proper use of language, but only occasions of sensation; and no one ever said that they were sensations. The terms, color, sound, hardness, etc., are used, however, to denote both our sensations and the qualities or activities of bodies which occasion those sensations. Some writers confound these meanings, and we need to bear the distinction carefully in mind.

The most common division of the qualities of matter has been into two classes, primary and secondary. This distinction may be said to date back to the earliest period of philosophy. Democritus distinguished between those qualities which are known by touch and all others, and denied that the latter give any real knowledge of matter.

Aristotle used the terms common sensibles or percepts, and proper sensibles or percepts, the former being magnitude (extension), figure, motion or rest, and number. According to Sir W. Hamilton "he anticipated Descartes, Locke, and other modern philosophers, in establishing, and making out by appropriate terms, a distinction precisely analogous with that taken by them of the primary and secondary qualities of matter." (Philosophy, ed. by Wight, 313.)

Descartes re-introduced this division into philosophy in the modern period. According to him our knowledge of the primary qualities is clear, that is, intuitive, self-evident; but of the secondary qualities we have only an "obscure and confused conception of something which occasions the appropriate sensation." (Porter, Human Intellect, 637.)

But as he taught that the essence of matter is extension, as the essence of mind is thought, the knowledge of extension and the qualities depending on it, was, for him, a real knowledge of matter as it is. And we shall find this doctrine of extension, as the essential attribute of matter, pervading subsequent classifications.

Locke's division, though some advance upon that of Descartes, is yet essentially the same, and accounted for in the same way; that is, the primary qualities are those which we perceive directly, intuitively, as they really are, while the secondary are merely affections of the mind caused by bodies. He says: "A power to produce any idea in our mind, I call quality of the subject wherein that power is;" and divides qualities into, "first, such as are utterly inseparable from the body in what estate soever it be," such as solidity, extension, figure, motion or rest, and number, and secondly, "such qualities which in truth are nothing in the objects themselves but powers to produce various sensations in us by their primary qualities, that is, by the bulk, figure, texture, and motion of their insensible parts, as colors, sounds, tastes, etc." (Essay on Human Understanding, Book 2, Ch. 8.)

However interesting or even useful this division may be, the reason given for it is unsatisfactory. We can no more conceive matter without secondary qualities than without primary. We can indeed imagine the sky to be green and the grass blue, but we must conceive every object to have some color (counting white and black as colors), if it is exposed to light at all, capable of emitting sound, if struck in the air; having some chemical reactions, similar to those occasioning smell and taste, having some degree of hardness or softness, heat or cold, elasticity or rigidity, etc.

Moreover, it is just as easy to conceive matter to be without figure and solidity as without color; the ether, if it transmits light, must be matter, yet it does not retard the motions of the planets; a gas diffused in another gas can hardly be said to have form. Again, number is not a quality of matter, but a logical necessity of the perception of different objects; we must know them as one or many, if we know them at all. And motion or rest is no quality of matter, though all matter, so far as we know, is in constant motion.

The advance of physical science since Locke's time leaves

little room for doubt that the primary qualities of matter depend as much on the "bulk, figure, and motion, of their insensible parts," or molecules, as do the secondary. When we feel a body as heavy, pressing down on the hand, the sensation results from an activity of the body, pulling itself toward the center of the earth. The atoms of matter are supposed to be in constant vibration, and the regularity and continuity of these vibrations define its form and solidity. In fact, it is now a common theory that the very essence of matter is the activity of its "insensible parts," which are in themselves only centers of force, having a merely supersensual existence.

The most complete and elaborate classification of the qualities of matter is that of Sir W. Hamilton. His division is three-fold, primary, secundo-primary, and secondary. The primary qualities are deduced "from the simple datum of substance occupying space," and fall into two divisions, the property of filling space, or geometrical solidity, and the property of being contained in space, or physical solidity.

Geometrical solidity which is defined as "the necessity of trinal extension, in length, breadth, and thickness," is developed into three qualities, divisibility, magnitude, and figure. Physical solidity, defined as ultimate or absolute incompressibility, is really equivalent to being or existence; he calls it impenetrability. The attribute of being contained in space is explicated into two, mobility or motion and rest, and situation or position. The author well says that these "primary are less properly denominated qualities, and deserve the name only as we conceive them to distinguish body from not body, corporeal from incorporeal substance." They are indeed deductions from the conception of matter as reality whose essence is extension, and not properly qualities at all.

The secundo-primary qualities "are all contained under the category of resistance or pressure." Resistance or pressure may have three sources, co-attraction, repulsion, and inertia. The first involves gravity and cohesion; gravity gives the qualities heavy and light, cohesion gives hard and soft, solid and fluid, tough and brittle, etc. Repulsion is developed into compressible and incompressible, elastic and inelastic. Inertia gives movable and immovable. The secondary qualities are such as color, sound, flavor, the feelings of heat, sneezing, shuddering, setting-the-teeth-on-edge, etc.

"The primary determine the possibility of matter absolutely; the secundo-primary, the possibility of the material universe as actually constituted; the secondary the possibility of our relation as sentient existences to that universe." "The primary may be roundly characterized as mathematical; the secundo-primary, as mechanical; the secondary, as physiological." (Metaphysics, Bowen's ed., 340.)

Our remarks upon Locke's division are also applicable to Hamilton's second and third classes. Considered as qualities of bodies, these are activities, powers of affecting other bodies; and since we can transform these motions into sensation, and interpret these sensations in perception and thought, the activity of objects toward us seems to differ from their activity toward other things, but it is not really different. All the qualities of matter, except those metaphysical qualities which are not properly so called, are similarly related to perception. Even impenetrability is declared by Lotze to be, not a property but an activity of matter, somewhat, we suppose, as the pressure of gases is due to molecular vibration. "Bodies do not react on one another because they are impenetrable, but they are impenetrable because they react on one another." (Dictate Naturphilosophie, §19.)

Mr. Herbert Spencer's classification differs from Hamilton's only in terminology. He calls the three classes "body as presenting statical, statico-dynamical, and dynamical attributes." This nomenclature is not more felicitous than Hamilton's; for all qualities of bodies which appear in perception must be dynamical, must exert force or influence of some kind; and all must be statical, must have continuous, independent existence.

SUBSTANCE AND ATTRIBUTE.

When we speak of qualities the question necessarily arises, Qualities of what? The term quality, or attribute, implies substance. The two are really inseparable, like the correlative terms, husband and wife, triangle and three sides. Are qualities, then, one thing and objects another? Are qualities something which the object may have or not have, and which may exist by themselves, apart from objects? Mr. Mill replies that qualities only exist, there is no substance, or substratum, matter is only a permanent possibility of certain sensations. Berkeley is generally, though erroneously, understood to have held the same view. Hume distinctly denied the existence of the real thing to which the qualities belong. Kant maintained that there is such a real existence, or noumenon, but that it is unknowable. In this he is followed by Herbert Spencer and many others. Other philosophers have in general held to the reality of substance.

Undoubtedly the constitution of our minds is such that when we perceive an object we perceive it as really existing; our minds act in this relation under the category of being, and we can never practically accept the belief that the object is nothing but a set of sensations. No argument can make this any clearer. But there is not in nature or in comsciousness anything corresponding to the separation of the object into substance and attribute, real thing and quality. This separation is purely logical, and has an effect somewhat like dividing the mind awkwardly into different faculties.

Substance apart from quality is only an abstraction, for there is no real being without attributes. Being without attributes is equivalent to non-being. To say that the noumenon is unknowable apart from phenomena is mere platitude, for of course we can only know what is in relation to us, and know it by those relations. We know the object as related to us by its qualities or activities, and there is no object without qualities or activities. "Sensible qualities," says Lotze, "show us how things act, not what they are." (Dictate, Metaphysik, §16.) Not what they are, that is, apart from their action; but they are just as they act.

"The 'underlying substance' of the schools, the 'thing in itself' of Kant, are mere names, which signify either being in the abstract or being in the concrete. If it is being in the abstract, then it must be synonymous with matter as knowable, that is, it is only a concept, which can be separate from its relations in thought but never in fact. If it is being in the concrete, then this must be known with its relations and never apart from them. In either case the substance or thing in itself cannot be known by itself." (Porter, Human Intellect, 632. See also Bowne's Metaphysics, 48.)

CONSCIOUSNESS.

This important subject may be said to be transitional, between topics connected with perception, and the necessary elements of perception.

Every perception, feeling, or act of will, is accompanied by a knowledge of self as the perceiving, feeling, or willing agent. This is called consciousness, a very appropriate designation, since by its etymology it means a with-knowing. It can be separated from other acts of the mind only logically, not practically. It is an inseparable element of every act of perception, omitted hitherto in our discussions, in order to avoid complication, and because its importance demands separate and fuller treatment. "We know and we know that we know; these propositions," says Hamilton, "logically distinct, are really identical."

The facts of memory make this clear. When we remember anything, a former perception, or feeling, or action, the element of self is perfectly clear. All philosophers are agreed that there is here an irresistible belief in the identity and continuity of the past perception and the present memory, however they may explain it or try to explain it away.

Professor Ferrier has most ingeniously based a whole system of metaphysics on the postulate, or ultimate datum, which he considers self-evident, that consciousness of self accompanies all knowledge. "All cognition is a knowledge of self plus an object."

It would be well if the term could be confined to this meaning, self-knowledge, as implied in all mental action. But general usage gives it a wider meaning, and we cannot hope to make this useful restriction. It is commonly used in the sense, of "introspection, or introspective attention," (Bain); "the power by which the soul knows its own acts or states," (Porter); "the immediate knowledge which the mind has of its sensations and thoughts, and, in general, of all its present operations." (Morell.)

Hence consciousness is often spoken of as a faculty of the mind. Such phrases are almost inevitable, and yet they are misleading; for consciousness is parallel with all the faculties, a condition of them all, not properly to be considered a faculty, co-ordinate with, for example, perception, or imagination. If the power of knowing that we know is a faculty, parallel with preception, imagination, etc., then we are required to suppose another and higher faculty to embrace both in one unity of feeling; but this faculty would be consciousness in the usual sense, hence the first is a useless supposition.

Less positively incorrect, but still objectionable and to be avoided, are all figurative ways of speaking of consciouness, as a witness (Cousin), a light (Hickok), a dry light (Coleridge), a revealer, etc.

Consciousness is often said to be the source of all our knowledge of the operations of the mind, and psychology has even been called "an inquiry into the facts of consciousness. All that we can truly learn of mind must be learned by attending to the various ways in which it becomes conscious." (Fleming.)

Cultured consciousness, or introspection, is indeed an important source of knowledge in psychology, but not the only one; much may be learned by observation and comparison, and these are important checks upon the errors and deceptions of introspection. John Locke deserves credit for calling attention to this source of knowledge, under the name of reflection. He taught, however, that what we know in consciousness is the operations of the mind, not the mind itself. Among his followers, says President Porter, "it has passed into a positive dogma that the soul in consciousness cognizes the operation only, and nothing besides."

The correct formula is, we know the ego as modified in its changing states, whether of perception or feeling or action, limited by whatever relations. We place the ego first because it is "unchanged and permanent," while the "states are varying and transitory," to quote the words of President Porter, who continues, correctly and clearly: "It is of the very nature and essence of a psychical state to be the act or experience of an individual ego. We are not first conscious of the state or operation, and then forced to look around for a something to which it is to be referred, or to which it may belong; but what we know, and as we know it, is the state of an individual person. . . . The fact of memory proves it beyond dispute." (Human Intellect, 95.)

On the other hand, some have denied the possibility of this philosophical consciousness. Comte dogmatically asserted that consciousness is one state, perception, or feeling another, and two such cannot exist together; an absurdity which every one's experience disproves. Herbert Spencer says "no one is conscious of what he is, but of what he was the moment before." It is a sufficient reply to this, that all other philosophers are agreed to call this kind of knowledge, characterized by the element of past time, by the name of memory, not consciousness; and that it rests on the same assumption with Comte's, that the mind cannot do two things at once, which is entirely gratuitous.

We do not intend to affirm that consciousness is always equally clear and forcible in every act of the mind, nor that it is intuitive in the sense of being incapable of culture. The infant has blurred and inaccurate perceptions and confused feelings, and of course its consciousness is equally blurred, yet real and easily demonstrated. It cannot tell you that it knows the ego from the non-ego, neither can it tell you that it has a pain in its stomach. Yet it knows that the pain is in its own stomach, not in yours; knows that its mother is not the same being as itself; knows, in some dim way, itself as a separate being or entity. Before even this dim state of knowledge arises, we may say that the child has not consciousness in the full sense of the term. "As long as the sensations are confused together, and are not discriminated, . . . the soul remains in this elementary condition of comparative unconsciousness. This is the condition of the infant [at birth]. It is also the condition into which the developed man relapses in swooning, distraction, intoxication, or approaching sleep." (Porter, Human Intellect, 100.)

But as soon as discrimination begins, and the actions are no longer quite automatic, consciousness is real, though its content may be slight and dim. The philosopher, accustomed to introspection and familiar with abstract terms, can argue better about himself, and describe his feelings better than the ignorant laborer; but he is not any more certain of his own identity, more sure that it is he himself, and not another, who experiences all his sensations.

Even the brute, though he cannot express any distinction between the ego and the non-ego, has consciousness more or less developed. The dog knows whether you whip him or another dog, knows whether it is he or another dog that has a bone. In the lower orders of the animal creation it is not easy to say how far down consciousness can be traced, but we may say confidently that it cannot exist where the actions are demonstrably automatic, as in the oyster, etc., noticed under the head of sensation.

"It is probable," says President Bascom, "that sensibility to physical pain and pleasure, and the appetites, were the first mental facts to appear in consciousness. . . . This also is the order of development in human life. The infant enters on a conscious activity first through the sensibilities, the appetites, and is trained for months in this school. . . . But the appetites must almost immediately be supported in consciousness by the special senses. . . . . There seems to be good ground to believe that consciousness arises slowly with the increase of that unity in the nervous system which puts it under the control of a single center, gathers the senses about that center, and knits the organic life as closely as does consciousness our intellectual activity; . . . that consciousness becomes the specialized function of the cerebrum, from a previously weak, vague, and confused form. . . . . . The clearest proof of consciousness in doubtful territory is memory. This faculty is the basis of experience, and not till it has been obtained can the facts of consciousness, if any are present, be organized into knowledge. The action of memory is also more readily discriminated from automatic action than is the conscious from the unconscious use of the senses." (Comparative Psychology, 180–188.)

Recent observations by Sir J. Lubbock, Kirby and Spence, etc., go to show that the intellect of the insects, ants, bees, wasps, etc., has been greatly overestimated, that memory is almost lacking to them, and hence consciousness must be dim and vague, and those actions which seem so wonderful, almost entirely automatic.

Philosophical consciousness, or careful introspection, is as capable of culture and improvement by education as any other power of the mind. "Men differ more widely in respect to the energy and effect with which they use this power than in respect to any other." (Porter, Hum. Int., 87.) By directing the attention to the various elements of perception, the object, the sensational process, the element of self, we learn to observe ourselves, the action of our senses and minds.

The uncultured consciousness does not distinguish between mind and body. To the child or the savage his self is his body, with all the powers he has, mental and physical; and when he has the feeling, "it is I who perceive this object," he has no notion of an immaterial self, distinct from the body. Socrates is represented by Plato as going through a long explanation, and asking many questions, before he can make the distinction between the two kinds of ego clear even to his grown-up pupils. After many comparisons, such as that of a shoemaker's knife, and a shoemaker's hand, as equally instruments, he at length extorts an apparently unwilling concession of the point.

Under religious and moral instruction especially, the feeling may be very early aroused; but it is essentially an acquired one, a product of the cultured consciousness. We are conscious of self as the subject of thought, feeling, and action. If we have not learned that thought is not a function of the body, or that the soul is a distinct entity from the body, then consciousness cannot present to us such an ego.

Some strange opinions concerning the ego have been held by philosophers, in their anxiety to carry out preconceived theories. Mr. J. S. Mill held that the mind is a series of sensations and feelings. But he was compelled to admit that it must be conceived as a series of sensations which is aware of itself! Such a mind would be like a string of beads without any string. Again, on reaching the subject of memory, Mill saw the impossibility of explaining it without a person or entity of some sort to be the continuous subject of a continuous action, and frankly declared that memory was the final inexplicability which he could not manage on his system. The nature of self will be more conveniently discussed when we come to speak of the soul.

AUTHORITY OF CONSCIOUSNESS.

Consciousness is necessarily the court of final appeal in all matters that come within its range. "The facts of consciousness are the most certain of all facts. The objects which consciousness presents are, if possible, more real and better attested than the objects of sense. . . . We may doubt whether this or that object be a reality or a phantasm, but we cannot doubt that we doubt." (Porter, Hum. Int., 115.)

The difficulties which arise about this matter turn on false assumptions as to what consciousness can do, or false reports of what it really does, or else are mere verbal disputes. If an insane man tells us that he is conscious of being made of glass, he is mistaken; but he would be equally mistaken if he said that he was conscious of being made of flesh and blood and bones. No such subject comes within the range of consciousness. If a man tells us that he is conscious that two straight lines cannot enclose a space, we reply, it is impossible, and it would be dangerous to admit such language, for it opens the door to endless dogmatism. The mind has no organ for truth, though it has command of certain tests by which truth may be tried. When the mind is conscious of being in a certain state, of receiving certain sensations, or experiencing certain feelings, there can be no reasonable doubt about the truth of it. But some abnormal condition of the body or mind may have originated the state or impression. The insane man is conscious that his limbs feel hard and smooth, like glass, to him. He is right, but his perceptions originate in his own mind, dominated by a "fixed idea." The mathematician has an immediate perception that two straight lines cannot enclose a space; but what he is conscious of is the perception, not the fact.

One of the most celebrated dicta in the history of philosophy is Descartes', "*Cogito, ergo sum.*" It was intended as a refutation of absolute skepticism. Whatever I doubt, I cannot doubt that there is something which doubts and thinks; to do so is to destroy the doubt itself and render all reasoning impossible. When Descartes was asked to explain his dictum he substituted for *ergo, scilicet, c'est-à-dire,* showing that this is the correct interpretation of his words. "In consciousness I am confronted, not with a thought, but with a being. Whatever else may be unreal, whether idea, phantasm, or speculation, this acting and suffering self is a reality, not a mere phenomenal as contrasted with a transcendental ego, nor an ego inferred or suggested, but an ego directly known to be." (Porter, Human Intellect, 99.)

UNCONSCIOUS PERCEPTION.

An interesting question arising in connection with the subject of consciousness, is the extent to which mental action may be unconscious. The phenomena called by Dr. Carpenter "unconscious cerebration," and by Sir W. Hamilton "latent modifications of consciousness," will be discussed under the head of Association. We have already seen under the head of Sensation that some writers use the term "sensation" of impressions which are entirely automatic, and do not appear in consciousness, but the more general and better usage is against this.

In some cases, however, the point may be a doubtful one. When a student, absorbed in his book, does not notice the clock striking in the same room, he afterwards, in some cases, recalls having heard it. In such a case he may have had the sensations, occasioned by the sound, at the time, but, attention being intently directed elsewhere, no perception was formed, and the sensations were automatically recorded. More probably, however, the supposed remembering of the sound is an imagination, a phantasm, suggested by the fact being learned that the clock really has struck. Some remarks made under the head of Attention are applicable to this point.

Sir W. Hamilton applies the term, Unconscious Mental Action, to the elements of compound sensations. For example, the roar of the ocean at a distance is made up of the noise of many waves, each one of which, by itself, is inaudible. Hamilton contends "that they produce a certain modification, beyond consciousness, on the percipient subject." But no proof can be given of such a view. It is far more probable that each impulse by itself is too weak, in compound sensations, to affect the sense-organ.

Psychology "is unable to advance any proof of unconscious elements or processes in the human mind. Such proof is, indeed, in the very nature of the case, unattainable." (Sully, Pessimism, 192.)

USES OF THE TERM CONSCIOUSNESS.

A subjective division of consciousness has been adopted by President Porter, into two kinds, natural or spontaneous, and reflective or philosophical. But these are really different stages in the cultivation of introspection, and are not distinct enough to deserve separate mention as different kinds of consciousness.

An objective division may be mentioned, into, first, the feeling of self as a necessary element in perception, and second, the knowledge of the mind and its states, of the mind as modified.

Sir W. Hamilton used the term consciousness sometimes in the usual sense, a knowledge of the mind and its states, sometimes in a wider sense, as "a comprehensive term for the complement of our cognitive energies." He says that "consciousness and immediate knowledge are terms universally convertible." He extends the term consciousness to knowledge of the external world, and says "I am conscious of the inkstand." Worst of all, he does not strictly adhere, in all cases, to the same meaning of the term throughout the same argument. The extended use of consciousness as equivalent to knowledge, he probably derived from the German word "bewusstsein," which denotes, as President Porter remarks, rather a be-knowing, than a with-knowing, and is commonly used to mean knowing in general. It is not too much to say that Hamilton lent his great influence to confuse the nomenclature of philosophy in English on this important topic, by thus teaching the duality of consciousness.

Mr. Herbert Spencer also uses consciousness as equivalent to knowledge. He also speaks of being conscious of space, of time, and of motion, and even says in one place, "we are scarcely at all conscious of the space behind us." He also calls dreaming "sleep-consciousness." This use of the term has some advantages with reference to space and time, but it is better to call these necessary elements in perception than to say we are conscious of them.

Dr. Cocker carries this confusion still farther by making two cross-divisions, each threefold. He divides consciousness subjectively considered, somewhat as President Porter does, into spontaneous, representational, and reflective; objectively into knowledge of self, of the world, and of God.

The terms Christian consciousness, and God-consciousness, have been borrowed from the German by some writers. In place of the latter term, "intuition of God" is in better English usage, and even better expresses the real meaning of the German; "necessary idea of God" is also frequently used in this meaning.

NECESSARY ELEMENTS OF PERCEPTION.

I. Space.

We have seen, when discussing the senses separately, that through sensations of sight, under certain conditions, we know external objects as extended in two directions, as having surface-extension; and that through sensations of touch and muscular motion, under certain conditions, we know objects as extended in three directions, as having solidity. This obviously introduces a new subject, that of Space, which we could not delay at that point to examine, and whose importance demands separate treatment.

The question what space is in itself, belongs to metaphysics, and we shall only discuss it so far as it is incidental to our present purpose.

As to the cognition of space, two great theories divide philosophers. On the one hand it has been held by the majority that our knowledge of space is previous to all experience of things in space, so that we bring to our perceptions of the external world this a priori concept, or intuitive idea of space. On the other hand, John Locke attempted to show and his followers still hold, that all our knowledge of space is derived entirely from sensations. The first school, holding that our ideas of space, time, cause, etc., are necessary elements of cognition, not derived from experience, are called intuitionalists, a priori philosophers, or various other names of similar significance. Those who derive all these from experience are called sensationalists, experientialists, experience philosophers, etc.

John Locke's polemic against intuitive ideas had great force against the crude way of viewing the subject at that time in vogue, and has resulted in a change of the entire situation. It is no longer held by the intuitionalists that the mind is equipped with ready-made knowledge previous to experience, nor that this knowledge springs up in completeness on the occasion of the first experience; but these principles are generally considered, with more or less clearness and consistency, to be conditions of thought, formulas or categories under which the mind acts, necessary or primary elements of cognition. To this point we shall return.

It is often overlooked, however, by the intuitionalist philosophers, that our objective knowledge of space as a quality or relation of actually existing bodies, is a product of experience. On this point Sir W. Hamilton has suggested a useful distinction. He says that space is known a priori, extension a posteriori; that is, the term extension should be applied to space as filled by bodies, or measured by the distances between bodies, while the term space should be reserved to mean an eternal condition of the existence of the material universe, the abstract something which makes these concretely-known relations possible. It would be well if the terms could be used in this way, but the attempt so to restrict them would be hopeless, especially as so many recent writers purposely confound the two, and attempt to reduce all space to extension.

When we begin our mental life we first learn the space-relations of the objects close about us; then the parts and furniture of the room and house; then the trees, houses, etc., objects which we see from day to day; next cities, mountains, seas, the globe on which we live. The moon, too, is comparatively easily reached by this space-construction, its distance being easily comparable with those which we have already learned. Thence we ascend to the planets and the stars, where, for any real understanding, we must use a new standard of measurement, no longer miles but diameters of the earth or of its orbit. Thus we "place ourselves" in the universe, and learn our space relations (extension-relations.)

But on the other hand the experience-philosophers overlook the most important point, that not a single object can be perceived as extended, not a single distance can be compared or estimated or imagined, not a single step taken in this process of so-called generalization, which does not involve space as an element in cognition. If I see a tall and a short man together, I cannot tell in what the difference between them consists, unless I have at the time of comparing them, in and with the act of comparison, and as a kind of category which I apply in that act, a knowledge, in my mind, if not in words, of bigness or size. So, if the points of a pair of compasses are placed upon my skin, not too near together, so that the two sensations are exactly alike except in place, I could not know that this is the particular in which they differ, if I had not, in and with my double sensation, some cognition of what difference in place depends upon, that is, space. So, also, if I look upon a colored object and feel around it with my eyes, following its outline by rotation of the eyes, I perceive the points and parts of the object as extended, that is, under space-relations, implying, as before, some cognition of space.

It is not meant by this that in the process of perception space is perceived as a third thing, different from self and the object, yet known by the senses. We do not see, hear, smell, or feel space; it is not sensible, but intelligible, knowable by a direct, inexplicable act of the intellect. When an object is perceived at all it is known under this relation, a space-relation.

Nor is it meant that the mind clearly distinguishes, and says to itself, "I know this object as in space, and I know space;" this is the end of mature reflection, not the beginning of perception.

The reason why our perceptions of material objects are thus conditioned is that the objects themselves exist under space-relations, and cannot exist in any other way. It is impossible for us, while in this semi-material state of being, to conceive any other kind of existence, that is, not under space relations. We cannot imagine to ourselves a pure spirit, that is, one without parts or distances, existing outside of all space-relations. Nor can we imagine space as infinite, but when we remove its boundary in thought, another forms itself beyond.

Space may thus be said to be a necessary form of all our perceptions, and may even be said to be a form latent in the mind, by which it knows the external world; for the mind does not, at first, consciously and explicitly recognize space as a separate entity, but nevertheless cannot think the material world without it; much as one cannot speak without grammar, even though he does not know what the word grammar means. The knowledge of space may thus be said to be a priori, in the Kantian sense, that is, prior to experience, because it is implied in the very first experience of the actual world; it is a condition of experience, logically antecedent, though practically simultaneous; the mind has an aptitude, a capacity for knowing objects in this way, a necessary, innate power of perceiving things under this form, and in no other way, because things actually exist under this form and in no other way.

It has been held by many philosophers that space has no real existence by itself, but is a mere relation among objects, or a product of the mind. Leibnitz taught that space "is only the order of things coexisting, as time is the order of things successive." Mr. H. Spencer, if we understand him correctly, adopts the same view. He says:—"The idea of space involves the idea of coexistence, and the idea of coexistence involves the idea of space." (Psychology. II, 201.) But space cannot be the mere sum or abstract of the relations of things, or the mere order of things, for it is that which makes all these possible; "the principle, without form, order, or relation in itself, which makes possible an infinite number of forms, orders, and relations of things." (Lotze, Dictate Metaphysik, §51.)

Kant taught that space is ideal, a mere subjective form imposed by the mind on things. In this view;—"The idea of space has no objective validity, it is real only relatively to phenomena, to things in so far as they appear out of us; it is purely ideal in so far as things are taken in themselves, and considered independently of the forms of the sensibility." (Fleming, Vocabulary of Philosophy.)

Herbart taught that space is an idea, necessarily arising in every mind from the conflict of other ideas. (Lotze.) But all ideal deductions of space, says Lotze, "smuggle in the specific quality of space (spatialness, räumlichkeit) among the abstract concepts out of which they deduce it, though it is the very thing to be deduced." (Dictate, Metaphysik, §55.)

Since Kant's time some form of the ideal theory of space has been held by nearly every German philosopher. But this theory of what space is in itself is not a necessary result of Kant's theory of the cognition of space. He was, rather, forced into this position by his arbitrary assumption "that there is no correspondence between things as they really are and things as they appear to us. . . . We can admit the positive portion of Kant's theory, then, namely the a priori cognition of space and time, without accepting the skeptical doctrine which he has needlessly and unreasonably appended to it,—the doctrine, that is, that space and time in themselves are unreal, and illusions." (Bowen, Modern Philosophy, 279.)

The reality of space and time rests on the same basis as all the ultimate principles of knowledge,—namely, necessity. We cannot think of matter without space, or events without time, any more than we can think of a plurality of objects without number.

Sir W. Hamilton says that Kant has demonstrated the a priori nature of space, to the conviction of every one capable of understanding the subject. We accept this with the limitations suggested above. We prefer the formula that space, subjectively considered, is a necessary element in perception, and objectively considered is a necessary condition of the existence of matter.

Lotze has endeavored to escape the difficulties of the ideal theory by holding space to be a product of the inner states of things or elements. These elements act upon one another and upon us by virtue of their inner states; which actions cause them to be related to one another as though in space-relations, and to appear to us in the same way. "According to the common view space *is*, and things are *in* it; according to ours, things *are*, and there is nothing between them, but space is in them." (Dictate, Metaphysik, §55.) This is evidently only a refinement of Leibnitz's doctrine that space is a relation of matter. It also ascribes occult, if not supernatural, powers to the atoms of matter.

A real definition of space is impossible. All the so-called definitions are either synonyms or but partial descriptions. If we say that space is a condition of all material existence as extended, this is mere tautology, for "extended" implies space. If we leave out the word "extended," we have no definition of space, but a fact, perhaps the most important one, about space. Space, like force, life, motion, is a word which is incapable of further explication.

Many striking remarks have been made about space, which really do nothing toward defining it. Dr. Clarke held that space is an attribute of the Deity. Sir Isaac Newton was charged with saying that space is the sensorium of God. Lotze said that a blind man's space, (not merely his knowledge of space), is different from the space of those who can see.

A curious speculation has been indulged in some quarters, that space may have more than three dimensions, and "m-dimensional space" has become a not-uncommon phrase. This theory evidently depends upon the doctrine that space is ideal. If space is a real thing, or even a real relation between real things, all directions and distances can be reduced to three co-ordinates. Lotze, though himself holding to a modified ideal theory of space, answers this notion of m-dimensioned space conclusively. "The relations of things which such minds," (namely those minds to which space has more than three dimensions,) "would perceive, would be entirely different from those which we observe. Such an intuitive form would have no similarity to our space, and it is only by an illogical play with conceptions that it can be called any kind of a modification of our space-intuition." (Dictate, Naturphil. §31.)

The exposition of the abstract relations of space constitutes the science of geometry. The discussion of the postulates of geometry belongs to metaphysics.

The above doctrine concerning space receives strong confirmation from the phenomena of dreams. In dreams the perceptions through which we generally cognize space being absent, space-relations are wanting to our thoughts. We spend an hour climbing a familiar stair-way, and then suddenly find ourselves transported to a distant city, with no sense of incongruity. We leap over a wall, but cannot step over a gutter. The somnambulist can walk over roofs and cliffs, because, his sight being dormant he has no perceptions of the depths around him, and so his equilibrium is not disturbed by fear, and he is guided by the sense of touch. Blind persons often exhibit the same strange security.

Our view of space, both objectively and subjectively, is also confirmed by what is known of the lower animals. They evidently have empirical knowledge of space; that is, they perceive objects under space-relations, and adjust their actions to those relations. Yet they have no intuition of its abstract relations, and no power of constructing a geometry. The hare and the dog both know which is gaining on the other, whether the distance between them is increasing or diminishing, and the perceived fact automatically produces eager impulses and intense exertions. But neither knows that a straight line is the shortest distance between two points, or that velocity must be measured in terms of space and time; nor has either any capacity of acquiring such truths. The lowest intelligences, however, which are capable of perceiving objects at all, have plainly the power of perceiving them under space-relations.

"There is no more mystery," says President Bascom, "in the animal's fitting his action to spaces without distinctly considering them than there is in man's doing the same thing. The apparently voluntary movements of the animal are as automatically co-ordinated to spaces as are its stages of digestion to the length of the intestinal canal." (Comparative Psychology, 231.) . The adjustment of our own actions to space-relations is also to a great extent automatic, either originally or by long practice. When we throw a stone or strike with an axe, space-relations are necessary conditions of the action, and some latent cognition of space is implied in the perceptions concerned. But abstract reasoning about space, or the dis covery of its abstract properties, or the description of the cognition or intuition of space, are things which only the philosopher has within his reach. They are unintelligible to the uninstructed man, the brute has no capacity even of acquiring them.

"These truths, instead of being the first which are consciously possessed and assented to, are the last which are reached, and by only a few of the race are ever reached at all. . . . . The mind must be exercised to some extent in philosophical studies before it can comprehend their import and application." (Porter, Human Intellect, 502.)

II. Time.

Time and Space are usually spoken of together, and are indeed inseparable in experience. We can only measure each by the other. Yet time, as an element in perception, does not resemble space either in itself or in the method of our knowledge of it. Time has been called the form of our inner experience, as space is the form of our outer experience. But it is involved in all our experiences, and especially in memory. Perception, as we have seen, takes place by means of discrimination, and discrimination implies a succession of impressions and succession involves time.

The schools of philosophy differ concerning time precisely as they do concerning space. The empirical philosophers teach that time is a generalization from observed succession of events. This is true of our empirical knowledge of time; we learn to know a minute, a year, a century, and in this knowledge time, space, and motion are inseparably connected. When we say: "I can run so many yards, or repeat so many words in a minute," we mean, " I can do this while the clock-pendulum swings a certain number of times," or use some similar standard of measurement, thus comparing times with motions and with times, and the subjective succession with the external one.

But the possibility of knowing these successions as such, and of making these comparisons, is the very thing to be accounted for; and we could never perform these mental actions, if we had not some native endowment in correspondence or congruity with the nature of things, beyond the mere ability to perceive one thing and then perceive another. To know two events in succession and compare them, requires consciousness and memory; but memory is knowledge of the past, and hence the first act of knowledge involves some obscure knowledge of what time is, or at least some action of the mind under the category or form of time.

Kant taught that time, like space, is a form which the mind imposes on the events which it knows, empirically valid, but in itself an ideal existence only. The difficulties of this theory have been noticed under the head of space. Lotze attempts to escape these by denying that events are necessarily successive. He says that our ideas (presentations, vorstellungen) of events are necessarily successive, and so we get an irresistible impression that the events themselves are in succession, that is, under the form of time. (Dictate, Metaphysik, §57.)

But this is only ingeniously begging the question; no reason why events are successive to us can be assigned, except that they are really in succession. When we cognize a change in any object we know it as having a beginning and an end, and the parts in irreversible order, so that those which are last cannot be known as first. To say that this is a form imposed by the mind, and the events are not really, perhaps, in succession, is entirely gratuitous.

Time has an onward flow, and can never run up stream, but must always run onward. This we know directly, and this is the intuition or a priori cognition of time. Our impression that events, when known, are real, and real in the succession as known, is irresistible and correct. Our estimate of the proportion of comparative time may be distorted by disorder of the brain, or by defect of perception, as in dreams, but such facts only render plainer the fact that time remains through all, a real relation, an eternal reality. The contrary cannot be proved, but is merely assumed by the ideal philosophers.

That time is not ideal is shown by the following considerations:—

1. We have decided that space is real, and, if so, time cannot be ideal. The same arguments apply for the most part, and the connection of the two is so intimate that one alone cannot be ideal.

2. The same event may be perceived by many different minds, and by them known to be contemporaneous with subjective experiences or with other external events; and events are thus irresistibly and necessarily felt to have a common measure of duration, which is capable also of division and comparison, and therefore is objective.

3. Time is, indeed, in one sense, a form or quality of the inner experience of the mind. But this experience is conditioned in the main by external events, and is directly known to be so. When our experience is not controlled by constant impressions from the outside world, but runs its own course, as in dreams, all proportion of time-relations is lost, though the general intuition or concept of time remains. In a dream we

seem to be an hour crossing a street, and no longer time in crossing the ocean. De Quincey, in his opium-reveries, seemed to live a hundred years in an hour. A long dream is often interpolated between a sensation which awakens us and our awakening, though to an observer the awakening seems instantaneous. Time then must be real, since the mind is ordinarily dominated by events in this regard, and when it is not so, its experience becomes fantastic and irrational.

4. Memory, the most inseparable quality or power of mind, requires and implies time.

5. The lower animals exhibit phenomena of the same order with reference to time, though incapable of idealism or abstraction. A dog, if you strike him several times knows that the blows are not simultaneous. He knows time-relations in physical events, and knows nothing about time beyond these. "By no one fact," says President Bascom, "is the intellectual progress of man from the animal to the rational plan of life more clearly indicated than by the length of the periods he takes into consideration in his daily conduct. It is difficult to induce the savage to put forth exertions which provide for wants beyond those of the hour; while the civilized man is only too much disposed to forecast the wants of remote years, and weigh down the present with the work of providing for them." (Comparative Psychology, 234.)

Like space, time is incapable of being defined. The definitions usually given are tautological or incomplete. If we say;—"Time is that which makes events possible as successive," this is mere tautology, for succession is the very thing to be explained. If we say;—"Time is an idea or form in the mind," it cannot be proved that it may not be this and also something more. We cannot define time or space "because the very attributes which we must employ imply both. . . . Every object and event has properties or attributes which imply the existence of these entities. In knowing that these objects exist, we know that time and space exist as their actual conditions." (Porter, Hum. Intellect, 566.)

Aristotle defined time to be the measure of motion. Dr. Reid said;—"We may measure duration by the succession of thoughts in the mind, as we measure length by feet and inches, but the notion or idea of duration must be antecedent to the measurement of it, as the notion of length is antecedent to its being measured."

Dr. S. Clarke said;—"Space and duration are immediate and necessary consequences of God's existence, and without them his eternity and ubiquity would be taken away."

"Sir Isaac Newton maintained that God, by existing, constitutes time and space." (Fleming.)

Schopenhauer has with great ingenuity drawn up a list of axioms showing the curious parallelism between space and time, in twenty-eight pairs. We select a part of them from Professor Bowen's translation. (Modern Philosophy, 179.)

1. There is but one time, and all times are parts of this one. Space, the same.

2. Time cannot be thought away, but everything in time can be thought away or imagined as non-existent. Space, the same.

3. Time has three divisions, past, present, and future. Space has three dimensions, length, breadth, and thickness.

4. The present moment is without duration. The mathematical point is without extension.

5. Time makes arithmetic possible. Space makes geometry possible.

6. The indivisible (single) of arithmetic is the unit. The indivisible (single) of geometry is the mathematical point.

7. Time has no beginning or end. Space has no limits or boundaries.

8. Time has no rest. Space has no motion.

9. Time itself has no duration, but all duration is *in* it. Space has no movement, but all movement is *in* it.

10. Movement is possible only in time and space.

11. Time is everywhere present. Space is eternal.

12. Time in itself is empty or void, being perfectly indeterminate. Space, the same.

13. Time makes the change of attributes possible. Space makes the persistence or unchangeableness of substance possible.

14. We know the laws of both a priori.

Time cannot be seen, felt, or heard; it is intelligible, not sensible, is known directly, like space, by an inexplicable act of the intellect.

III. Cause.

When our perceptions are conditioned by our own activity, not merely moving the organ to receive the sensation, as in sight and touch, but actually creating the condition of the sensation itself, as in the case of muscular resistance or pressure, a new element is here introduced; the consciousness involved is different from what we have previously discussed. When we undertake to lift, or move, or compress any heavy or hard object, we receive from it muscular sensations due to its weight or solidity. But we also have a sense of effort put forth, a feeling of voluntary power, quite different from any consciousness involved in any other class of sensations. And, especially if we succeed in moving the object, there is a feeling that our voluntary effort has done something, has made a change in the external world, has exhibited power of efficiency, in a word, has become a cause. Cause, then, is a necessary element in some of our perceptions.

But this is not all. The idea of causation necessarily and irresistibly arises in the mind on every similar occasion. For example, if I push a book along my table, I know that my hand exerts force, power, efficiency, and actually causes the motion of the book. Now, suppose I roll a ball along the table. Its motion continues after the motion of my hand has ceased; yet I know intuitively, that is, directly and irresistibly, that this continued motion was caused by my hand. Again, suppose that the rolling ball strikes against another ball, and sets it in motion. In this case also I know, intuitively, irresistibly, that the change of state of the second ball from rest to motion, was caused by the first ball, as the motion of the first ball was caused by my hand.

We do not mean that our knowledge of cause is derived entirely from the case of voluntary activity, and then carried over by inference or analogy to other cases. This is an error to which we shall refer later on. But the case of voluntary causation is easier to understand, because a part of the process appears in consciousness.

We affirm that in every case where causation is simple enough to be readily traced, the conception of efficient cause is equally a necessary element of all such perceptions. For example, if I see a croquet-ball moved by a blow from another one, I cannot help believing that the first ball caused the motion of the second. But a good deal of mechanical knowledge is required to trace the motion of a locomotive to the chemical energy of combustion; a child or a savage might well suppose its motions voluntary. Yet when any complicated machine is once understood, we cannot help tracing causation through every one of its parts.

"In our ordinary observation," says Lotze, "it is completely intuitive that a new motion is *produced* by the impartation of motion through a blow or impulse." (Dictate, Naturphilosophie, §17.)

We admit that we cannot perceive the efficient force going over from the cause to the object of its activity, nor explain how it goes over. "The nature of efficiency," says Lotze, "is inexplicable." We cannot hear, feel, or taste causation, any more than we can see, hear, or feel time or space; all we perceive, in the plainest cases, is the cause in action, and the effect. Causation is intelligible, not sensible. But it is not for that reason any the less real. "The concept of efficiency" [*Wirken*], says Lotze, "is indispensable to our comprehension of nature [*Weltauffassung*], and all attempts to deny the reality of efficiency and yet conceive the course of nature [*Weltlauf*] are abortive." (Dictate, Metaphysik, §46.)

This "intuition" is irresistible because it is correct. This "necessary element of cognition" is a law of the mind because it corresponds to a law of the universe; and the mind, if it knows the world at all, must know it as it really is. Just as the mind perceives objects under space-relations because they exist under space-relations.

A cause is an efficient antecedent, or an assemblage of such antecedents (for causes are rarely if ever single), not simply an inseparable antecedent.

But this is not all. Not only is causation real, but it is uniform. The same causes, under the same circumstances, always produce the same effects. This axiom may be considered as a deduction from the axiom that causation is real efficiency, under the operation of the logical principle of identity. Whatever a thing is, that it will of course continue to be under the same circumstances. Whatever efficiency, active force, anything may have, that it will of course continue to have, under the same circumstances. If we see one ball pushed by another we cannot help believing that the first ball exerts actual power on the second, and that it will continue to do so, all things remaining the same; that if the motion of the first continues, the motion of the second must continue also; that if the operation be repeated under the same circumstances, the same results will be repeated.

This axiom is stated by some writers as a second "necessary cognition" or "intuitive idea," parallel with the first. Some also make it universal, referring to all events whatever President Porter, for example, says: "we assert that the mind intuitively believes that every event is caused, that is, every event is produced by the action of some agent or agents." But he directs his argument chiefly toward proof of the reality of causation, and does not keep the two points rigidly separate, but sums up thus: "If it [causality] cannot be resolved into some other relation equally general or more general than itself, we must conclude that it is original, and intuitively discerned and believed." (Human Intellect, 572–73.) This does not discriminate between the two axioms.

It seems to us a decisive objection to this second axiom that it is a statement of a supposed general fact. According to our view of the necessary elements of cognition, the mind acts under them in connection with specific perceptions or thoughts. The mind knows space by knowing a material object under space-relations, because it cannot perceive such objects any other way. But it does not have intuitive knowledge of the fact that all matter exists under space-relations. We afterwards infer that fact as a ground of our knowledge of space-relations. So with causation; when we perceive a simple case of causation, we necessarily know that there is efficient activity being exerted, and that this will continue to be exerted and will produce the same results, under the same circumstances. Our own view is that this is involved in the "intuition" or "necessary idea" of causation as a real, active, efficiency; and that the universality of causation, or the truth that every event has a cause, is an inference on this basis from our experience.

Now it is admitted by philosophers of all schools that our belief in the reality of causation is original and irresistible to primitive thought. But many of them have held that this belief, though irresistible, is fallacious. The whole sensational school, led by Hume, Brown, Mill, and Bain, declare that there is no more in causation than we perceive by the senses; that efficient causation is a figment of the mind; that invariable connection of antecedent and consequent is all that really exists under that name in nature.

"When a spark falls upon gunpowder," says Dr. Brown, " and kindles it into explosion, every one ascribes to the spark the *power* of kindling the inflammable mass. But let any one ask himself, what it is which he means by the term, and, without contenting himself with a few phrases that signify nothing, *reflect*, before he gives his answer, and he will find that he means nothing more than that, in all similar circumstances, the explosion of gunpowder will be the immediate and uniform consequence of the application of a spark." (Lecture 7, p. 68.)

Similar words might be quoted from many other writers. But the common-sense of mankind rejects the theory as inadequate and idealistic, and will never accept it. Such skepticism will always be confined to philosophers, and even among them it is far from universal. Those who are not driven by the exigencies of a pre-assumed system, generally admit that the human mind is in some kind of correspondence with the universe, so that its normal action with reference to things must be correct.

The fact is that Hume, having determined beforehand to account for everything by experience, without any a priori or necessary principles of cognition, and finding the problem of causation insoluble on that theory, was obliged to discharge cause of all its real meaning in order to bring it within the scope of his theory.

So Dr. Brown, in the words of Sir W. Hamilton, "professes to explain the phenomenon of causality, but, previous to explanation, he evacuates the phenomenon of all that desiderates explanation." Their successors have pursued the same easy method. But even Mr. Fiske, the celebrated evolutionist, admits that they have gone too far.

"That matter, as objectively existing, may exert upon matter some constraining power, which, as forever unknowable by us, may be called an *occulta vis*, I readily grant. Thought is not the measure of things, and it was therefore unphilosophical in Hume to deny the existence of any such unknown power." (Cosmic Philosophy, I, 155.)

Writers of this class, however, usually bring back implicitly that which they have explicitly denied and expelled. For they all admit that the sequence of antecedent and consequent is invariable in nature, so that the course of nature can be understood and predicted. Mr. Mill says in his Logic: "To certain facts, certain facts always do and as we believe always will succeed. The invariable antecedent is termed the cause, the invariable consequent the effect."

Now this invariability must have a ground or reason, and no ground for it can be conceived except reality of causation; all attempts to find another ground have failed. We shall refer to some of these attempts hereafter.

Having degraded "uniform causation" to "uniform succession," these writers have sought for another formula for the ground of induction, the final axiom of all reasoning, and have found it in the phrase "uniformity of nature." Professor Bain declares that the uniformity of nature is known intuitively, and makes it the ultimate principle and postulate of all reasoning. Mr. Mill derives it from experience, though he makes it the basis of induction. But by thus leaving out causation from the axiom of causation, they have destroyed its validity. The complete uniformity of nature is by no means intuitively true. "That nature is uniform in her different departments and throughout her domain is by no means an instinctive belief. As intelligent and scientific, man has reached particular uniformities, as of the seasons, of tides, of comets, only after such induction as each case seems to demand. This he has done, not on the ground of uniformity of nature, for the question in each particular case was whether nature would be uniform in that case, but solely on the ground of the uniformity of causation." (Hopkins, Outline Study of Man, 169.)

Mr. Mill, perhaps because his candor and fairness enabled him to see some of the difficulties of this subject which are lightly passed over by others of his school, seems to have fallen into some confusion of thought. Mr. Lewes mentions a remarkable instance of this. "That Mr. Mill was somewhat confused on this point, may be seen in his surprising conclusion that the orbital movement of a planet is not a case of causation." (Problems of Life and Mind, II, 340.) Again, Mill says in his Logic;—" The uniformity in the succession of events, otherwise called the law of causation, must be received not as a law of the universe, but of that portion of it only which is within the range of our means of sure observation, with a reasonable degree of extension to adjacent cases." But the "uniformity of nature" is a very different thing from the "law of causation." In the words of Dr. McCosh;— "The grand metaphysical question is not about the uniformity of nature, but about the relation of cause and effect."

On the subjective side of this theory, namely its method of accounting for our belief in causation, we find these writers generally agreed in attributing it to association.

Hume bluntly calls it the result of use and custom. Dr. Brown admits that there is an "original principle of our nature," which he calls "intuitive expectation," and that we believe in the causal connection of two events if we see them occur together only once, not merely from custom, but that the association is immediate and original.

Mr. Mill derives the belief by induction, and denies that it extends further than induction carries it. "In distant parts of the stellar regions," he says, "where the phenomena may be entirely unlike those with which we are acquainted, it would be folly to affirm confidently that this general law prevails." But he bases induction in the last analysis on inseparable association, and so does not differ essentially from Hume.

We may perhaps admit that association and induction are competent to account for the idea of causation as these writers understand it, mere invariability of succession in nature, without prejudicing the argument for real and uniform causation. And it is not always easy to determine in which sense the term causation is used by them. What they attempt to account for by association, however, is the instinctive belief, which they declare to be fallacious, in the reality of causation.

The association-theory on this point is open to a similar objection with their theory of space. It overlooks the most important point, containing the real thing to be explained, that every one of the experiences from which they say this belief is derived, really implies its existence in full force. If we see a ball move after being struck by another ball, the belief that the first has caused the motion of the second and would do so again in like circumstances, is just as irresistible on the first occasion as after a thousand repetitions.

Dr. Brown, indeed, escaped this difficulty, but since he denied the reality of causation, he was left in the position of affirming an intuitive principle of our nature, and yet denying its validity, a contradiction which should lead to universal skepticism; for if the very powers of the mind are fallacious, all knowledge and all reasoning must be impossible. Or rather, if any philosopher declares that the faculties on which and with which he has built his system are deceptive, he can claim no value for the system.

Causation, then, subjectively considered, is a priori in the sense that it is a power and an irresistible tendency in the mind to cognize objective causation on proper occasion, as real and uniform; a congruity in this respect between the mind and the universe.

"A careful analysis of the causal judgment, as it is styled, reveals the fact that it is not a necessary inference, but a positive affirmation of a fact. Its true test is self-evidence, and nothing but a perceived fact can be self-evident." (Professor Ormond, Princeton Rev., 1882.)

And Mr. Lewes says;—" All believe irresistibly in particular acts of causation. Few believe in universal causation; and those few not till after considerable reflection."

It may also be truly said, in a certain sense, that our knowledge of causation is derived from experience, for it is only in and through experience that we know anything about it, and when we say that causation is universal or that nature is uniform, we are generalizing from experience.

We have said that our knowledge of what causation is, as involving real efficient power, is derived from or rather given in our own sense of voluntary muscular exertion. Some writers, especially the Frenchman, Maine de Biran, have attempted to show that our belief in the reality, necessity, and uniformity of causation, is derived by inference and induction from this subjective experience, that is, our volition. But this theory is open to the following objections.

(1) Induction itself must rest on some axiom not derived from experience; namely, as we shall show in the proper place, the axiom that causation is uniform, which is either a part of the "causal judgment" or an immediate deduction from it. But the theory professes to account for this very axiom by induction. (2) This theory, if adopted, is inevitably pushed to the conclusion that all causation is spiritual and there are no

material causes; that matter has no inherent forces; hence that there is but one agent in the universe, the Creator, who causes all events directly and voluntarily,—conclusions almost universally rejected by philosophy as well as common sense.

(3) Muscular exertion, or "volition," is a case of physical causation, and subject to the "causal judgment," the "intuition" of the reality and uniformity of causation, as much as any other. If I roll a ball against another, and the second ball is moved, I have an "intuition" or "necessary judgment" that the motion of the second ball is caused by the first, and that the motion of the first ball is caused by my hand, and that the motion of my hand is caused by myself, *ego;* how the motion passes over through the series is unknown. The only difference between the cases is that in one the process is given partly in consciousness and partly in perception, in the other it appears only in perception. The spiritual principle of volition or "choice," has nothing to do with either. This runs up into a higher realm, and introduces to us a new kind of causation; where the effect is a spiritual state and the cause an inexplicable act of personal will.

Some celebrated theories concerning causation demand a brief·discussion. Sir W. Hamilton has discussed the theories of causation with his usual learning and vigor. He has made a list of eight possible theories; but as (according to President Porter) the division is more ingenious than correct, we do not copy it. His own doctrine is derived from that of Kant, and is too abstruse to be given fully here, but belongs rather to metaphysics. According to this view, when an object is presented to us, we necessarily know it as existing, and cannot conceive of it as non-existent in the past or the future; yet we know from experience that it did have a beginning in its present form. It is impossible to conceive either the beginning or annihilation of any part of the complement of existence possessed by any object. "But to say that a thing previously existed under different forms, is only in other words to say, that a thing had causes." (Metaphysics, Bowen's ed., 554.)

It is evident that this doctrine of the constancy of the sum of existence, either in the universe or in one object, is a vast assumption. It is only another form of one of the latest and most sweeping, not to say most doubtful, of the inductions of modern science. (See Bowne's Metaphysics, 107.)

Again, this theory assumes, as Hamilton expressly declares, two intuitive ideas or forms of thought, existence and time. It also requires the principle of the impotence of the mind, and the law of the conditioned, "the law that the conceivable has always two opposite extremes, and that the extremes are equally inconceivable." If causation really exists in nature, it is far more simple and natural to suppose that it is intelligible, knowable by the human mind directly.

Hamilton's own "law of parcimony," otherwise known as "Occam's razor," "which forbids, without necessity, the multiplication of entities, powers, principles, or causes," cuts down his theory of causation. It is simpler to assume it at once, as a fourth necessary element in cognition, with being, time, and space, than to assume so much from which to derive it.

The most ingenious attempt to explain away the reality of efficient causation is the monadology of Leibnitz. This theory, indeed, was intended to explain also the union of soul and body, the nature of animal and vegetable life, and all the other mysteries, physical and theological, of the universe. A monad, according to Leibnitz, is one of the ultimate elements of existence, either physical or spiritual; a supersensual entity, neither a pure, hard atom, nor a mere idea, nor an immaterial spirit, but partaking of all three natures. These monads were created by the Supreme Power all different, and each one endowed with active force. "The Deity conferred upon his creatures from the first a certain measure of efficiency, which is the ultimate principle of all the various phenomena that they produce." Hence the career of each monad is predetermined, and it pursues its own course from the beginning, with the appearance of exerting and receiving efficient activity, but without the reality of it.

Monads, on this theory, are of different orders, corresponding to different orders of being, from a stone to a human body and soul. In a crystal, or a plant, or an animal body, there is a governing monad, or one which is said to govern, because "all the others act together harmoniously, *as if* they were directed by one central power." In the lower orders sensation and thought are latent, "in the human soul they rise to full consciousness."

This strange mixture of physics and metaphysics seems too fantastic to be seriously offered as an explanation of causation or of the relation between soul and body, and is indeed no longer so put forward. But it contains some very remarkable anticipations of recent scientific theories. It rests on the doctrine of continuity; each monad pursues its career without a break; there can be no leaps or sudden transitions in nature. "What is called the uniformity of physical law is never broken." But this is equivalent to modern evolutionism. Again, the recent doctrine of heat as a mode of molecular motion presupposes molecules like Leibnitz's monads, full of spontaneous, active force. And Darwin's "cell-gemmules" and Herbert Spencer's "physiological units" are only Leibnitzian monads of a higher order. "They are now held up as the most advanced results of inductive science, or, if you will, as the supposed limits or goals, toward which the sciences depending on observation and analysis are tending and preparing the way. But to the eagle-eyed thought of Leibnitz, they were necessary deductions from the single axiom, first propounded by him as dominating the universe of existing things, the principle of sufficient reason." (Bowen, Modern Philosophy, 118–125.)

"Pre-established Harmony" is the phrase which describes Leibnitz' substitute for causation.

Another celebrated theory to account for all things, and especially the interaction of bodies with one another, and of mind with matter, is that of Monism. This is the doctrine that all real being is one, and all apparently separate entities, or elements, or atoms, are but manifestations of this being "which alone is self-existent, and in which all things have their being. . . . This being, as fundamental, we call the infinite, the absolute, and the independent. In calling it the infinite we do not mean that it excludes the co-existence of the finite, but only that it is the self-sufficient source of the finite. In calling it the absolute, we do not exclude it from all relation, but deny only external restriction and determination. Everything else has its cause and reason in this being." (Bowne, Metaphysics, 131.)

Lotze (whom Professor Bowne follows rather closely), says that it is impossible consistently to conceive of interaction between two elements which are independent of one another, self-existent. "The states of a cannot go out to b, and *vice versa*. . . . If action at all is to be made to seem possible, this assumption of the self-existence of things must be utterly denied. . . . And this can only be accomplished through the assumption that all individual things are substantially one, . . . that they are from the beginning modifications of one single being, which we provisionally designate by the names, the Infinite, the Absolute. . . . Action between two finite beings is thus only apparent, not real. In reality the Absolute acts upon itself." (Dictate, Metaph. §48.)

This theory is evidently at the opposite pole from that of Leibnitz, and incurs the danger of lapsing into pantheism. In this extreme form its most celebrated modern supporters have been Spinoza, Schelling, and Hegel. Many, however, profess to hold it in a sense consistent with the personality of God.

Aristotle divided causes into four kinds, a distinction often referred to in philosophy, and with which the student should be familiar. They are (1) material cause, or that out of which anything is made; (2) formal cause, or the form, idea, archetype, or pattern of a thing; (3) efficient cause, or the principle of change or motion which produces the thing; (4) final cause, or the end or purpose for which a thing is made. (Fleming.)

Efficient cause, the third in the order above, is of course that which we have been discussing. The fourth, final cause, or design in nature, must be briefly noticed.

TELEOLOGY.

The doctrine of final causes, or design in nature, commonly called Teleology, has been the subject of much discussion in recent years. Formerly, nearly all philosophers held that the adaptations found throughout nature, by which the parts of the universe minister to one another, working together in a chain of causation, are proof that the scheme of things has been planned by intelligence as well as upheld by power.

"I had rather believe," said Lord Bacon, "all the fables in the Legend and the Talmud and the Alcoran, than that this universal frame is without a mind. . . . For while the mind of man looketh upon second causes scattered, it may sometimes rest in them, and go no further; but when it beholdeth the chain of them, confederate and linked together, it must needs fly to Providence and the Deity." (Essay 16.)

In more recent times, the progress of physical science, introducing the conceptions of law, uniformity, development, and evolution, has weakened the belief in design, and has been supposed to weaken the argument for it. Indeed, some scientific men have undertaken a polemic against the teleological conception, which they have carried on in a spirit that has merited and received the name of "teleophobia."

No doubt there have been some crude statements of the theory of design in nature. Sometimes the whole universe has been subordinated to human interests, and sometimes a specific purpose has been assumed, such as a mere display of power, or the pleasure of the Creator, in creative action. But "it is especially necessary that those who oppose teleology should deal with its scientific [well-reasoned] forms, and should not waste their attacks upon forms which have never kept up with the advance of the investigation." (Euken.)

A correct statement of the doctrine of design is not at all affected by the progress of science, the extension of the realm of causation, or the hypothesis of evolution. But rather, the more all natural events are seen to be joined together in a single scheme, the more wonderful does that scheme become, and the more the mind "must needs fly to Providence and the Deity." The old view of nature saw in it a number of separate kingdoms, and a series of separate creations. The modern view, after extending the boundaries of each one of these kingdoms almost indefinitely, joins them all in a vast unity. But the vastness of this unity, does not, as some seem to suppose, make it self-existent, without an intelligent design or Cause; nor does this remove it from human thought any further than before.

Teleology has nothing to do with efficient causation, but belongs to a higher sphere of thought. The positive argument for design in nature, as for the existence of an intelligent, personal Creator, belongs to Natural Theology.

IV. Identity and Similarity.

The fact was mentioned in introducing the subject of sensation that the activity of the mind in sensation is a discriminating one. The very process by which an impression becomes known to the mind, that is, becomes a sensation in the full sense of the word, is a change in consciousness, in other words a conscious change in the sentient organism. But this implies two states, not identical but different, and either similar or dissimilar; involving not only an impression occasioned by some object, but a knowledge of something about that impression.

"We know that if the idea of red and at the same time the idea of blue are excited in the mind, the two do not combine to form the idea of violet. . . . Every comparison, especially every relation between two elements, presupposes that both points of relation remain separate, and that a representing activity passes from one to the other, and the mind becomes conscious of the change which it experiences from the idea of a to that of b. We do this when we compare red with blue, and there arises the new idea of qualitative similarity which we ascribe to both. If we see at the same time a strong light and a weak one, we do not have the sensation of a single light which is the sum of both; but both remain separate, and, passing from one to the other, we are conscious of another change of state, a quantitative more-or-less of the same impression.

"Finally, if two exactly similar impressions are separately made upon us, they do not blend into a third; but because we compare them as before and in the transition from one to the other find no change of state, there arises in us the new idea of identity.

"These new ideas which we may consider as of a higher order, are by no means resultants of the interaction of the original simple ideas, as in mechanics a third motion is compounded of two others. The first ideas, as mere impulses, arouse in the mind a reaction, through which arise the new ideas of similarity, identity, and their opposites." (Lotze, Dictate, Psychologie, §21–22.)

These two principles, identity with its inseparable correlative diversity, and similarity with its inseparable correlative dissimilarity, are necessary forms of all knowledge, in its most rudimentary form of simple sensation, or the elaborately combined and associated form of acquired perception. "Saying what a thing is, is saying what it is like, what class it belongs to." (H. Spencer, Psychology, II, 131.)

Simple perception may know an object as distinct from self, as having real being, and as existing under space-relations. But complete perception knows an object as the same or different, similar or dissimilar with others; recognizes it as belonging to a new class, or as a new object hitherto unknown.

This is often called the relativity of knowledge, a phrase which is used, however, in a great variety of meanings. Mr. Mill means by it the doctrine, "that we only know anything as distinguished from something else; that two objects are the smallest number required to constitute consciousness; that a thing is only seen to be what it is by contrast with what it is not." But we hold it self-evident that the mind can perceive one object alone, distinguished only from the ego.

Sometimes the relativity of knowledge means the doctrine that we can only know objects so far as they are related to our faculties, and so far as we have faculties of knowledge. This no one will deny, but it should be called, as Dr. McCosh suggests, "the limited knowledge of man," not "relativity."

Sir W. Hamilton applies this name to the Kantian doctrine that we can never know the ultimate reality of things, the thing-in-itself, but only phenomena, which phenomena may, for all we know, be partly due to the action of our minds. This is sheer assumption. The thing-in-itself, apart from its phenomena or attributes, is not only unknowable but impossible. We do know the true reality of an object, through its qualities, so far as we know it at all. Again, "To suppose that in perception or cognition proper we mix elements derived from our subjective stores, is to unsettle our whole convictions as to the reality of things. By assuming this middle place between Reid and Kant, this last of the great Scottish metaphysicians has been exposed to the fire of the opposing camps of idealism and realism." (McCosh, Defence of Fundamental Truth 234.)

The last-mentioned meaning of "relativity of knowledge" is probably the most common one, and the most appropriate. But some writers confuse this meaning with the one first mentioned, and it would be well if so ambiguous a phrase could be banished from philosophy.

Many writers also confuse the application of the principles of identity and similarity, to sensation, as being a change of consciousness, and their application to perception, as a cognition of an object that is different from self, and similar or dissimilar with other objects. The distinction is a clear one and is worth making.

These principles are necessary laws of intelligence, so far as we can know anything about intelligence in our present state of being. Accordingly we find that the minds of the lower animals act under the same conditions. If you strike a dog several blows, he knows that they are not all one and the same blow. There are involved here, then, time, number, and identity-diversity. If the dog sees you or any one else pick up a similar stick on another occasion, he knows this stick is like the other one, and expects the like pain, which he runs away to avoid. His knowledge may be merely association, but it involves the principles of similarity and of self, just as truly as the feelings of pain, fear, and hatred.

In short, all sensations and perceptions which take place in a material organism and give knowledge of material things, take place under the relations of identity-diversity or similarity-difference; which, therefore, viewed in connection with the mind, may be called categories, or a priori concepts, or intuitive ideas; and viewed in connection with things may be called relations. (The word relation, however, is often used in a quite different meaning, as when gravity is said to be a "relation" between two bodies.) Not conditions of the existence of things, but conditions of things as related to us. We call them, with space, time, and cause, necessary elements of cognition, but do not assign precisely the same origin or scope to each.

Professor Bain has founded his entire system on these principles. "The primary attributes of intellect are (1) consciousness of difference, (2) consciousness of agreement, and (3) retentiveness. Every properly intellectual function involves one or more of these attributes and nothing else." (Mental Science, 82). He elsewhere defines agreement by similarity, and uses the term identity, while he develops "retentiveness," into the power of association. He strives, with great ingenuity, to show how, with these, the whole structure of knowledge is built up.

We have seen reason to believe that he has but little success in accounting for space, time, or cause, as subjective principles. But it is especially to be remarked as an important inconsistency in this scheme, that it really assumes original and necessary principles just as truly as the opposite theory, which Bain so vigorously combats. The only difference is that it does not assume so many of them.

The question in what identity consists, has received a good

deal of attention. Different kinds of identity have been distinguished; as identity of a stone or any inorganic substance, of a tree, an animal, of a person. It is plain that identity of an organized being cannot consist in absolute sameness of material particles, for these are constantly changing; besides, a tree may lose many of its branches and leaves, and yet be the same tree, and a man who has lost an arm or a leg is still the same man.

John Locke held that identity in plants and animals consists in continuance of the same organization, and that life consists in that organization in which all the parts minister to one another. (Essay, Bk. II. C. 27, §4.) This comes very near to the modern doctrine that "the phenomena of living bodies can be explained by the mechanical and chemical forces belonging to matter." It also approaches the modern definition of an organism as "a structure in which all the parts are mutually means and ends."

Personal identity is still more difficult of definition. Consciousness, in connection with memory, testifies to the reality of personal identity, and declares that the subject of past experiences is the same with the subject of present memory and present experience. "As the knowledge of personality is given in consciousness, that of personal identity is secured by the aid of memory." (Calderwood.)

Locke makes personal identity to consist in consciousness. But this is insufficient, as is shown by the extravagances into which he is led by it. For he says: "It must be allowed that if the same consciousness can be translated from one thinking substance to another, it will be possible that two thinking substances may make but one person." . . "But if it be possible for the same man to have distinct, incommunicable consciousness at different times, it is past doubt that the same man would at different times make different persons." He also argues that if we suppose two distinct consciousnesses acting in the same body, one by night the other by day, the day-man and the night-man would be two as distinct persons as Socrates and Plato. (Essay, Bk. II, C. 27, §23.)

The fact is, everybody knows by his own experience what is meant by identity, though nobody can define it or say exactly in what it consists.

The relation of Similarity is capable of analysis, and has been divided by Mr. Herbert Spencer, and provided with a characteristic nomenclature. His disciple, Mr. John Fiske, states it as follows. Similarity and dissimilarity are divided into: (1) "cointension and non-cointension, as when we perceive that two sounds are equal in degree of loudness," or that two temperatures are different; (2) "co-extension and non-co-extension, as when" the color of an orange is recognized as accompanied "by sweetness and not by viscidity;" (3) "connature and non-connature, as when greater warmth is mentally assimilated to less warmth, but distinguished from blueness or roughness." (Cosmic Philosophy, II, 118.)

General Remarks on the Necessary Elements of Cognition.

Next to the theory of vision, that department of psychology which has made the greatest progress is this, the doctrine of "a priori concepts," "intuitive ideas," or, as we prefer to call them, necessary elements of cognition. It is also to be noted that this is the border-land between psychology and metaphysics.

The doctrine of "intuitive ideas" was vigorously assailed by John Locke. But the mode of the attack, and also of the defence, shows how ill-reasoned, vague, and incorrect were some modes of thought current at that time, and, indeed, not wholly unknown even at the present day.

One of the so-called intuitive truths on which Locke spends his strength most freely, is the fact that a thing cannot be and not be at the same time. To the modern reader this proposition, however true, seems of a very different rank. For it is plainly a logical rule, amounting to this, that contradictory attributes are not to be predicated of the same subject. Locke proves that the rule does not exist consciously and formally in the mind of the ignorant, the child, or any but a philosopher; which is not at all the same thing as proving that they do not think under the rule, when they think correctly.

The argument for the a priori cognition of space, time, and cause, as at present understood, is not affected by Locke's reasoning. He himself, moreover, in the positive, constructive, part of his Essay, tacitly assumes principles of thought which are called a priori or intuitive by more modern and more systematic writers.

Locke's polemic was of vast importance in philosophy, and was in a sense completely successful. But, far from settling the question, it led the way to better definitions, more careful thought, and deeper study. The two schools still keep up their traditional opposition, but each has partly shifted to the other's ground, and sensationalism must be said to have lost the battle.

The more recent empirical philosophers, who consider themselves the special followers of Locke, have attempted to account for space, time, and cause, subjectively considered, without admitting any necessary or a priori elements of cognition. We have already examined this attempt in connection with the subjects of causation and space.

It is important to notice that writers of this school, while denying intuitive ideas, yet rely upon some principles of thought which are really of the same order. Professor Bain not only, as we have seen, admits a knowledge of identity and similarity as original to the mind, but also declares that the uniformity of nature is an innate principle. "We can give no reason, or evidence, for this uniformity, and, therefore, the course seems to be to adopt this as the finishing postulate. And undoubtedly, there is no other issue possible." (Logic, 671.)

Mr. Mill cannot perhaps be quoted so specifically to the same effect; but in his Logic his statements are often qualified by such phrases as "it is more rational to suppose," and "with a reasonable degree of extension to other cases." And "the observant student notices that in the most important portions of his discussions he is ever and anon introducing, with a *naïve* innocency of bearing, at once refreshing and irritating, under the names of 'belief,' 'persuasion,' 'natural prompting,' and the like, the very a priori, universal, organic, rational, and recreative element, which he would exclude, and which he then seeks to make it appear that he has deduced, either strictly, or, in his phrase, (a strange phrase for a logician to employ) 'as far as any human purpose requires,' from pure observation and 'objective,' physico-psychological 'experience.'" (Morris, British Thought and Thinkers, 325.)

Mr. Herbert Spencer recognizes the impossibility of accounting for these principles by association alone, and advances the theory that they are the product of association and inheritance combined. This has been called the "psychogenetical hypothesis," by Mr. Lewes who speaks of "inherited intuitions," and "laws of thought registered in modifications of structure which have been transmitted from parent to child." But this theory does not escape the chief difficulty of the theory of association pure and simple. It only gives a longer time for association to work in, and does not at all show how it can have any power at any time to evolve a necessary principle of thought. What is to be accounted for is not the concrete knowledge of space, time, cause, etc., but the fact that the mind cannot help acting under these forms and categories in perception and thought, even in the lowest stages of mental life.

"In the contest over this concept, the question is not about something known previous to experience. . . . Just as little do we dispute about a something ready-made in the mind, for we recognize here only a striving activity. . . . But we discuss as the main question, not only of philosophy, but of all science, and of psychology especially, the fact that in mental activity something essential, original, and legitimate is recognized. It shows that one is behind the times in his knowledge of modern philosophy, if he presents the dilemma whether knowledge is furnished ready-made in the mind or is created from without, for he thus leaves out of consideration the question to the development and defence of which the most prominent thinkers of the last century have devoted their strength." (Euken, Fundamental Concepts, translation, 90.)

Association can do nothing to account for these principles of cognition, thus received and defined, even though it be prolonged backward through the endless ages of evolution. The limits of association were tacitly admitted by Mr. Mill when he admitted that on that basis two and two might possibly equal five.

In short, there is no safe ground between the bold sensational theory of Condillac, which resolved all states of the mind into sensations by simply calling them such, and a reasonable recognition of a necessary element in thought and perception; "for Hume did certainly show that a consistent empiricism must become sensational, and Kant, that experience, in Locke's sense, involves a multitude of a priori elements." (Bowne, Metaphysics, 508.)

On the other hand, the so-called a priori school have greatly changed their ground since the time of Locke, made important concessions and introduced valuable distinctions. The more recent method is thus expressed by President Porter. "While these truths stand first in the order of thought, they are last to be reached in the order of time. This implies that we are, in some sense, indebted to experience for their acquisition. It is equally clear that experience does not give them authority." (Human Intellect, 504.) First unconsciously but necessarily used in concrete perception and thought, they are afterwards abstracted and generalized into laws or principles.

It was formerly the custom (and some traces of the custom still remain), to treat these principles all in a lump, assuming that they are all alike in origin and nature. We have shown above how, in our opinion they should be treated each by itself. We append a table of these principles, with the connection in which each is first exercised and known.

1. Being, or substance, or real existence;—Through any perception that gives knowledge of the external world. We spoke of this under the Qualities of Matter.

2. Self;—Through any mental activity. We spoke of this under Consciousness.

3. Space;—Through any real perception involving voluntary exertion.

4. Time;—Through the series of states of consciousness.

5. Cause;—Through resistance and the perception of action.

6. Identity and similarity are relations conditional to all knowledge.

Of the others which are frequently enumerated, number and quantity need no exposition, and are merely relations of objects; right belongs to ethics; the infinite and the absolute to metaphysics; the idea of God to theology; the idea of beauty to esthetics.

It will have been noticed that we are not satisfied with the usual names applied to these principles. The term "intuition" is objectionable because it has come to have a vague and semi-mysterious implication, as though intuition were a short road to knowledge, a superhuman way of attaining to truth. It is true, however, that the real meaning of the word intuition is not open to the same objections. It means, "immediate knowledge, direct perceiving or beholding of an object or principle" (Calderwood); "the immediate affirmation by the intellect, that the predicate does or does not pertain to the subject, in what are called self-evident propositions." (Hamilton.) The corresponding German word (Anschauung) is constantly used, since Kant, to denote perception under the forms of time and space. "Intuition," therefore, is a word liable to misunderstanding at best.

The term "a priori concept" has some evident advantages; but these principles are active in cognition long before they become concepts at all, which, indeed, they need not do to be useful, but only to become authenticated. The term "idea" is too vague and uncertain for use in philosophy, and has never recovered from being overworked by John Locke.

The term "principle" is perhaps without serious objection; but the phrase "necessary element" seems to suit better our view that the mind operates under certain conditions, some of which are imposed upon it by its intimate connection with a physical organism, some by the nature of the objects of its knowledge, and some by the nature of all thought.

Sir W. Hamilton has enumerated no less than twenty-three different names which have been applied to these principles by different writers.

IS THERE A "REGULATIVE FACULTY?"

Since the time of Coleridge it has been common among English writers to use the name of Reason for a supposed faculty of producing "intuitive ideas." Sir W. Hamilton employed the term Regulative Faculty.

If our analysis has been correct, this theory of a special faculty is untenable and unnecessary. The mind in each of its kinds of activity must act under certain conditions, and must evolve whatever products the conditions and objects of its activity require. When the mind knows an external object, it knows it in space, and cannot know it otherwise. There is no need of a special faculty to produce the space, nor is space a product of the mind, but a necessary condition of material existence, and hence inseparable from preception. So the mind when it judges, must judge according to the relations of identity and similarity, and can judge in no other way, for these are conditions of all judgment.

To find out what these principles are, and distinguish them, and show their universality, is the work of generalization and analysis, exercising the various other powers of the mind.

If any one affirms that he is conscious of forming these ideas or applying them by a special faculty, we can only say that we can detect no such power in ourselves, and, according to our theory, it is unnecessary.

CRITERIA OF FIRST PRINCIPLES.

We need some standard or rule of judgment by which to decide what principles are entitled to places on our list. It has already been intimated that the chief criterion is necessity. The intellect is "constrained by the spontaneous workings of its nature to receive them as true." (Porter.) It is not meant by this that their reality and validity are never denied in terms, but that those who deny them and try to disprove them, make use of them in the very process of their reasoning. Nor are these principles used only by philosophers. As all who speak at all must speak according to some kind of grammatical rules, even though they do not know what grammar means, so all who think or perceive must do so under the forms, laws, or categories appropriate to each act, whether they can or cannot define and describe them. Few reach that speculative stage where these principles become definite, generalized concepts, and most who do so are pledged to one school or another long before reaching so advanced a stage of thought. But "we are justified in appealing from the philosophy of men to their words and actions. What all men inadvertently confess in their casual assertions, what they imply in the very form of their language, . . what is assumed in all investigations and reasonings without the attempt to give any reasons for its truth,—these are all taken [by us] to be or to involve universal and necessary truths of Intuition, however difficult it may be to define them correctly, to reconcile them with the dicta of a received philosophy, or to show their place in any order of systematic arrangement." (Porter, Hum. Intel. 510.) We have applied this method of reasoning, to some extent, to the doctrines of Mr. Mill and Professor Bain.

We have attempted to show in discussing each of these principles that it is a necessary principle, and we judge that to be the only and sufficient criterion. Many writers, however, have laid down three or more criteria. President Porter gives three, universality, necessity, and logical dependence and originality. Dr. Cocker gives five, self-evidence, originality, simplicity, necessity, and universality. Sir W. Hamilton lays down but one, which he calls by the double name of universality and necessity, and says that it was first proved by Leibnitz. It is evident that necessity alone is sufficient if it can be proved; also that universality can hardly be susceptible of complete proof, though an approximation to such proof would go far to raise a presumption of necessity. Various other criteria are thus useful for proving necessity, and may be called tributary to the one true and sufficient criterion, necessity.

DOCTRINE OF PERCEPTION.

We are now in a position to state our view of perception in a connected way, with the proper limitations and distinctions.

The lowest and simplest form of mental action is sensation. Note the term, *mental* action. Some writers hold that sensations are impressions, which combine themselves, transform themselves, interpret themselves, evolve out of themselves not only knowledge but consciousness. We hold that the simplest sensation is an act, a function, and implies an actor, a subject; that knowledge pre-supposes some one who knows, who has interpreted sensations into knowledge under the necessary forms and categories of thought.

A sensation requires an ego as a condition of its existence, and involves a knowledge or feeling of this ego. Some writers use the term sensation in a narrower sense, to denote only the impression of the sense-organ, and say that we are conscious of our sensations, or unconscious of them, as the case may be, and that having a sensation and knowing that we have it are two different things. This use of the term is objectionable.

The method of sensation is discrimination between different states of consciousness, implying the action and the validity of the categories of identity and similarity.

It is probable that the adult mind never experiences a simple sensation, wholly separate from others and unaccompanied by associative suggestion. Our simple sensations become firmly connected with one another and with various ideas, interpretations, feelings, imaginations, etc., so that when they are repeated, or even when similar ones are experienced, a great deal of knowledge is revived or suggested by association, beyond that which is conveyed directly by the single sensation in point. This is called acquired or cultivated perception.

When the sense-organ is voluntarily moved or modified to

adapt it to the object, as in rolling the eye or moving the fingers, simple natural perception of the external world takes place. We perceive it directly, under the category of being, by an inexplicable act of the mind, as something real, existing outside of us. This is the true meaning of the term substance. What the object is in its qualities, what its properties are, we learn by interpretation of the sensations occasioned by it.

We also, in this kind of perception, know the external object under the form of space, under space relations, as existing in space. "External world" means, normally, objects external to the particular sense-organ; and the other parts of the body are at first perceived and explored just the same as other objects. Later on in our experience a distinction is established between the body and the rest of the external world.

When we exercise or resist force we recognize self or the moving object as a cause; that is, we know it as the cause of the change which has occurred, in addition to perceiving it as being and as being in space; and we know this cause not as mere succession, but as actual efficiency acting uniformly. Some writers hold that our belief in causation as real efficiency is a result of long-continued association. But they also hold that real efficiency is a delusion, that there is no connection of events in nature but invariable succession.

THEORIES OF PERCEPTION.

We shall now briefly describe some of the more noted theories of perception, in the historical method. But some preliminary remarks and definitions will be necessary.

A distinction must be drawn between the metaphysical part of a theory of perception and the psychological part, though they are in practice inseparable. The psychological part has been more backward in development, and has indeed been for the most part a late product. It is only in recent times that light and sound have been correctly understood, and hence a correct doctrine of the most important sensations has been beyond the reach of all but very recent philosophers. Indeed, the psychological part of perception may perhaps be all brought under the theory of vision. It has even been said that "theories of sense-perception are to a great extent theories of vision." (Porter.)

The sense of sight is so complicated, involving not only a special sensibility to light and color, but so many different kinds of muscular sensation, that it presents for study a wonderful combination of phenomena, optical, physiological, and mental. Accordingly, since the true theory of vision has been established and almost universally accepted, many important questions concerning perception may be regarded as settled.

But by the term "theory of perception" is usually meant, theory of the knowledge of the external world in perception. This has been in dispute among philosophers from the earliest times. How mind can come into contact with matter, how knowledge and thought arise in consequence of the presence of an external object, how much the mind contributes and how much the object,—these difficult, probably insoluble questions, constitute the metaphysical part of a theory of perception.

The solution of these questions has always been seriously affected by the condition of philosophy at the time, the reigning metaphysical and theological dogmas of an age usually permeating all its speculations.

A preliminary classification of theories is necessary. These fall into two great classes, theories of immediate or presentative perception, and theories of mediate or representative perception. This distinction refers to the psychological process, not to the physical one; to what goes on in the mind, not what goes on in the air or the ether or the nerve.

Immediate, presentative, or intuitive perception denotes a

direct knowledge of the object in perception. This object, however, may be held to be either real or ideal, a real external object according to the natural belief of men, or a subjective ideal object, a phenomenon in or of the mind. Those who hold the object to be externally real may be called realists, as believing in a material, external, extended object; or natural realists as holding the natural, primary opinion concerning the external world; or natural dualists as opponents of the theory of monism or absolute identity.

Those who deny the reality of the external object may be called idealists as opposed to realists, or as believing in nothing but ideas; or monists as believing in the absolute identity of the subject and object, the unity of the universal essence.

Idealists, again, may differ in various ways, holding that the mind and the object are both ideal, being correlated phases of the same essence; or that the mind is the author of all its own perceptions; or that all perceptions are infused in the mind by the immediate act of a supernatural power.

These two theories, natural realism and idealism, are, says Sir W. Hamilton, "the only systems worthy of a philosopher; for, as they alone have any foundation in consciousness, so they alone have any consistency in themselves."

The representative theory of perception may be said to be a mixture of the other two. Those who hold to it believe in the reality of the external world, yet deny that we can know it except by inference. They may thus be called cosmothetic idealists, or hypothetical realists. They all hold that the object in perception is not the external object itself, but a representation or idea or image of it in the mind. Obviously the source and nature of this image may be the subject of various subsidiary hypotheses.

Sir W. Hamilton has drawn out these distinctions to the last degree of tenuity. (Philosophy, Wight's ed., 264. Metaphysics, Bowen's ed., 352.)

HISTORICAL SKETCH.

It is important for the student to gain some acquaintance with the greatest names in philosophy and their relative greatness and position. Hence our sketch, though necessarily very brief, will not be confined strictly to theories of perception.

We pass over the earliest Greek philosophers, about whom little is really known.

PLATO, (429-347 B. C.) the greatest writer and thinker of antiquity, was not a system-maker, and it is not easy to decide from his dialogues what his real opinions were. He made a distinction between two kinds of knowledge, that of the senses, which he held to be illusive and untrustworthy, and that of the intellect, which he held to be certain, lofty, and rational. He has been called an idealist, but that is on account of his doctrine of ideas, and not with reference to his doctrine of perception; for he taught that sensation is a joint product of the action of the external object and the sentient agent. He did not, however assign a definite part to each of these elements in perception.

Plato is remarkable for the beauty and versatility and dramatic power of his style; for the vast range of his intellectual activity; for his surprising anticipations of modern discoveries and theories; for his insight into moral and religious truth, and his firm belief in the unity and goodness of God; and for his wonderfully stimulating power over many of the finest minds in all subsequent ages.

ARISTOTLE, (384-322 B. C.) made advances in the knowledge of the operation of the senses, especially vision, in which he approached wonderfully near to the modern theory that vision depends on the vibrations of an invisible medium. It has always been in dispute, however, whether Aristotle meant that perception is through a corporeal emanation from the object, thus anticipating modern scientific knowledge in the case of sight and hearing,—or that perception is through a mental form, an incorporeal impression, thus anticipating some of the modern representationists.

Aristotle held to a common or general sense, underlying all the special senses, for which some recent writers use, in English, the term "cœnæsthesis." He also taught that imagination (phantasy) pictures and retains before the mind the impressions of sense, thus being a condition of memory.

He opposed reason to sense, teaching "that sense is restricted and individual, thought free and universal; and that while sense deals with the concrete and material aspect of phenomena, reason deals with the abstract and ideal. But while reason is thus in itself the source of general ideas, it is so only potentially"—it requires sense-presentations which it "unifies and interprets." (Wallace, Outlines of Philosophy of Aristotle, 91).

Aristotle is remarkable as the author of the science of formal logic, which has received no substantial improvements since his day; for his interest in every department of physical science and the zeal with which he examined and classified natural objects; for his practical and political wisdom; for the wonderful ascendancy of his influence and the unreasoning deference paid to his authority throughout many centuries of the Christian era, after the re-discovery of his works.

The schoolmen, through the middle ages, for the most part followed Aristotle as closely as they could, though not always understanding him correctly, and being somewhat influenced too, by the less precise, less practical, more poetic spirit of Plato. Being largely absorbed in theology, and having scarcely any more scientific knowledge than Aristotle had possessed they were able to add almost nothing to his psychological doctrines, and could only dispute about "intelligible species" or "perceptible forms." We cannot give space to any of them.

DESCARTES (1576-1650), is commonly called the father of modern philosophy. Putting aside the authority of Aristotle and all others, he doubted everything. "There would have been little merit in such an assumption of independence at a later day, after it had become the fashion; but it was an unprecedented step at the beginning of the seventeenth century." (Bowen.)

His doubt, however, was not that of the skeptic; he did not doubt for the sake of doubting, but in order to test systematically the foundations of truth. "My whole design" he said, "looks to the attainment of certainty." He was "the prince of dogmatists;" his method was dogmatic or deductive, not inductive. He found the first basis of certainty in the axiom, *cogito, ergo sum;* thought, the existence of which cannot be denied, implies a thinker, a thinking being, an ego. This personal existence becomes "the type of all reality, and the measure of all certainty."

He afterwards developed this into a doctrine of innate ideas. But "by innate ideas he does not mean ready-made ideas, complete images or pictures, in the mind of the infant. He means that the mind infused by the Deity into every human body has certain natural predispositions which compel it to adopt certain beliefs, as soon as it begins to reflect and to exercise its faculties. Such are the ideas of God, of substance, of unity, and a host of others, which he never essayed to enumerate." (Mahaffy, Descartes, 165.)

He drew a sharp distinction between matter and mind, teaching that extension is the essence of matter and thought the essence of mind. The mind, finding itself the subject of certain affections called sensations, infers that external objects exist as the cause of these sensations. The body, however, is a part of the external world, a mere machine or automaton, acted upon by the qualities of objects, and undergoing changes which are interpreted by the mind. The medium through which sense-impressions are conveyed to the brain is the "animal spirits," an invisible, imponderable fluid. How these sensations are imparted to the mind he does not explain.

In thus assuming to know the essence of matter and mind Descartes opened the door to vast errors. The logical consequences of such assumptions would be too much for any system to support; and though he himself did not follow them to the end, his followers did so, and soon involved themselves in contradictions and fantastic theories, as we shall see. "There is scarcely a theory of sense-perception," says Pres. Porter, "in which some erroneous assumption of Descartes may not be traced."

He did not teach that perception is by means of representative ideas, but such is plainly the natural outcome of his system, and some of his followers soon began so to hold. He taught that in perception we only infer the existence of an external object, with the aid of habit and association. He did not himself push the natural implications of this further than to say that it is possible to suppose there is no external reality which corresponds to our ideas of matter. But it was not many years before Berkeley arose to make this dogma world-renowned.

Descartes was indeed a truly great man. Besides stimulating and directing several generations in philosophy, he led the way in physics and mathematics, being the originator of the modern application of mathematics to physics, and of algebra to geometry. "We to whom the scholastic theories are things long past, cannot now feel the novelty and the boldness of Descartes' conception, that all nature can be represented in algebraic formulae, and its laws expressed in definite equations." "He swayed not only his followers but his opponents for a whole century; and he gave to certain sciences, especially to optics, to physiology, and to physical astronomy, an impulse which has never been exhausted." (Mahaffy, Descartes, 69, 204.)

His followers in philosophy, accepting his opposition between mind and matter, began to hold that neither could ever act upon the other, and to devise theories to account for their apparent interaction.

LEIBNITZ (1646–1716), is usually mentioned in connection with Descartes, though the interval in time is somewhat great, and Leibnitz lived long enough to reply to Locke, and dispute with Newton the honors of the calculus.

To solve the great problem of body and mind, and other problems as well, he invented his celebrated hypothesis of pre-established harmony, already described. He held that God has pre-arranged from eternity parallel courses of events, so that, although matter and spirit cannot act upon one another, yet "a mode of one always coincides with a mode of the other."

This can hardly be called a theory of perception, but is rather a hypothesis of how to get along without perception.

Leibnitz' great influence in philosophy was chiefly through his metaphysical doctrines. His psychological suggestions were chiefly worked out by his followers, a few of whom we shall mention. But if this wonderful man did little for psychology it is because he did so much for almost every other department of human knowledge. Of him it was said that he drove all the sciences abreast. He shared with Sir Isaac Newton the glory of discovering the infinitesimal calculus, and the notation which he devised was far superior to that of Newton. His theory of monads seems like an anticipation of the modern atomic theory, of Darwin's cell-gemmules, and of Spencer's physiological units. His doctrine of space and time is almost the same with that of Kant. He seems to have seen that heat is a mode of motion, and that space is occupied by an imponderable ether. Matter, he taught, is nothing but force, which is now the latest theory of metaphysical physics. His scheme of optimism, embodied in a theodicy or vindication of the Divine government of the universe, though ridiculed by Voltaire in his "Candide," is celebrated and influential in literature and theology to this day.

He was a statesman, a politician, an instructor of princes, a man living in courts, acquainted with diplomacy, and familiar with affairs.

This brief sketch displays a marvelous genius, perhaps equaled in comprehensiveness by Aristotle alone among the sons of men. If such a man could find no way of explaining the interaction of body and mind but the fantastic hypothesis of pre-established harmony, it goes far to show that this knot, though anybody can cut it, is to be untied by no human mind.

The most immediate follower of Leibnitz was Wolf (1679-1754), who, in a mechanical way, developed some of his master's doctrines into a system of representational psychology. We only mention him as a transition to the next name.

HERBART, (1776-1841), may be called the next in this succession, developing and applying the hints of Leibnitz, though some call him a successor of Kant, to whom he owed much.

He was a very able and extremely ingenious thinker, and his speculations have not received, especially in this country, all the attention they merit. His psychology is derived from Leibnitz' monadology. "The soul is a simple, spaceless essence, of simple quality. It is located at a single point within the brain. When the senses are affected, and motion is transmitted by the nerve to the brain, the soul is penetrated by the simple, real essences which immediately surround it. Its quality then performs an act of self-preservation in opposition to the disturbance which it would otherwise suffer from the —

whether partially or totally—opposite quality of each of these other simple essences; every such act of self-preservation on the part of the soul is an idea. All ideas (representations) endure, even after the occasion which has called them forth has ceased. When there are at the same time in the soul several ideas, which are either partially or totally opposed to each other, they cannot continue to subsist together without being partially arrested; they must be arrested, that is become unconscious, to a degree measured by the sum of the intensities of all these ideas with the exception of the strongest." (Ueberweg, History of Philosophy II, 265.)

Herbart applied mathematics to the discussion of sensations and ideas, to a surprising extent. His philosophy may be called an attempt to combine idealism and materialism.

LOTZE (1817–1881), adopted some of the methods of Herbart, especially the use of mathematics, and certainly reached similar conclusions on many points, though he strenuously denied being Herbart's disciple. Lotze stands very high in recent German philosophy, and is noted for candor, breadth, acuteness, ingenuity, and moral purpose. He was perhaps more nearly a follower of Leibnitz than of any one else. We have already quoted him many times.

We must now ascend again the stream of philosophy to Descartes, and trace the development of his hints in Malebranche, parallel with Leibnitz, and in Locke, who took a decidedly different direction.

MALEBRANCHE (1638–1715), was another who pushed Cartesianism beyond itself. According to him, mind, having no extension, cannot be touched or affected in any way by matter; they are separated from each other by the "whole diameter of being." He accounted for perception by the "vision of all things in God," and this is the usual catch-word of his philosophy. What we perceive is not objects themselves but ideas or representations of objects. These ideas do not proceed from the object, nor are they produced by the mind, nor by the constant action of divine power, but they "exist in God, and human minds behold them there, through their union with him." (Bowen.)

If this be a theory of perception at all, it is plainly one of representative perception, with strong leanings toward idealism and Pantheism.

Malebranche was a great writer. "His writings, which are voluminous, had great popularity and success, for he was one of the founders and masters of ornate and eloquent French prose, the contemporary and rival of Pascal, Bossuet, and Fénélon, and perhaps superior to them all in lofty flights of the imagination, in the wealth and vivacity of his illustrations. . . . Perhaps no other writer, except Plato, suffers so much by cold analysis and abridgment." (Bowen, Modern Phil., 74.)

SPINOZA (1632–1677), a Spanish Jew by descent, whose family, exiled through persecution, had settled in Holland, developed the philosophy of Descartes in another direction. By an obvious step he reduced Descartes' two substances, mind and matter, to one substance with two fundamental attributes, extension and thought, thus becoming the leader of modern Pantheism. His metaphysics has had vast influence in the history of philosophy, but it does not concern us here, and his psychology is not of sufficient importance or clearness to occupy our time. We mention him as displaying the remarkable way in which the suggestions of Descartes were taken up and developed in many directions by the acutest minds of the age.

JOHN LOCKE (1632–1704), is usually thought of as a fine example of English common-sense, from his using common every-day language without technicalities. In this respect, however, his success has not been encouraging, for his neglect of terminology and technicality involved him in obscurity and contradiction, and has caused endless uncertainty and controversy.

The catch-word of his system is, "all knowledge is derived from sensation and reflection." The most important novelty of his great work, the Essay on Human Understanding, was the denial of innate ideas, which occupied the first book, and which was a direct reply to Descartes. His ablest critics hold, however, that he introduces under the head of reflection, those a priori concepts which, in a crude and unphilosophical form, he had disproved at the outset.

"He protests against innate ideas, but nevertheless admits all that Descartes had ever maintained,—viz., that the human mind must infallibly attain certain universal truths in the ordinary exercise of its powers. . . . Though he hardly mentions Cartesian theories except to refute them, his whole essay teems with assumptions taken from the system he decries." (Mahaffy, Descartes, 203.)

By "reflection" Locke is admitted to have meant introspective or reflective consciousness.

By his denial of intuitive ideas he has had an immense influence on subsequent speculation, and the whole modern sensationalist school dates its own origin from him and looks up to him as its great original. J. Stuart Mill calls Locke "the unquestioned founder of the analytic philosophy of mind." Like most of his followers, he misunderstood the doctrine of intuitive ideas, at least in the real intention of its supporters and the more careful statements of recent times.

He assumes that the mind resembles in the first place a piece of white paper, on which ideas are to be written by sensation, in which the mind is passive. But in fact "he finds it impossible to carry out his first fancy of the mind as a purely neutral tint, or as a mere faculty of passive receptivity. . .

. . Mind, for Locke, is like a mirror, conscious of the images reflected on its surface. The images do not explain the consciousness. Accordingly, the 'white paper' theory, so far as it seemed to imply that mind was blankly passive and receptive, and only that, is practically modified in the progress of Locke's inquiries. The 'white paper' turns out to be capable of 'operations,' and to possess 'powers.'" (Morris, British Thought and Thinkers, 196.)

Indeed he made these admissions in such a way that some have claimed them to be his true doctrine. His "prevailing tendency, however, is certainly not in this direction." His admissions are unconscious and his great work has proved a fountain of empiricism and skepticism. Yet it has greatly advanced the truth also by the controversies it has kindled, compelling better definition and statement.

Locke held that the objects of perception are the qualities of matter, the primary qualities being known directly and the secondary through them, the obscure idea of substance being involved. He did not probably hold a theory of representative perception by means of ideas, though much of his language seems to imply this, and he is so understood by many.

Though Locke embroiled himself with the clergy by declaring that the substance of the soul might possibly be material, and by rejecting the usual proofs of the existence of God, yet he was a man of irreproachable life, and a Christian believer.

BERKELEY (1684–1753), is known as the great idealist. Accepting Locke's theory or supposed theory of representative and passive perception, he saw that on this theory matter was an unknown and unknowable something, the occasion of our perceptions, and that it was not only impossible to prove that any such thing really exists, but absurd to impute causation to such an inert, passive unperceived substratum as this "substance," in which the qualities of matter were supposed to in-here. Matter, then, as the substratum of qualities, the cause of sensations, is, he says, an unnecessary hypothesis. Material substance, being an abstract idea, and its qualities existing only in the perceiving mind, the universe can only exist in the mind of the Divine Being, and can have no real separate being of its own. Thus Berkeley did not, as is usually stated, deny the existence of matter, but spiritualized, or idealized it.

Berkeley's positive contributions to the theory of perception have been spoken of under Vision, and their value is inestimable. But his theory has also proved fruitful in metaphysics, having been the source of the whole vast stream of modern idealistic philosophy.

Through Hume he awakened the mighty speculative genius of KANT, who taught that the mind, by a complicated process, constructs its own perceptions, the qualities of matter being relative to our faculties only, and the reality of matter a "*noumenon*," unknown and unknowable. This scheme of cosmothetic idealism, or ideal realism, soon became absolute idealism in the hands of his successors, (the greatest of whom was, Hegel) and was reared into the most extraordinary structure of abstract thought the world has ever seen. Thus philosophy, having made the tour of Great Britain, through Locke in England, Berkeley in Ireland, and Hume in Scotland, returned to Germany, enriched and strengthened, to run a wonderful course in its chosen land.

HUME (1711-1776), the prince of skeptics, applied Berkeley's mode of reasoning to the phenomena of mind as well as matter, and thus produced a system of skepticism the most thorough-going ever framed.

We must now return and trace the principal stream of philosophical tendency from the works of John Locke, namely, that which developed the sensationalistic or materialistic side of his philosophy. He was not a materialist, though he declared that matter might possibly think, and that the soul might possibly be made of matter.

But his doctrine that all knowledge is derived from sensation and reflection received a most unexpected development. It was not noticed that reflection with him was really introspective consciousness, finding or producing a priori concepts or necessary truths, and it was promulgated, on Locke's authority, that all knowledge is derived from sensation alone, that all the faculties of the mind are but transformed sensation and association.

This scheme is called empirical, as deriving everything from experience, a term introduced by Kant; or experiential, a term recently gaining ground (perhaps because the word empirical has another application, namely, to a physician who experiments on his patients, a quack); or sensational, as deriving all knowledge from sensations and all faculty from sensation; or associational, as accounting for the transformation of sensations by the law of association; or materialistic, as not really leaving room for any immaterial soul or mind.

This development of the more obvious and popular side of Locke has been the strongest current in English thought, and was almost the only current of French thought throughout the eighteenth century. A great similarity runs through this whole school of writers.

CONDILLAC (1715–1780), was the chief apostle of this new gospel of sensation in France. He taught that the mind is passive in sensation, that all ideas are but transformed sensation, and yet that bodies are only collections of sensations, being nothing but qualities, without any substratum of real being, and qualities being entirely subjective.

This curious combination of materialism and pseudo-idealism is common to many others of the school, even down to the present time. Huxley propounds it in the crudest fashion.

J. Stuart Mill confessed its difficulties as insuperable and yet adhered to it. Bain attempts to defend it, and Herbert Spencer takes it for granted.

DR. THOMAS BROWN (1778–1820), professor at Edinburgh, was strongly under the influence of this kind of thought. He was remarkable for the eloquence and enthusiasm with which he lectured, and the great popular reputation which he acquired throughout Great Britain and the United States.

Brown was the first properly to distinguish the muscular sensations, from which he derived our knowledge of space and of the external world. Like his school in general he confused sensation and perception and denied efficiency in causation. He had remarkable ingenuity as well as eloquence and great boldness. He was treated with great harshness of criticism by Hamilton, who, of course, had Brown greatly at advantage by his superiority of learning. Hamilton accused Brown of plagiarism; but if the sins of philosophers in this way should be marked, who shall stand? Not even, it is hinted, Sir W. Hamilton himself.

JAMES MILL (1773–1836), is chiefly known now as the father of John Stuart Mill, but his treatise is one of the best of his school, free from the prolixity of Brown, and less intended for the popular ear.

J. S. MILL (1806–1873), a great name in English thought, was not a special student of psychology. His greatest works are his treaties on political economy and logic. His inacquaintance with the history of philosophy led him into errors, and his criticisms of Hamilton were often ineffective. He is very remarkable in psychology for the frankness with which he acknowledged the inadequacy of his own, and his father's system, to answer the great questions of philosophy.

He defines mind as "a series of feelings, or, as it has been called, a thread of consciousness, however supplemented by believed possibilities of consciousness." But he admits that this theory of mind "has intrinsic difficulties, . . . which it seems to me beyond the power of metaphysical analysis to remove." And he adds, "if we speak of the mind as a series of feelings, we are obliged to complete the statement by calling it a series of feelings which is aware of itself as past and future." "The truth is, we are here face to face with that final inexplicability at which, as Sir W. Hamilton observes, we inevitably arrive when we reach ultimate facts." (Examination, I, 262.) It seems plain to us that Mr. Mill made this particular inexplicability for himself, though we admit that there are enough of them in the universe ready-made; but as stated by him it is more, it is an absurdity.

He declares that our irresistible belief in the reality of the external world is a product of association. (I, 237.) He defines matter therefore as a "permanent possibility of sensation. If I am asked whether I believe in matter, I ask whether the questioner accepts this definition of it. If he does, I believe in matter. . . . In any other sense than this I do not." (I, 243.) "The belief in such permanent possibilities seems to me to include all that is essential or characteristic in the belief in substance." (I, 246.) This assumes that the only thing to be accounted for is the power which matter has of occasioning sensations, and also implies a wrong conception of what a sensation is, a false use of the term sensation. Being is thus reduced "to less than its own shadow, namely, only to a 'permanent possibility' (whatever that may mean) of its shadow, projected in the form of feeling." (Morris, British Thought and Thinkers, 330.)

We have referred to Mr. Mill so often in the preceding pages that it is not necessary here to discuss his psychology further.

ALEXANDER BAIN (1818–), Professor at Aberdeen, an associate, disciple, and friend of J. S. Mill, is a voluminous writer on the phenomena of mind. Adopting the associational theory he has very ingeniously strengthened some of its weak points.

He insists upon a principle of spontaneous activity in human nature, which he makes a "primitive element of the Will." This may, perhaps, partly meet the objection against the sensational system, that it makes sensations active but the mind passive.

He teaches that it is natural for man to believe; that we are irresistibly impelled to believe in what we perceive or what is told us, until corrected by experience. The "intuitionist" form of this principle would be that the testimony of consciousness is correct beyond appeal, so far as it goes, and the errors of perception are to be explained in other ways.

He holds to three primitive principles, consciousness of agreement and of difference, and retentiveness; thus implicitly introducing two categories of the understanding, identity-diversity, and similarity-dissimilarity, and surreptitiously assuming, under memory, the principles of Self and Time.

He holds that the basis of induction is a belief in the uniformity of nature; but the only rational ground for such uniformity is reality of causation, which he denies, and the belief in which he derives from experience, having first reduced it to mere succession.

His system thus really rests upon necessary principles of cognition, and so shows, it seems to us, a decided progress in the school, though a progress under the surface and as it were, in spite of itself.

HERBERT SPENCER (1820–), has devoted his life to the elaboration and defence of the theory of evolution. His Psychology is more taken up with the development of nerves in a mass of organized matter, and the evolution of mind out of "nervous shocks," than with psychology in the usual sense.

His theories of the origin and nature of mind will be better discussed later on. His theory of perception makes it involve classification.

"Special perception is possible only as an intuition of a likeness or unlikeness of certain present attributes and relations [sensations] to certain past attributes and relations." (II, 132.) In another place this "intuition" becomes association. "The primary and essential association is between each feeling and the class, order, genus, species, and variety of preceding feelings like itself. . . . A feeling cannot form an element of mind at all, save on condition of being associated with predecessors more or less the same in nature." (I, 256.)

Every perception, he says, implies a judgment, a "saying what a thing is." "And the saying what a thing *is*, is the saying what it is like, what class it belongs to." (II, 131.)

He holds to the immediate knowledge of the external world in perception, "The thing primarily known is not that a sensation has been experienced, but that there exists an outer object." (II, 369.)

He admits that there is a real substratum of material existence, but affirms that this reality is unknown and unknowable The Cosmic Philosophy of Prof. John Fiske is a more luminous exposition of this system than Mr. Spencer's own, and comparatively free from tedious prolixity.

We must now turn to the succession of writers who have opposed both the idealistic and the sensational systems arising from Locke, and who belong chiefly to the school of the so-called Scottish philosophy.

THOMAS REID (1710–1796), Professor at Edinburgh, explicitly reintroduced those "intuitions" which Locke had implicitly assumed, under the authority of common-sense, or the necessary beliefs common to all men. He was a natural realist in his doctrine of perception, though not always clear or consistent. He taught that the mind is active in perception, but did not distinguish between natural and acquired perception.

He is chiefly known to the present generation through the elaborate commentary of his greatest disciple, Sir W. Hamilton, but his services to philosophy were important, though less brilliant and less renowned than those of some lesser men.

SIR WM. HAMILTON (1788-1856), was the foremost in learning and power of all the philosophers whom Great Britain has produced. He left no complete treatises, and his opinions have to be gathered from his lectures to students and his notes on the works of Reid, whose disciple he was in the main. His writings have been gathered up in Wight's "Hamilton's Philosophy," and Bowen's "Hamilton's Metaphysics."

His metaphysical theories were largely derived from Kant. His law of the conditioned he expressed thus: "All that is conceivable in thought, lies between two extremes, which, as contradictory of each other, cannot both be true, but of which as mutual contradictories, one must." To illustrate this he drew up a table of contradictions similar to Kant's antimonies.

In regard to perception, he was a natural realist, holding that we have a direct knowledge of the non-ego, yet there is some dispute whether by the non-ego he meant the qualities of matter only, or matter as being. He insisted on the distinction between sensation and perception, and thus did good service.

We have quoted Hamilton so often already that further notice here is unnecessary.

NOAH PORTER, President of Yale College, may be called the true successor of Sir W. Hamilton. Like him, he has great learning but is not a system-builder. Like him, he is a natural realist but qualifies this position as follows: "In original perception, the object directly apprehended is the sensorium as excited to some definite action." He does not explain, as we understand, how the change is made from perceiving the sensorium to perceiving the object through the sensorium. For he insists that the object in complete perception is not the qualities of matter, but the external world itself, as being. He makes prominent the distinction between sensation and perception, and also that between natural and acquired perception.

He teaches that the intellect is active in "sense-perception;" that sensation is always either pleasant or painful. He distinguishes two kinds of consciousness, and three non-egos. He uses, throughout, the word "soul," where others use "mind."

President Porter's great work, The Human Intellect, is of immense value for reference, and by far the greatest psychological work yet produced in America.

Many other names of great philosophers might be referred to, but we have preferred to select a few of the greatest, in the hope of impressing upon the student, (1) That philosophy has occupied many of the greatest minds of the race. (2) That its conclusions are of practical importance in life. (3) That psychology is not unprogressive, but advances from age to age in the definiteness of its problems, in the clearness of its conclusions. A vast deal of vagueness and obscurity has been dissipated, and men know, at least far better than of old, what they are disputing about. Moreover, on some topics, as the sense of sight, substantial unanimity has been reached; while on others great concessions have been made by the principal schools.

PART II.
REPRESENTATIVE POWER.

The representative power may be defined as the power which the mind has of entering into conscious states which are similar to its former states or to combinations of them. It is best treated under the heads of Memory, Association, and Imagination.

I. MEMORY.

Memory has by some been subdivided. Sir W. Hamilton divides it into three separate powers, called Conservative, Reproductive, and Representative. But of these three the first two are only auxiliary to the third, and by themselves useless, even if really existing.

It would be of no use to preserve knowledge if it could not be reproduced, that is, brought up again by the unconscious power of association; it would be of no use when thus associated, if it could not be represented, that is, brought fully into conscious possession. Moreover, the way in which retention takes place is so wholly unknown, and so entirely out of consciousness, that it is a gratuitous assumption to say that there is a separate power of the mind for this purpose.

It is better then to use "retention" or "retentiveness" of the simple capacity of not forgetting, which is not an *act* of the mind at all.

The word "memory," if used in psychology, ought probably to be restricted to this meaning. "Recollection" and "reminiscence" are commonly used of the act of recalling any fact formerly known, by means of association, and are generally defined as voluntary reproduction. But strictly speaking there is no such thing as voluntary reproduction; all we can do is to set in motion the automatic, unknown machinery of association, and wait for it to produce the result.

Memory, in the full, complete sense, or Recollection, implies four things. (1) A state of consciousness in past time. (2) The return of a representation of that state to consciousness, not exactly the same state itself. (3) The intuitive knowledge that this new state is a representation of something past, involving the element of time. (4) The recognition of the past state as having belonged to the same ego, involving the element of self.

Some would place between the first and second another condition of recollection, namely the retention of some trace or sign of the first state by which it may be recalled. But of such a trace we really know nothing. All we know is that we experienced a certain state, and when a proper stimulus occurs, starting the right train of association, a representation of that state appears in consciousness. but not the state itself.

It is taught by some recent writers that memory is a reproduction of the same state, only weaker. This is an error. We insist upon the self-evident fact, that the state of mind called memory is not the same in kind as that called presentation, or perception, or any original experience, but is a representation, as different from presentation as the "idea" of a tree is from a tree, or the picture of a man from a man.

It is often stated by recent writers on the subject that memory is the renewal of past sensations and the ideas they have excited. But memory does not reproduce sensations. If a sensation be really reproduced, in the literal meaning of the term, it is even then a new sensation, not the same one; and if it be represented, the product is not a sensation at all.

Thus, if you are nauseated on seeing a friend go on board a ship, that is because the sight of the ship, with all the associations of sea-sickness formerly experienced, excites reflex sensations just like the former ones. But they are new sensations, not identical with the old ones; and they are real sensations, not mere representations of old ones. Memory proper has nothing to do with such a case.

If the name of an absent friend is mentioned, and you picture his face before you in the mind, that is imagination, not memory. But neither is it sensation. If the representation of his face becomes so vivid as actually to excite reflex sensations, so that you think you see him before you, that is hallucination, not memory. The number of persons who have imagination strong enough to recall a face so as to paint it, is very small; though very many can compare the image so produced with "memory" (in the popular sense) and decide as to the faithfulness of the picture. It is easier, too, to recall the expression of a face than to picture in the imagination a representation of the features, because the expression is a mental product in the first place.

When we wish to recall a smell, a sound, a taste, etc., we "recall" first the object which produced it, and sometimes the representation excites reflex sensations very distinctly.

It is very difficult to recall a word by the mere sound of it as heard, or the looks of it as seen, if the meaning is unknown. Few can do it at all, and they seem to do it by imagination, reproducing the sound or form of the word "before the mind's eye or ear."

It is the "idea," the mental product, the presentation, which is reproduced in memory, in the form of a representation. If this is strong enough it may excite a reflex sensation, like the original one, not identical with it. The representation of a sensation or group of sensations is imagination, an imaging forth by the mind to itself. (Carpenter, Mental Physiology, 431.)

All the products of the representative power are subjective, thought objects, subject-objects. They cannot be compared with object-objects of any kind; they cannot be described. They may be compared with other subject-objects, sensations, perceptions, emotions, as men may be compared with trees, houses, beasts, birds. But the two classes of objects are incommensurable.

It has been remarked by various writers, including even Hamilton, that the wonderful thing and hard to account for, is not remembering, but forgetting. This remark springs from the physical analogies which have long been common in connection with this subject, and which modern science has not weakened. The memory used to be compared to a receptacle, a casket; to shelves and pigeon-holes. At the present day we hear much of nerve-vibrations, of traces left in the brain, of permanent combinations of brain-cells, etc.

No doubt there must be some physical machinery of memory, as there is of sensation and emotion. Physiology and pathology have done something, and may do much more, towards tracing out the process in the brain, and explaining the mechanical part of the problem. But if all this were made as plain as the optical part of vision has been made by modern science, this would not go one step toward solving the real difficulty of the case, namely, how a trace in the brain can be transmuted into conscious memory, or how permanent connections of brain-cells can appear in consciousness as associated sensations or "ideas."

The problem is the same which confronts us in studying sensation. If we can no more tell how a nerve-thrill can occasion a state of consciousness than how the Djinn appeared when Aladdin rubbed his lamp (Huxley), we are equally unable, of course, to tell why a trace in the brain should occasion a representation of consciousness, and why a connection of such traces should cause ideas to adhere together, or why the decadence of such traces should cause disappearance of these representative states. The question of forgetting is no more difficult and no easier than that of remembering, and both are utterly inexplicable.

Many of the facts, however, which tend to show the dependence of memory on the brain, and which are relied on to explain memory by some writers, who are forgetful of the above considerations, are very curious and instructive.

Disease affects the memory most strangely. In the delirium of fever, an ignorant woman once repeated long passages of Hebrew which she had heard many years before, and of which she had never understood a word. Many foreigners, long settled in America, having nearly forgotten their native tongue, have been known to return to its use on their death-bed. Dr. Scandella, ill with yellow fever, spoke on the first day French only, on the second English only, but on the day of his death only Italian, his native language. (Ribot, Diseases of the Memory.)

Sir Henry Holland, when overcome with fatigue at the bottom of a mine in Germany, forgot the German language completely; but it was restored to him by rest and food. Sir Walter Scott, having composed his romance of Ivanhoe in illness, could not afterwards recall a single incident or character in it. A person has been known to forget, after a violent illness, all his acquired knowledge, which however returned to him instantaneously, some months afterward. After a severe injury to the head, the patient usually forgets not only the accident itself but all events which occurred within several hours previous. A well educated man, after an attack of fever and ague, lost, it is said, all knowledge of the letter f. (Winslow.)

Somnambulists often remember during one fit of somnambulism what they did, or suffered, or where they hid articles, during the previous attack, but cannot so remember in the intervening time.

It is quite certain that there are different kinds of memory, corresponding to the different kinds of mental aptitude, or to peculiarities of sensation. Some persons, nearly idiotic, have had a wonderful memory for words. Some remember words best, some principles, some events, some numbers; some recall sights best, some sounds.

Led by such analogies some writers have maintained that there is no general faculty of memory, but that each of the senses has its own memory. This of course involves the sensational view of the mental functions. But even on that view it would be more consistent to say that memory is a general function of the nervous system.

There can be no doubt that memory is as much dependent on the nerves and brain as other mental functions, but there is no reason to suppose that it is more so, and no satisfactory hypothesis has yet been constructed of the manner and extent of this physiological dependence.

To the theory that memory is a function of the immaterial part of the mind, the soul, it has been objected that it is inconceivable that the soul, which is an undivided unit, existing in a single point of space, can retain a vast number of distinct impressions, and be able to reproduce a corresponding number of states. But this is an argument *ex ignorantia*. We do not really know anything about the mode of existence of the soul, whether it is an absolutely unitary being, or has parts and powers; whether it exists in one or many points of space, or inhabits the whole brain. Lotze holds that the soul is a single element, and of simple quality, but yet may be present at more than one point of space at the same time.

The same argument may be retorted against the materialists. It is inconceivable that the almost infinite number of separate elements which go to make up the series of our mental life, should be each one represented by a combination of brain-cells. Each spoken word, for instance, has several sounds, and each sound is produced by several impulses of the vocal organs. Each written word also has several letters, and the combinations between the sounds and the letters form another vast series. Yet many persons have at command as many as ten thousand words. Some can use fluently three or more languages, with command of three or four thousand words in each. Then, a prodigy of learning occasionally arises who knows twenty languages, is familiar with a hundred authors, can repeat whole volumes, and knows a dozen sciences. Add to this the vast number of elements of knowledge comprised in our daily life, all our knowledge of places, persons, facts, the properties of matter, etc., and the number of separate things remembered will be seen to be vastly greater than the four hundred million nucleated cells, computed to exist in the brain.

But each act of the brain must involve more than one cell, probably many thousands; they cannot leave their places to enter new situations, and if they could do so registration would thereby be lost. Thus even the physical difficulties of this scheme are insuperable, and we conclude that the fact of retention is inexplicable.

The process of reproduction is capable of some further elucidation through the principle of association, under which head we shall recur to some phenomena of memory.

II. ASSOCIATION.

This principle accompanies or pervades nearly every activity of the mind. We have already seen that different sensations, occasioned by the same object, cohere together, so that any one will suggest all the rest, and occasion a complete presentation of the object; also, that a sensation, being once found by experience to be a sign of distance or solidity, ever afterwards suggests that perception, when it is repeated. So, peculiar sensations may be associated with certain perceptions, as nausea with the sight of a ship, in the example cited above. Or, perceptions and emotions may be agglutinated. A dog is filled with fear at the sight of a whip. A timid person shudders at seeing a gun. A familiar tune may excite emotions of joy or of sadness according to the circumstances of the hearer.

Professor Bain has described various modes of association, with remarkable minuteness and concreteness; showing, for example, how it applies to the use of language, to mechanical inventions, to the fine arts, to oratory, to poetry, to business, to handicrafts, etc. This has been called a "natural history of the human mind." It is ingenious, instructive, and interesting, but it throws no light on the law or cause of association.

The operation of this principle can only be observed in connection with representation. We cannot know whether sensations or presentations cohere together, until they are represented together in memory or imagination. Hence the laws of association are always stated in a form which implies representation.

The most general law of association is this:—Ideas tend to be represented together which were formed together or near one another in any sense, that is, in time, place, interest, emotion, action, dependence, cause, or any relation in which they can coexist. The principle on which this depends is that the mind acts more readily in the same manner or a similar manner with any in which it has acted before.

Sir W. Hamilton, following St. Augustine and others, states the law as follows;—"Thoughts suggest each other which had previously constituted parts of the same entire or total act of cognition." He calls this a law of redintegration. But if literally interpreted this law does not include all the phenomena. Mere similarity is often the connecting link between ideas, and so is contrast; but these are not naturally or easily included under redintegration.

Aristotle laid down three laws of association, namely, that ideas are associated by contiguity in time or space, by resemblance, and by contrariety. Other schemes have been proposed. Hume gives resemblance, contiguity in time and place, and cause and effect. Dr. T. Brown introduced a twofold classification of primary and secondary laws. For the first he adopted Aristotle's three laws; by the second he attempted to show why, when several ideas are in equally close association with the suggesting idea, according to the primary laws, only one is actually suggested. The secondary principles are such as vivacity, frequency of repetition, recentness, the amount of interest or emotion involved, the natural predisposition of body or mind, of which he gives nine. But obviously such a list could be drawn out indefinitely, for any object may have a vast number of associations. For example, if gems are spoken of, we think of the diamond as the finest; if hardness is mentioned, we recall the diamond as the hardest of minerals; if combustibility, we recall the diamond, and Sir Isaac Newton's prediction of its combustibility from its refracting power; if refracting power, the same; if preciousness, we recall the diamond in that connection, and so on. It is not worth while to attempt to classify these. One example is as good as a thousand.

We must beware of attributing efficiency to the laws or rules which have been discovered in association, or the principles on which it may be supposed to act. Laws, rules, and principles of action in nature, are only abstractions from actual phenomena, not real beings which guide events. The error is one not infrequent in all science, and needs no special attention in psychology. A relation between two ideas is an abstraction, and can have no real efficiency. Ideas do not appear in consciousness together because there is a relation between them, but the mind, which formed them in the first place, recalls them, and for some unknown reason recalls those more easily which it first formed together, and this we call a relation between the ideas.

Association throws some light on the process of reproduction. Obviously the simplest case of reproduction, would be one in which the whole series of our past ideas was recalled successively, being associated by the principle of contiguity in time, until that idea is reached which fits in with our present experience.

Something like this has occurred to persons in extreme danger, as while falling over a precipice, or when almost drowned. In such cases the sufferer sometimes sees, as it were, all the events of his life sweeping before him with inconceivable rapidity, so that he seems to live over again his whole life in a moment of time. In repeating a "piece" one is often obliged to begin again at the beginning, and can then go through without hesitation. Dr. Leyden, who was celebrated for his extraordinary memory, could repeat an act of Parliament, or any long document, after once reading it. "But when he wished to recall any particular point in anything which he had read, he could only do it by repeating to himself the whole" from the beginning to that place. (Abercrombie.)

Now, taking a case of this sort, as the simplest one, suppose the series of ideas to be represented by A b C d e F g H i j K, etc., where the large letters stand for the more important ideas, and the small letters for the less important ones. Then the less important ideas, serving only the office, in that particular series, of connecting together the more important ones, might be dropped out, during frequent repetitions of the series, and only the latter would remain, and would be associated together, so as to recall or suggest one another. We may suppose this process repeated until A is connected directly with Z, and, the next time Z comes into consciousness, this new coherence being established, A will be suggested immediately.

Or we may suppose that a new principle intervenes and supersedes that of contiguity in time, when the series is repeated. For example, some of the ideas, A C F H, etc., may refer to the same subject. Then, on repetition of the series, the next step would be to drop out such steps as do not belong to that subject, and the new series might be A C F H R Z, from which would result after a few more repetitions, the so-called immediate coherence of A and Z.

Something like this seems to occur when we try to think of a name and are at first unable to do so, because we cannot get hold of any short series of links between the present idea and the past one. In such cases what is needed is time for the machinery of reproduction to operate. Guided by experience we always say, "no matter, it will come to me," and remove our attention from the matter. Very often the automatic apparatus of suggestion does actually reproduce the name after a time, and, if the process is repeated with the same name after a few hours, it is much shorter, and finally the connection becomes "immediate."

Another indication of the correctness of this analysis is the fact that some past events, having become established in consciousness by frequent reference, owing to their importance for our life, are far more distinctly and exactly placed in our recollection than others. Hence we use them as reference-points for more quickly reproducing the latter. Thus we say, "I remember the storm of May 3, 1874, because it was the day before I was married." Old people commonly reinforce their statements in this way: "Brother Joshua came to visit us in the year 1865; because he was here when the news of Lincoln's assassination arrived." In courts of justice those witnesses are always esteemed the best who remember events in their connection, recalling them by several threads, and giving parallel, associated events, by which to check the correctness of the principal ones. Shakespeare understood this. Dame Quickly says, in Henry IV, "Thou didst swear to me upon a parcel-gilt goblet, sitting in my dolphin chamber, at the round table, by a sea-coal fire, upon Wednesday in Whitsun-week, when the prince broke thy head for liking his father to a singing-man of Windsor; thou didst swear to me then, as I was washing thy wound, to marry me, and make me my Lady thy wife."

According to Mr. Herbert Spencer, memory, when it is "immediate" or perfect, is automatic, like instinct, a part of organization; and only associative or suggestive memory really deserves the name. "Instinct may be regarded as a kind of organized memory, memory may be regarded as a kind of incipient instinct." (Psychology, I, 445.) "Memory necessarily comes into existence whenever automatic action is imperfect." (448.) "As fast as those connections among psychical states which we form in memory grow by constant repetition automatic, they cease to be a part of memory." (450.)

If we correctly understand this distinction, it agrees with the view already given. The real difference in the two kinds of memory is in the length of the process, the number of intervening suggestive links. When these are all dropped, as explained above, the connection "between psychical states" becomes immediate, that is, automatic. But, properly speaking, all associative suggestion is automatic or unconscious.

Associative representation is the chief activity of the mind in dreams, somnambulism, hypnotism, and hallucination, making a transition to the subject of the imagination. In these, association has its own way, unrestricted by either the will, or the actual facts of the external world.

1. Dreams.

In sleep the circulation of the blood in the brain is checked and almost suspended; hence there is not enough activity in the nerve-centers to produce motion in response to a stimulus either of the sense from without or of the mind from within. All the senses are partly dormant, and the sensations which are received become so feeble that they only recall past ideas. Since communication with the external world is suspended, the ordinary checks upon representation, furnished by the relations of space and time are wanting, and the various elements of our experience are combined in lawless, fantastic fashion. We have no sense of incongruity, in dreams, when we suddenly find ourselves in a distant city, nor when we spend an hour in crossing a street or ascending a stairway.

That the will is dormant, and the mind wholly under the sway of association, is shown by the fact that dreams are sometimes inspired by whispering in the ear of a sleeping person. A young military officer was once caused in this way to fight a duel in a dream. He thought that he was insulted, challenged, taken to the field, and that he killed his antagonist. But, being told to fly, his efforts to do so awakened him.

Nearly every one knows the terrible night-mare sensation of being unable, in a dream, to move, in order to escape from danger. This is undoubtedly a real experience, expressing the actual fact. The representative power is active, but the sluggish brain cannot respond to it by moving the limbs. Homer compares the pursuit of Hector by Achilles around the walls of Troy, to such a dream. (Iliad, Bk. 22, Line 200.)

It is a wonderful part of the phenomena of dreaming that we remember our dreams. This is largely an acquired power. Persons who tell their dreams, soon learn to remember them and to have them oftener. Those who never tell them seldom remember them.

The cause of dreaming and the cause of the particular dream which occurs, may be quite distinct. Thus one may dream, perhaps, because he ate too much supper, or because he is lying on his back, or because the wind makes a gentle noise; but he dreams of being at sea because he read about a ship the day before; or dreams about home because he is away from home. Dr. Gregory relates that once, having a bottle of hot water at his feet, he dreamed that he was walking on Mount Etna. A person who had a blister on his head dreamed that he was scalped by Indians.

Since all outside distractions or checks are removed in dreams, if any one subject or train of thought has excited the mind while awake, to such an extent that the mind spontaneously dwells upon it, excluding other suggestions, some very surprising results appear, though really no more inexplicable than any dream. Thus, Coleridge composed the poem of Kubla Khan in a dream. Dr. Franklin often unraveled political combinations in his dreams. Condorcet habitually solved mathematical problems in his sleep. This kind of dreaming runs into somnambulism; for the dreamer sometimes rises and writes down the problem or stanza in his sleep, though he does not remember, when he awakes, that he has done so.

This phenomenon has been called "unconscious cerebration" (Carpenter), " unconscious mental modification " (Hamilton), "insensible perception" (Leibnitz), etc. Various theories of brain-action have been devised to explain it. Great numbers of wonderful examples have been accumulated, and may be found in easily accessible books. But there can be no proof that this kind of mental action is unconscious, at the time; but only that it is not remembered.

There is no necessity for assuming any new principle, other than associative suggestion, in connection with dreaming or somnambulism. The facts all come under these. In some cases a dream of this kind is forgotten, while the results remain in the mind, and a problem can be solved or a thought expressed which could not be before. But this does not show that the activity of the mind was unconscious at the time.

Some writers have failed to distinguish between this phenomenon and ordinary associative recollection, and have confused together the examples of both. "Unconscious cerebration" is only mysterious and inexplicable in fact, just as all association, and indeed all mental action is so. On dreaming, in general, see also Sully, Illusions, Chapter 7.

2. Somnambulism.

Somnambulism is an acted dream. In this the motor centers and nerves have sufficient circulation to support activity, while some of the senses are still dormant. Representation goes on and is acted out, and the patient's consciousness is the same as in a dream.

In this state many strange occurrences take place, due to concentration of the mind on one topic. Those senses which are not dormant are in a state of exalted activity, and the patient performs so many actions, guided by touch alone, or touch and hearing, with eyes firmly fixed and sightless, that observers feel certain he can see through a wall, or see with the back of his head or with his hand.

No extravagant supposition of new senses or strange spiritual powers is necessary. The somnambulist is like a blind person, who learns more by touch than other people do because he concentrates his attention upon it.

3. HYPNOTISM.

The state called somnambulism can be induced artificially, and is then called hypnotism, or mesmeric sleep. In this state the phenomena of sleep and somnambulism are curiously blended. The will being entirely dormant, the patient's actions are a dream suggested by the operator, like the duel described above. He sees flames of fire issuing from a magnet, sees them where the operator says there is a magnet, even if none be really there. His thoughts and actions are at the mercy of associative suggestion.

This state may even be voluntarily assumed by some persons. It has been known in many countries and ages in the form of religious trance or extasy. The spiritualistic trance-speaker, if not an imposter, is in this state. He speaks much more fluently than he could in his natural condition, because his attention is concentrated on his language, and all distractions are excluded. But he says nothing new, nothing which he did not know before, and nothing of any importance. Persons in this state, however, sometimes recall things which they had forgotten and could not recall in their normal condition. Many of these phenomena are best discussed in connection with the subject of the Will.

4. HALLUCINATION.

Hallucination is a waking dream. Owing to some disorder of the brain, caused by disease or the action of opium, alcohol, haschish, etc., the ideas called up by association, as in dreams, excite the nerves and centers of vision, and produce subjective or reflex sensations of sight. Nearly all patients in violent fever suffer in this way.

The case of Brutus has been mentioned. The case of Nicolaï, a bookseller of Berlin, is famous and typical. But the phenomena are too common and too slight in psychological importance to justify further attention here.

Representation here goes on, and excites a reflex activity of the visual centers, as somnambulism of the motor centers. For further details and examples, see Sully on Illusions.

III. IMAGINATION.

By all these abnormal phenomena of association the transition is made to the imagination, which is association, guided by the will and watched by consciousness, and thus having the appearance of a creative power. Two observations were long ago made which confirm this explanation. (1) Imagination produces nothing absolutely new, but only combines objects in new ways, or parts of objects to make up new wholes, or changes the properties of objects, or alters the degree or proportion of their different qualities. (2) Imagination is confined to material things, objects of sense. This last is only true of the ordinary, established use of the term imagination. It is often used now in a figurative, extended sense, as we shall see.

In imagination the wider excursions of the suggestive power are restrained by the will, the relations of space and time are not lost sight of, because the senses are not dormant, and all is normal. As already said, imagination, in its usual meaning, is the power of representing objects. To recall a face so that you can paint it, is an act of imagination in the ordinary sense. To form from this face a different one, by heightening the expression, improving some features, adding beauty or any peculiar character, is called an act of creative imagination, and the face thus produced is called an ideal face.

The different activities of the imagination have often been distinguished and classified. Sir W. Hamilton limits the word to its literal meaning, and says that the terms productive and creative are very improperly applied to the imagination. President Porter distinguishes three offices of the imagination, (1) the combining and arranging office, (2) the idealizing office, (3) the office of forming standards of action. But he adds four special applications of the imagination,— the poetic, the philosophic, the ethical, and the religious. And it must be noticed that he treats of the phantasy as a separate division of the representative power, including some things which most writers place under imagination.

We propose the following division of the field of activity of the imagination into five parts. (1) Imagination in the common, literal meaning. (2) Reverie. (3) Poetic or artistic imagination. (4) Mechanical or scientific. (5) Ethical or moral. In every one of these the imagination produces the ideal by combining the real. It has but one method.

1. Ordinary imagination is the representation of objects when they are out of actual sight, so that they appear before the mind's eye just as they really are. The difference between this and the activities of associative representation noticed above, dreaming, hypnotism, etc., is that they are all abnormal, some part of the mental force being dormant, while this is perfectly normal and regular.

This view is confirmed by the following definitions. "The image-making power. The power to create or reproduce an object of sense previously perceived." (The Webster Dic.) "The faculty of representation by which the mind keeps before it an image of visible forms." (Calderwood.) "Mental representation of the absent object, 'passive imagination.'" (Krauth.) "Imagination as reproductive, stores the mind with ideal images, constructed through the medium of attention and memory, out of our immediate perceptions." (Morell.) Shakespeare compares it with the poet's pen.

> ". . . as imagination bodies forth
> The forms of things unknown, the poet's pen
> Turns them to shapes, and gives to airy nothing
> A local habitation and a name."

Simple imagination has decided limitations. (a) It is confined to things actually seen or known, either directly or through descriptions and pictures. A person born on the prairie, who has never seen a mountain, cannot imagine one. One who has never been at sea cannot picture to himself the raging deep. The dweller in the tropics cannot imagine the arctic ice. But all can body forth before the mind, to some extent, the descriptions they have heard and the pictures they have seen.

(b) It is limited to natural objects and qualities. It cannot produce a new color, present an object out of space, an event out of time, or a pure unembodied spirit. But it can combine arbitrarily all natural forms and qualities; it can create centaurs, the heads of men on the bodies of horses; or mermaids, part woman, part fish; or angels, beautiful women with wings; mice as large as elephants; diamonds as large as houses; a nation of pigmies, or of giants, or of fairies; a Titania, a Caliban, a Satan, all the heroes of romance.

Imagination sometimes interferes with the correctness of narrative, making it untruthful by interpolating objects transplanted from other senses or evoked by association. Old persons sometimes relate having seen events which occurred before they were born, the descriptions heard in childhood being reproduced by the imagination as actual experiences.

2. Reverie is a voluntary, waking dream. The subject of it gives himself up to the power of association, and imagines himself passing through a series of events or experiences of various kinds. This power may be cultivated by practice until reverie becomes as capricious, as absorbing, as apparently real as a dream. It may become a confirmed habit, a luxury,

a dissipation. It produces new experiences by combining events known or heard of, in a series, making personages, themselves the creation of a similar process, pass through pleasing or diverting scenes, like a stage-play. The poet and the novelist can use this half-conscious play of associative representation to weave their tales, as the kaleidoscope is used by designers of new patterns for carpets and wall-papers.

3. In the poetic or artistic imagination we approach more nearly what is called the creative power of this faculty. Shakespeare says,

> "The lunatic, the lover, and the poet,
> Are of imagination all compact."

Here the ideal element begins to be felt. It is not easy to define the ideal. Some have even denied its existence, and held that the imagination only combines the *disjecta membra* of experience. But the testimony of the most elevated, noblest minds is very general to the existence, value, and force of an ideal element.

We do not indeed affirm that the ideal is a product solely of the imagination, nor would we say that it is formed or constructed by any faculty. It is a way of viewing certain subjects, a method of thought and a style of feeling, a product of the emotional and reasoning powers, combined with the imagination.

The painter, the sculptor, the poet, the orator, have lofty views of the value of their respective arts, deep feelings excited by great excellence, strong desires to attain what is worthy, a thorough conviction that great success is attainable in these arts. Now a wide knowledge of art and literature, gained under the impulse of such feelings and convictions as these, not merely furnishes the imagination with a stock of materials, and supplies the mind with the loftiest standards of comparison for the artist's own work, but impresses him with a belief in the nobility of true excellence, and with a passion for success. Under these influences he is never satisfied with what he has done, always feels that he or some one else can do better, and never gives up striving for a higher success.

This mode of thinking and feeling is called a love of the ideal, a worship of the ideal, a service of the ideal, the formation of ideals; not because the imagination forms a definite standard of excellence, for if definite it would not be ideal; but because all the concrete examples which furnish its stock in trade are seen to be imperfect and surpassable. Thus the popular phrase is perfectly justifiable, that we judge ideally, or by an ideal standard; but it is not strictly accurate to say that the imagination constructs such a standard.

Under this head may be placed another remarkable combination of the representative and reasoning powers, the so-called mathematical imagination. A line without breadth and perfectly straight, a surface without thickness and perfectly plane, may be said to be ideals, which can never be realized in fact, but which the imagination supplies to every geometrical construction. So number is never really abstract, but always concrete, and when we speak of three, or ten, alone, we exercise an abstracting imagination.

The power to isolate a relation of space or of number, remove it from the concrete, and make this abstraction seem real to us, may well be called imagination, and requires culture in this peculiar line to make it available, as does the artist's feeling of the ideal.

The solution of problems in or by mathematics often comes under the next head, of the scientific imagination.

4. The scientific imagination is used in the framing of hypotheses. The scientific investigator, seeking the explanation of a phenomenon, frames a supposition; "What if it be thus and so?" All his knowledge of natural laws, and all possible

suppositions which seem to him reasonable, as to new laws of nature, form the material out of which his imagination forms a hypothesis. He then tests this by experiment, calculation, any means in his power. If the result is unfavorable, the process has probably suggested a new supposition, which can be tried in like manner. Thus Newton formed the hypothesis that the force which binds the moon to the earth, and the earth to the sun, is the same as that which attracts bodies on the surface of the earth, giving them weight. His calculations failed to confirm the supposition. He calculated that the moon would be deflected fifteen feet in a minute, while it is really deflected but thirteen. He laid his calculations aside. Thirteen years afterwards Picard measured an arc of a meridian, and found a new value for the earth's diameter. Newton then went over his calculations again, with this new value inserted, and found them correct. The result confirmed his theory and made him famous. (Fiske, Cosmic Philosophy, I, 111.)

"Without an active imagination, philosophical invention and discovery are impossible." (Porter, Hum. Intel., 369.) Prof. J. Tyndall's essay on the Scientific Uses of the Imagination is valuable in this connection.

Every great mechanical invention is the result of a similar process; only, when the first guess proves to be right, it seems an inspiration, though really the result of long mechanical practice or study, supplying the imagination with a fund of materials. But in fact every great mechanical triumph has been the outcome of a vast number of hypotheses constructed in iron and wood, often laid aside and altered, perfected by many steps. The power-loom, the spinning-machine, the locomotive, the sewing-machine, the reaper, the thresher, the chronometer, the blast-furnace, the iron ship,—have each been developed by successive efforts of the scientific or mechanical imagination.

5. *The ethical and religious imagination.* Some of the remarks made upon the artistic imagination are applicable here. The literary artist may produce an ideal character, just as the painter produces an ideal face, by improving, heightening, strengthening, in a word idealizing, an actual one. But he cannot do this unless he has an "ideal standard" already in his mind; but as in art, so here, this does not mean a definite, detailed standard, but an aspiration, a love of moral beauty. The details of the creation will be supplied by the imagination out of the experience, habits, education, observation, etc., of the author, in more or less accordance with public opinion and the tastes of the time.

Moral ideals and rules, however, are difficult to carry in the mind and apply correctly to all actions, in the various and complicated circumstances of life. They are best presented, therefore, concretely, in the person of some one who inspires our admiration, and whom we can imitate. Nearly all religions have their great heroes or founders, whom the people are bidden to imitate. The Christian religion has this great advantage, that it satisfies this longing of the human heart far better than any other religion, and presents in the person of Christ an ideal which abounds in divine perfections, and yet is not perfect in such a way as to repel and discourage the believer, but attracts him with a deep sympathy and arouses him to the best thoughts, feelings, and actions.

The "creative imagination" may find ample play in applying the teachings of Christ and his example to all the circumstances of modern life, answering the questions;—What would He command if He were here? What would He do if He were in my place?

The imagination has no application to spiritual beings. It is limited to the analogies of our present life. Our attempts to imagine pure, unembodied spiritual beings, only result in human forms made of thin, transparent matter. Still less can we imagine the Infinite Spirit, the Divine Being. We may form concepts of power, wisdom, and goodness, perhaps of infinity. We may attempt to join all these together. But for us to imagine a Being of infinite wisdom, power, and goodness, would be for the finite to represent, to image forth, the infinite. We believe that such a Being exists, but that does not imply that we can image to ourselves his mode of existence.

The words "conception" and "conceive" are sometimes used in connection with the imagination. This may be allowable in popular language or conversational discourse, but in philosophical language these terms have long been applied in the best usage, to the reasoning power, the faculty of thought-knowledge, of abstractions, and should not now be changed. Dugald Stewart is the only philosopher of note who has used conception in the sense of imagination.

The critics of Mr. Herbert Spencer affirm that he neglects this distinction, and uses the term "conceive" in the sense of imagine. "To think a thing as possible," he says, "is the same as to imagine it." (Psychology, 11, 179.) This obviously injures the cogency of his celebrated antinomy of the reason, his doctrine that anything must necessarily be true if we cannot "conceive" the opposite; a doctrine which, however, we should reject on other grounds.

PART III.
THE REASONING POWER.

The reasoning power is also called the Understanding by Coleridge, Hickok, and many others; the Elaborative Faculty, by Hamilton; Discursive Reason, by Whewell; Dianoetic Faculty, by Aristotle; etc. The correct term should be Reason corresponding to "reasoning," which is used to express what the faculty does. But "reason" has been used by so many writers since Coleridge, to define a supposed faculty of regulation which produces a priori concepts or intuitive ideas, that we cannot hope to restore its proper use. We keep as near it as possible in the term "reasoning power."

The functions of the reasoning power may be divided into judgment, abstraction, generalization, and reasoning proper. A product of the Judgment, when actually expressed, is called a judgment, and the phrase in which it is expressed is called a proposition. A product of abstraction is called a concept or notion. A product of generalization is a class. Reasoning proper is of three kinds, analogy, induction, and deduction. The judgment is by some called the faculty of comparison, and considered a separate division, co-ordinate with the understanding and the reason. (Kant.)

One cause of the confusion of nomenclature on this subject, is the influence of Locke's Essay. "This work is quite as much a treatise on logic and metaphysics as on psychology. It scarcely professes to give a complete and systematic view of the powers of the soul, but is chiefly occupied with the analysis of ideas. . . . Locke gave a direction to all subsequent writers, even to those who differ from him most materially. Even Reid, in treating of the higher powers, groups them all under Judgment, which he treats quite as much from a logical as from a psychological starting-point." (Porter, Human Intellect, 381.)

JUDGMENT.

We place Judgment first because it is concerned in all the activities of the intellect. In logic the phrase, an act of judgment, is used in a more restricted sense, and means the comparing of two notions which are already formed. For example, when I say, "grass is green," the concepts "grass" and "green" are both furnished, and the logical judgment only unites them in a judgment, and the phrase expressing this is called a proposition.

But in psychological usage, the judgment is active also in perception. I cannot perceive the grass as green without distinguishing green from other colors. Discrimination, as we have seen, is the very basis of knowledge. A judgment is then, psychologically, an act of the mind, which applies the categories of identity and similarity. For example, suppose I see a distant light in the midst of darkness; I perceive it as something different from the darkness. If it continues for a time, I judge it to be the same, identical, not different. If it changes to a red light, I judge it to be qualitatively different, not identical, but similar. If another light of the same color appears, I judge the two to be not identical, but different,—separately existent, but alike in one thing, color.

All knowledge implies judgment; we can not know any object except in some relation. "The secondary, comparative, and logical judgments are all founded on those which are primary, natural, and psychological." (Porter, op. cit., 432.)

When we see a red light, as above, if we know by previous

experience that the name of this peculiarity is "red," we apply that knowledge at once, and form the proposition, expressed or implied, "this light is red." If we have never learned the name "red," we can only say, "it is like the other light, like the one I saw last night," and begin the process of forming concepts, classifying, and making names. But if some one tells us, "the name of that color is red," the process is abridged; we attach the name to the concept, and have it ready in the memory for the next similar occasion.

Ordinarily, we learn the name when we learn the object, and the classifying judgment is made for us. When this is not the case a tentative process of naming and classification necessarily begins. When Captain Cook landed some goats on an island of the Paciffc, the natives called them horned hogs; on a similar occasion horses have been called large dogs; the hog and the dog being the only beasts known to them, and the cloven feet of the former classing them with goats. The Romans at first called the elephant *bos lucanus*, lucanian ox, having first seen them in Lucania. Children often classify in the same imperfect way, calling a cow's horns handles, the gums the fat of the teeth, etc.

In perception we also distinguish the object as different from self, which involves a knowledge of self as different from the object, and is a true act of judgment.

Judgment, therefore, can hardly be called a separate faculty or mental power; or at least the fact should be noticed that it does not isolate itself from other activities. We have already remarked upon the inseparable connection of the various powers of the mind. Each one involves others, and perhaps, if our knowledge were wider and deeper, we might see that each involves and depends upon all the others. It would hence be far better to say, "the mind in perception acts under the categories of identity and similarity, under the condition of consciousness, under the form of space, under the limitations of the senses," than to say—"the mind has a faculty of judgment, another of consciousness, etc., and all together make up the power of knowledge." But convenience and common usage compel us to adhere to the ordinary names.

The further discussion of the judgment and its operations belongs to the science of logic. We shall discuss briefly the concept, and the operations of generalization and reasoning, so far only as they seem to require mention as psychological processes. Their complete treatment is far more in keeping with the subject of logic. The logical text-book of President McCosh is especially noteworthy and valuable for its full and clear treatment of the concept.

THE CONCEPT.

The concept is a product of abstraction and generalization. Let us take a simple example, a red apple. We can, by an act of "analytic attention," called abstraction, think of the quality or attribute "red," apart from the other attributes which make up the mental object, apple. Lotze uses the instance of a tree, which we see at one time covered with green leaves, and at another after it has lost its leaves, and so find that we can separate the attribute, green, from the object tree. (Dictate, Logik, §20.) To the same effect Mr. Herbert Spencer says that we have the "power of recognizing attributes as distinguished from the objects possessing them, . . . a power to recognize attributes in themselves, apart from particular bodies." (Psychology, I, 344.)

This process is called abstraction. The quality or attribute of redness, for example, when we separate it in thought from the being of a single object, is called an *abstractum*. This does not imply that we can imagine the quality really to exist by itself, apart from any substance to which it belongs, or that we can imagine an apple or a tree without any color. But, suppose there are several red apples, we can compare them, by an act of judgment, and know that they agree in this respect, know that they all have the same attribute of "red," that is, they all have a like power of occasioning the sensation called red.

This quality, when viewed as the common property of all the members of a class which makes them to be a class, is called a concept. The concept is therefore a "general," a "universal." Now, in what sense this universal really exists, and what its nature is, has been the object of dispute among philosophers and logicians for many centuries. It is not a part of our present plan to give a history of these disputes.

But we affirm that the concept is a mental product, resembling in this respect a percept, or a representation. "The concept is a purely relative object of knowledge. . . . As a mental product and a mental object, it is purely relative, being formed by the mind and understood by the mind as indifferently common to single objects as so to speak, held ever ready by the mind to be affirmed of, and restored to, the single object to which it relates." (Porter, Human Intellect, 392. See also Bowne's Metaphysics, 30.)

Professor Jevons defines concept as;—"That which is conceived; the result of the act of conception; nearly synonymous with general notion, idea, thought." Mr. Spencer's remarks, quoted above, are of the same tenor. Lotze compares mere sensations to round bodies out of which no building can be reared; as only prism-shaped bodies can be formed into a wall, so sensations must be formed into classes, concepts, mental products, before we can think with them. (Dictate, Logik, §6.)

We may remark here that the logical term "notion," and the German "*begriff*" are generally used in a wider meaning than that given for "concept."

Concepts may be classified in various ways. We mention only the division into simple and complex concepts. Those called simple contain but a single attribute, as redness, sourness. Those called complex comprehend many attributes, as man, horse. So we may rise from one order of abstraction to another, until we reach such complex objects of thought as nation, civilization, religion, education, nature.

The term classification is used oftener in a higher and wider meaning, of the systematic arrangement of natural objects under higher and lower genera. This operation depends on analysis and comparison. An object is presented to the mind in perception as a complex of properties, parts, and relations. It is impossible to compare two objects without separating in thought these properties and relations. We may then, on comparison, form a class of those objects which agree in every observable attribute. Such a class would be in most cases very small. Or, we may form a class of all those objects which agree in only one given attribute, and such a class would usually be very large.

This introduces the distinction between the comprehension and the extension of concepts. The former denotes the number of attributes in which the objects agree, the latter the number of individual objects which belong to the class. The two are therefore always in inverse ratio; for, the slighter the resemblance the larger the class, and the more exact the resemblance the smaller the class.

We must now briefly describe the three great schools of opinion on this point. We quote the graphic description of Professor Bain. "It was believed by a certain school of philosophers, deriving from Plato, that there exists, in the universe of being, a circle in general, or circular form without substance, size, or color; that in like manner, there are archetypal forms of man, of just, of good, etc. After a severe controversy which raged in the scholastic period, this view was abandoned."

This was the view called realism, and its catchword was, *universalia ante rem*.

"Another mode of regarding the fact of community in diversity, is to suppose that the mind can represent to itself, in a notion, the points of agreement by themselves, and can leave entirely out of sight the points of difference. This is conceptualism." The catchword of this theory is, *universalia in re*.

Professor Bain then goes on to describe his own view, which is nominalism and the catchword of which is, *universalia post rem*. "The final result of the generalizing process is the *abstract* name. Such names as motion, weight, breadth, whiteness, melody, roughness, polarity, wisdom, justice, beauty, are called abstract names, as signifying qualities or attributes without reference to the things that possess the qualities. They seem to separate the points of community of agreeing objects themselves, an operation impossible in fact, and even in thought, but supposed by a kind of fiction to be possible." (Bain, Logic, 52.)

We grant that it is impossible so to separate the qualities of objects in fact, and even in imagination, but deny that it is therefore impossible in thought. Yet the quality, when thus thought separately from the object, is not a concept, but only an abstract; it becomes a universal, a concept, when thought as the common quality of several objects, that which makes them a class.

"It is said," says Lotze, "that the unlike parts of our ideas destroy one another, and the similar parts are simply left behind, and form the universal. But the simple ideas are not lost; they remain, alongside of the universals, which are added as a new product. Moreover, the general concept is not something which can be represented, pictured, like the examples from which it is derived. Thus, 'color in general' cannot be represented in the mind. Neither can 'animal in general.'

"Such general concepts are not, then, products of a coalition of many single ideas, for then they would have the same character [be of the same order] with their components. The names we give them, 'color' for example, merely summon up a series of single impressions, but with the added thought that we mean, not them, but that in them which is common, though it can never be separated from them as a distinct representation." (Lotze, Dictate, Psychologie, §23.)

Lotze is usually called a nominalist; but the above passage may fairly be understood as agreeing with the quotations from President Porter, and with our own view.

It is plain, however, that Bain and Mill were required by consistency to be extreme nominalists. For, on their view of the mind, universals must be formed by the automatic action of sensations. Sensations that are more frequently repeated make a deeper impression on the brain, so that when a series of objects occasion sensations, those which are alike are strengthened, while those which are unlike are crowded out and forgotten. Of course on such a theory there is no mental product, no elaboration by the active power of the mind in perception, and hence none in conception. Conception is reduced to imagination, the power of imaging forth real objects.

But those who hold that the mind is active, interpreting and combining sensations, and forming a mental product by means of them, a percept,—should have no difficulty in believing that the mind can superinduce upon this a still higher stage of mental products, the concept.

It is admitted that names are essential to the effective use of concepts, perhaps even to the formation of all but the more simple ones. Still analysis and classification of objects can undoubtedly go on to some extent without language. The lower animals can form classes of concrete objects, can classify men as different from other animals, sweet grasses as different from bitter herbs, etc., but they cannot form concepts of the higher degrees, or true *abstracta*. Such concepts as justice, truth, beauty, are unknown to them, for these require language to deal with them and make them useful, as well as a higher abstractive power of thought to make them possible.

The general name is really a different product, as is admitted by Bain himself. "The abstract name is not absolutely required for ordinary speech, nor indeed for science. . . . Justice expresses the same thing as just actions. . . . The term signifies just actions in so far as just, or viewed solely with reference to their being just." (Logic, 53.)

But this would be the forming of a concept as a mental product, not a mere name, and would inevitably become conceptualism. "What the mind considers is not the name but the meaning or import of the name." (Porter, Human Intellect, 416.)

The conceptualist, in like manner sometimes glides into the territory of the realist, by treating concepts as existing by themselves, apart from the objects from which they are derived, forgetting that they are but mental products, symbols. President McCosh says: "Conceptualism has often taken a wrong form. It does so when it regards the conception combining the objects as an idea in the sense of image. This was the mistake of Locke. . . . But if it avoids these mistakes and oversights, which are not parts of the doctrine properly understood, conceptualism is the true theory. For in general notions, [concepts] the 'essential element is the grouping by the mind of objects by common properties, and putting in the group all objects possessing the properties." (Logic 92.)

Dr. McCosh adds the following striking statement of the

real truth contained in each of these theories, realism, conceptualism, and nominalism. "There are *universalia ante rem* in the Divine Mind. There are *universalia in re* in natural classes. There are *universalia post rem* in human concepts and terms."

REASONING PROPER.

Reasoning may be called mediate judgment, or the comparison of simple judgments. For example, returning to our red apples, if we judge concerning them that they are red, or round, or small, or that they agree or disagree in any way, this is an immediate or simple judgment. If we say, "red apples are good, therefore these apples are good," this is a mediate judgment, that is, one with a middle term, a comparison of judgments.

The two chief forms of reasoning are Deduction and Induction. In the first, as in the example given above, the middle or general term is supplied, with which the first simple judgment is to be compared. In the second the general term is to be found. Thus, if I eat a good many red apples and find them all good, I may infer that all red apples are good, and this would be induction.

A complete deductive argument is called a syllogism. The following is an example of the simplest form of syllogism. All men are mortal; the king is a man; therefore the king is mortal. Three judgments are involved; the one we have placed first is called the major premise, the second the minor premise, the third the conclusion. The middle term (here man) appears in both premises. The minor term (here king) appears in the conclusion and in one premise. The major term (here mortal) appears in the conclusion and in one premise. Without a middle term, or with two middle terms there can obviously be no valid conclusion.

There are many forms of syllogism, but they can all be reduced to this simple form or its corresponding negative, as is shown in any text-book of logic.

Now what is the principle on which this kind of reasoning depends? Why are we obliged to admit the conclusion when we have admitted that the premises are correct and that the process is regular. Take the simple form, A is equal to B, B is equal to C, therefore $A = C$. Here the principle of reasoning evidently is, things which are equal to the same thing are equal to one another. But this form, though it resembles a syllogism is not one in reality, for all its terms have exactly the same extent, and there is no middle term. But its resemblance may aid us in seeing what kind of a principle or axiom is to be sought.

Strange as it appears, this axiom has been the subject of much dispute. The best known form of the axiom is Aristotle's *dictum de omni et nullo*, which is: "Whatever is true of a class is true also of whatever comes under the class."

Sir W. Hamilton has endeavored to reduce the relation to be expressed to one of extent, and gives the axiom as follows: "Whatever is part of a part, is part of its containing whole." This, though useful for advancing Hamilton's peculiar theories, does not differ, so far as our purpose is concerned, from that of Aristotle.

J. Stuart Mill, at the opposite extreme, reduces the relation to one of content, and gives the axiom thus: "Whatever possesses any mark possesses that which it is a mark of." He says that a middle term may be dispensed with, and that we really reason from particular to particular, without using any general. This, however, does not settle the question; every one knows that we actually reason in that way, but the question is, Is not the middle term implied when it is not expressed? Mr. Mill would say "The king is a man, and therefore mortal. I know that he is mortal immediately, since he belongs to the human race."

But evidently the middle term is implied, and the ordinary syllogism is only the full expression of the implication. Prof. Bain says: "We have to prove that some object is mortal, not expressly named a man, but designated by some other title, as 'king.' We cannot say, 'men are mortal,' therefore 'kings are mortal;' such an inference can be made only through an intermediate assertion, 'kings are men.'" (Logic, 156.)

Mr. Herbert Spencer denies that any axiom which it is possible to frame can be "capable of expressing the ratiocinative act." He says: "Reasoning is the indirect establishment of a definite relation between two things. . . . Every ratiocinative act is the indirect establishment of a definite relation between two things, by the process of establishing a definite relation between two definite relations." "Reasoning presupposes classification, and classification presupposes reasoning. . . . . They are the different sides of the same thing, the necessary complements of each other." (Psychology, II, 115, 118.)

This implies, evidently, the "relation-view of propositions," which is, "that every proposition really asserts the manner in which two 'nameble things' are related to each other." Both terms, that is, of the proposition, are subjects. Mr. Sidgwick says that this theory was suggested by Mill and really appears in parts of his logic, though not avowed by him. (Fallacies, 53.)

The theory seems to be merely an attempt to eliminate abstraction and the concept, like that of Bain and Mill mentioned above, but pushed a little further. It is a result of nominalism, an attempt to use real things in argument, without mental products. The full discussion of it belongs to logic. We subjoin a few authorities.

"Syllogism in the strictest sense is inference from the general to the particular or individual, and in all its forms, inference proceeds from the general." (Ueberweg's Logic, translation, 333.)

"A syllogism is a combination of two judgments, necessitating a third judgment as a consequence of their mutual relation." (Mansel.)

"A syllogism is an enunciation in which, certain assertions being made, by their being true it follows necessarily that another assertion, different from the first, is true also." (Aristotle.)

The general term is, then, necessary to the syllogism, which is the test-form to which all forms of deductive reasoning can be reduced.

It is sometimes objected that the conclusion of the syllogism does not advance beyond the premises, but is really affirmed in them. Indeed it is a formal canon of books of logic that the conclusion must contain nothing which is not already included in the premises. This is often called a *petitio principii* and said to destroy the value of this kind of argument. Its value is certainly reduced by this consideration below the claims of many logicians, but not by any means destroyed.

"It does not follow that the deductive process is therefore superfluous, inasmuch as it may be necessary to develop or draw out that which is already implied or folded up in the premises." (Whately, Logic.)

"Deductive inference may be described as a process of interpretation. . . . The deductive inference that the pope is mortal, presupposes an examination of the pope's personality. If this resembles the usual type of humanity, we identify him with the subject 'men' in our general proposition." (Bain, Logic, 211.)

Complete or syllogistic statement of an argument may often be more convincing, or its fallacy may be more easily detected, from bringing the terms more distinctly before the mind. By supplying the major premise in each of the following arguments, its validity or fallacy will be more clearly seen.

"A slave is a human being, and therefore ought not to be held in bondage."

"He is not thirsty, and therefore is not suffering from fever."

"No war is popular, because a war increases taxation."

"The Reformation was accompanied and followed by many disturbances, and is therefore to be condemned."

"All plants contain cellular tissue, hence no animals are plants."

The value of deduction for enlarging our real knowledge is seen to best advantage in the mathematical sciences. No doubt, in a sense, all the truths of geometry are wrapped up in its postulates and axioms; and all the truths of speculative astronomy are contained in the law of gravitation. But the interpretation, unfolding, explication, of these facts in a shape fit for the human mind to grasp, is a task for the ingenuity and ability of generations of mathematicians and astronomers.

A further question arises;—How do we know the major premise is correct, that its statement is true? In mathematical reasoning the truth of the major premise may be contained in the definitions or previously deduced from them. In geometry, if we define a line as the shortest distance between two points, we may rightly take as a major premise, "all straight lines are shorter than bent ones." Or, if the definition of a triangle implies that it has three sides, we may correctly assert this universally in the major premise.

But in most reasoning there may be room for doubt at this point. How do we know that all men are mortal? Unless we know this on certain grounds, it is not valid to say that the king is a man and therefore mortal. It is plain that we cannot prove it by simple enumeration, for all men are certainly not dead yet. This introduces us to reasoning by induction.

INDUCTION.

Induction is the deriving of generals from particulars. "That part of the reasoning process which proceeds from particulars to generals." (Calderwood.) "The arriving at general propositions by means of observation." (Bain, Logic, 231.)

"Induction is a kind of argument which infers, respecting a whole class, what has been ascertained respecting one or more individuals of that class." (Whately.)

"Induction is the process by which we conclude that what is true of certain individuals of a class is true of the whole class, or that what is true at certain times will be true under similar circumstances at all times." (Mill.)

The following is the best definition of induction as actually employed in science: "The legitimate inference of the unknown from the known, that is, of propositions applicable to cases hitherto unobserved and unexamined from propositions which are known to be true of the cases observed and examined." (Fowler, Inductive Logic, 9.)

Sir Isaac Newton correctly stated the nature of induction in the following passage: "As in mathematics, so in natural philosophy, the investigation of difficult things by the method of analysis ought ever to precede the method of composition. This analysis consists in making experiments and observations and in drawing general conclusions from them by induction. And although the arguing from experiments and observations by induction be no demonstration of general conclusions, yet it is the best way of arguing which the nature of things admits of, and may be looked upon as so much the stronger by how much the induction is more general." (Quoted by Lewes, Problems, I, 51.)

To reason by induction, then, is to take certain facts, as found by observation or experiment, and place them as representatives of the whole class of objects to which they belong, assuming that what is true of these few objects is true of the whole class. Obviously the cogency of all arguments founded on such a basis depends on the accuracy and extent of the observations, or else on the nature of the experiments.

For example, if I find that a shilling and a feather fall in the same time in a vacuum, I do not need to try a thousand experiments on different objects, gold, paper, wood, lead, before I admit the universality of the fact. A few repetitions with the same objects, simply to eliminate possible errors, are as convincing as a hundred, and I am prepared to declare the general truth that all bodies, not merely silver and feathers, fall with the same speed in a vacuum.

"When the chemist has shown by a single experiment that nitrogen will not support combustion, we believe it will be just the same through all future time. If we withhold our assent it is from a doubt whether the experiment was properly made." (Fiske, Cosmic Philosophy, I, 55.)

But when the argument concerns more complicated subjects, politics, morals, or even animal life, the danger of mistake is vastly greater, and the number of instances must be proportionately larger. A negative conclusion also introduces difficulty and doubt. For example,—

Aristotle mentioned it as a curious fact that no animal ever died on the sea-shore at the ebbing of the tide. Pliny said this was a mistake, and the statement was true only of man.

The delusion was scientifically disproved only so recently as 1727, and probably still lingers in popular superstition.

To prove the effect of a medicine in disease, as quinine in ague, would evidently require a careful elimination of disturbing causes, and many observations. But when a barometer was carried for the first time to the top of a high hill, the pressure of the atmosphere in all places and times was proved at a stroke, never again to be doubted by any one capable of reasoning and acquainted with the subject.

There are some who declare that the step taken by the mind in induction is from particular to particular, not from particulars to generals. For example, if I take a barometer to the top of a mountain and the mercury falls, I infer that if I take it upon yonder mountain the mercury will also fall, or that if I bring another barometer upon the same mountain it will fall. But there is just as much ground for drawing the conclusion of one mountain as another, one barometer as another, just as much ground for applying it to all as to one. The general term is therefore latent, if not expressed.

The axiom on which induction rests has been stated in many forms. The most usual form is that given by Professor Bain, the "Law of the Uniformity of Nature," which he calls the "most fundamental assumption of all human knowledge." "This axiom," he says, is the common ground of all inference, whether avowedly inductive, or induction disguised under the forms of deduction. Without this assumption experience can prove nothing. . . . This must be received without proof; it can repose on nothing more fundamental than itself. If we seem to offer any proof for it, we merely beg it in another shape." (Logic, 227.)

We must call attention to the fact that Bain here distinctly assumes an intuitive origin for this axiom. Mr. Mill, while accepting the axiom as the basis of induction and as true in itself, insists that it is itself derived from experience.

Mr. Herbert Spencer resorts to the law of contradiction as the ultimate test of truth; that is, the law that anything is true if we cannot conceive [imagine] the truth of the opposite. But the contradiction or non-contradiction is to be perceived by human faculties, whose correct and continued operation is thus taken for granted. The dictum can attain no higher certainty than its source. But the correct and continued operation of the human faculties is a part of the uniformity of nature, and therefore this axiom seems to rest upon the other, and to have no higher certainty.

President Porter does not base induction on any one axiom but mentions six principles or assumptions "which are a priori to the ordinary processes of inductive inquiry." These are, (1) The relation of substance and attribute. (2) The reality of causative energy. (3) The relations of time and space. (4) That nature "is consistent with herself, or uniform in her methods of revealing or suggesting what man is prompted to interpret or explain." (5) That "physical forces are regulated and controlled by design." (6) "That the rational methods of the divine and human intellect are similar."

Many writers accept the uniformity of nature as an axiom, without noticing that in thus making the unchangeableness of nature an intuitive truth, they exclude the possibility of miracles and of creation, if not of intelligent design. It is not at all surprising that evolutionists should rest everything upon the uniformity of nature. Moreover, sensationalists and others who disbelieve in the reality of causation, naturally adopt the same axiom, for they cannot rise higher, to the really intuitive axiom of causation, having excluded it by their assumptions.

But we affirm that the principle or fact of the uniformity of nature is not an axiom in any proper sense of the word, but a generalization from the facts of nature. It is but another name for the reign of law, the fact that all physical phenomena are subject to law, that is, certain uniformities of causation which men observe, and classify, and call laws. This conception of universal law is a late one in the history of the human mind. Early man supposes the fact to be that all unusual phenomena are the work of supernatural causes. And even in an educated and scientific generation, there are thousands who believe in magic of various kinds, by which disease is cured, and other effects are produced without means.

Again, if the world has had a beginning, or if miracles have ever interrupted the chain of causation, or if the world is guided by infinite intelligence toward a moral end, then the assertion of the uniformity of nature, the universality of law, is not correct.

As we have shown when discussing causation, the true axiom is, the uniformity of causation. President Hopkins, treating of the axiom underlying induction, says: "There is none, except the uniformity of causation. By this we mean that the same causes, operating under the same circumstances, will produce the same effects. Instead of this, modern science assumes as the axiom of induction that nature is uniform. . . . This is the one postulate of mere scientists on which their whole structure rests. But so far is the general proposition that nature is uniform from being at the basis of our induction that it is itself the result of induction." (Outline Study of Man, 168.)

This principle of the uniformity of causation evidently depends on the reality of efficiency in causation. Indeed, it amounts to this axiom or intuition, that cause is real efficiency, plus the logical principle of identity.

Mr. Lewes states the latter thus: "The validity of conclusions rests on the preservation of homogeneity in the terms and the identity of their ratios." (Problems I, 91.) It is always understood as a necessary condition of reasoning that the terms of a judgment remain the same while the judgment lasts. For example, if I say, "Water quenched my thirst yesterday and to-day, hence water has always this property of quenching thirst," I assume that the state of my system will be the same, in any future experiments, that no fever will be present disturbing my circulation, that the properties of water will remain the same, that it will not be impregnated with salt or poison, and will not be lukewarm, etc. All these are really identical propositions, as much so as, *a* equals *a*, or, what is is, or, water is water, or, thirst is thirst; while they are so, they will be so.

Indeed, as we showed under causation, if the " uniformity of nature" is true, and so far as it is true, it must have its rational ground in real efficiency of causation.

But much that is called induction is not really so. For example, if I find that water quenches my thirst to-day, I shall probably resort to water to-morrow when I am thirsty. But this does not necessarily imply induction. It may be mere associative expectation, and we find it constantly exercised by the lower animals. It is not induction unless a general truth be derived by the mind, as, in this case, that water always quenches thirst, the circumstances remaining the same.

Of course, the reduction of all reasoning to association or associative expectation is favorable to the hypotheses of evolution and sensationalism. And we contend that the only escape from what is false in these theories, is to be found in the true doctrine of causation. We also contend that this is the only solid basis for induction. Mill bases induction on another induction, as the Hindus found the earth on an elephant, which stands on a tortoise; and Bain is obliged to assume an intuitive axiom, contrary to all his principles.

Further elaboration of the theory of reasoning does not seem necessary to psychology, but belongs to the science of Logic.

THE LOWER ANIMALS.

The curious differences and more curious resemblances between the intelligence of the lower animals and that of the human race, have led to many speculations. Most philosophers have been content, however, to ignore the whole subject, and therefore, we cannot quote many great names in support of our conclusions. The truth on this subject lies between two extreme parties.

On the one hand, it was formerly the custom to consider the intelligence of the brutes of a totally different kind from that of man, something mysterious and inexplicable, more the result of divine guidance and implantation than human reason.

On the other hand the evolutionist writers of the present day minimize the difference between man and the brutes, and teach that both forms of intelligence are of the same character, differing only in degree of development and in the nature of the environment.

Mr. H. Spencer has elaborately endeavored to show that there is a gradation by insensible degrees from the lowest forms of sentient existence to the highest achievements of human thought; that there is no break in the progress, no place where a new principle comes in to give a new meaning to association and sensation. He is therefore obliged to undertake to demonstrate that all reasoning is only comparison, induction is only association, concepts are not mental products but brain products or images, and all the realities of things are unknowable.

We affirm that the reasoning power is the special endowment of man, and constitutes, with the knowledge of moral distinctions, his crown of supremacy over the creation. Even Mr. Lewes sees this truth, and states it as follows.

"When it is said that animals, however intelligent, have no intellect, the meaning is that they have perceptions and judgments, but no conceptions, no general ideas, no symbols for logical operations. They are intelligent, for we see them guided to action by judgment; they adapt their actions by means of guiding sensations, and adapt things to their ends. Their mechanism is a sentient, intelligent mechanism. But they have not conception, or what we especially designate as thought, that is, that logical function which deals with generalities, ratios, symbols, as feeling deals with particulars and objects." (Problems, I, 142.)

Mr. Lewes proceeds, it is true, to explain this away to some extent, by saying that language is the necessary instrument of these processes of conception and reasoning, without which man would be a mere animal. "Language is the creator and sustainer of that ideal world in which the noblest part of human activity finds a theatre." (154.) This contains an important truth and one often overlooked. The necessity of language to abstract thought is often underestimated. But language is a possession of man, not a faculty. It is the intellect of man which requires language, not language which produces intellect.

Many of the brutes have organs well enough adapted for some kind of articulate speech, and some can imitate very well the sounds of the human voice. They could learn to speak if they had any occasion to do so, but they have no thoughts that need any expression beyond the power of cries and gestures. "There is no occasion for language proper, and no ability to acquire it, without the power of abstraction. . . .

So long as the mind deals only with concrete things, their images and the impressions left by them on the memory, they themselves serve as a sufficient attachment to experience, and the only attachment of which it can avail itself. The moment, however, the mind reaches an abstract relation, separates the place, time, and causal dependencies of things from the things themselves, it requires language to designate, retain, and impart these products of thought. . . . Speech is the supreme instrument of abstract thought, and all thought proper is abstract." (Bascom, Comparative Psychology, 214.)

The lower animals have no abstract ideas, can form no concepts, and can thus have no material of reasoning in the true sense of the word. It is true they perform many actions which are often attributed to reasoning; but in this matter three points should be remembered. (1) There is much confusion in the way in which such words as reasoning, induction, thought, etc., are used, and the observers of animals are seldom trained to accuracy and carefulness in the use of logical and philosophical terms. (2) There is much looseness of description current on such subjects, although a mere unnoticed trifle may be of fundamental importance toward a right or wrong theory of the subject. There is also much exaggeration. (3) Most writers are somewhat under the influence of prejudgment, naturalists in favor of evolution, philosophers in favor of the glory of abstract thought.

The mental life of the brutes is associative, and association is an automatic coherence of impressions. They are capable of what some call induction, but that kind of induction is really associative expectation, as we have seen. Real induction results in a universal.

A careful inspection of the most wonderful instincts and feats of intelligence authentically recorded of animals, shows that in many cases association and automatic action are sufficient to account for what has been called the work of reason, and it may fairly be said that probably in all such cases the real difficulty is no greater.

Instinct is a kind of automatic intelligence. "Instinct," says Mr. Herbert Spencer, "may be regarded as a kind of organized memory." (Psychology, I, 445.) It has grown up with the organism, and is really a part of the organism. This is shown by the fact that those animals most remarkable for instinct are incapable of changing their habits, or learning anything new, or adapting themselves to new circumstances. A nation of ants or bees is like the Chinese nation. Superstitions, habits, customs, ingrained in the brain by centuries of stupid repetition, become so nearly automatic that such a people cannot conceive of a change, of an improvement, of a different order of society. So the ants and bees, having become fully adapted to their environment remain the same even when the environment is changed, with instincts as unchangeable as the superstitions of arrested civilization.

Bees, though taken to a tropical climate, continue to lay up honey, where it is useless to them. Hens often set without eggs. Beavers in captivity sometimes build dams in the corners of the room. Sir John Lubbock tried to make ants build a bridge, but they would not even lay a bit of straw across a crack in the ground, could not learn anything new. He also showed that "ants and bees communicate little with each other, far less than has been supposed; that they do not report directions and plans, and have but a limited knowledge of them, and move chiefly by scent. They are inattentive to sounds, guide themselves but little by vision, and have very acute scent and touch. These are the senses which favor organic development, while vision, and above all hearing, minister to reflection." (Bascom, op. cit., 154.)

"Parasites on bees that could be easily removed by com-

panions are allowed to remain, the sufferer receiving no aid.
. . . If we compare bees and ants with birds, we shall find the latter more free and variable in their constructive methods, not because they show more skill than the insects, but because a larger share of intelligence and a smaller share of instinct go to their composition."

The automatic nature of instinct may also be seen directly. Many instincts are the result of structure, or at least correlated with a peculiar structure. The bee could not build cells without the power of secreting wax; the two capabilities are correlative. The silk-worm and the spider must be able to spin, and the hornet to make paper, the fighting-ant to secrete poison, and the beetle to generate a strong odor, or their wonderful instincts could not be shown to exist. "The organ and the function correlate, and find their simple expression in the instinctive action. . . . Nor is it easy to understand how the two could have arisen otherwise than together as parts of the same organic development. . . . The organs can hardly be supposed to have existed without the function, waiting for experience to impart it; nor could experience direct its use till the function was present." (Bascom, op. cit. 157, 175.)

A multitude of examples might be quoted of the stupidity of animals, showing their inability to learn, to form new habits, to adapt themselves to new circumstances. The number of such anecdotes is hardly inferior to the stories of their wonderful instincts. A young chicken cannot learn from a young turkey the useful art of catching flies. "A hen will adhere to her empty nest, even after violent dissuasion." "After bringing a caterpillar to her nest, the wasp always leaves it before the entrance and goes in to see if everything is in order within the cavity. During this absence of the wasp Fabre removed her booty to some distance, forty times in succession. Forty times the wasp brought it back, but each time examined her nest afresh before she attempted to put her prey into it." (Brehm, in Bascom, 225.)

The training which men sometimes bestow upon the brutes never develops reason, but only forms new associations. Hamerton remarks of a wonderfully trained company of dogs, that when their master died, no one else could get them to do a single trick. "When the ox obeys a word of command, there is in this obedience no more comprehension of language than when he is quickened by a goad."

If instinct were of the same nature as reasoning, it would be of a vastly higher degree, and would show a stage of knowledge in the bee and the spider far above, not below, that of man. If the comb of the bee were planned and made as a man's house is made, it would imply an amount of mathematical knowledge attainable by few men even in this developed age. Such an argument would prove too much. Accordingly, the usual attempt is to reduce the intelligence of man to association, or automatic action.

Man does not have these strange unreasoning actions, in so far as he does not need them, being guided by a higher associative power, or by true reason. The new-born child cries when the cold air reaches his lungs, and sucks when his lips feel the breast, and these are automatic actions, like those of wasps and bees. But beyond these he has hardly a trace of instinct proper.

Yet men do actually lead, to a great extent, an associative life, similar to that of the highest of the brutes. Many of our actions and series of actions are guided by habit, require no reasoning, and exhibit no mental activity but association. Who has not heard even a long conversation without a trace of intellect, in the sense of reasoning power? Instinct and real intelligence, are always in inverse ratio, as also are association and reasoning. When the mind of a nation becomes stereotyped in superstition and custom, it forgets to a great extent its privilege of true thought, and lives an associative life, little above the brutes.

Beast-minds must of course act in the same manner as the human mind, so far as they are conditioned by the nature of the objects of knowledge. Since the external world exists in space, and cannot otherwise exist, it must be known, if known at all, under relations of space, both by men and by brutes. But the abstract idea of space, the generalized concept, is something which no beast-mind can frame.

There is no approach in the animals to any such capacity. To affirm that they form abstracts and concepts implies a false idea of what abstracts and concepts are, confusing them with images, representations. These two theories are logically inseparable;—(1) That the mind of man is a gradual development from the intelligence of brutes, without any difference in kind. (2) That concepts and abstracts are the result of the action of a series of objects on the mind, not of the mind on a series of objects.

As to the question, whether the mental life of the animals is a manifestation of an immaterial principle, nothing is really known about it. Some reference will be made to it under the next head.

NATURE OF THE MIND.

Having studied the phenomena of intellect we are prepared to ask understandingly the question:—What is the mind, the subject of these phenomena? Is the term mind only another name for the brain, acting in certain higher relations? Can the phenomena we have described be accounted for on the supposition that thought and feeling and choice are products of the interactions of nerve-cells in the brain? Or are the powers we have discussed too peculiar, too wonderful, too different from the properties of matter, to admit such a supposition? Must we pass over into the realm of the inconceivable, the immaterial, the spiritual, in order to find an agent capable of these functions?

A theory of the mind not uncommon in ancient times, is that the mind is a product of the harmonious blending of all the powers of the body. The favorite illustration was that as a musical instrument produces music when all its parts are attuned and proportioned, so the body produces the soul or mind. But this comparison really favors the opposite theory, for a musical instrument requires a player, or it makes no music, the soul corresponds not to the music, but to the player. But dropping this unfortunate comparison, the soul cannot consist in a mere *consensus* (*inbegriff*) of all the atoms of the body. The materials of the body are constantly changing. Several times in an average life, it is supposed, they are all removed and replaced, yet the personality remains the same. Limbs may be lost, senses destroyed, yet the mind not seriously impaired. The whole body therefore cannot be the producer of the mind.

A somewhat similar view is the modern theory that the mind is a series of sensations and feelings. This is rather held dogmatically than attempted to be proved by the sensationalist school of writers. Especially since Mr. Mill admitted that this series of sensations must be held to be aware of itself as past and future, and that "this theory has intrinsic difficulties which it seems to me beyond the power of metaphysical analysis to remove," the theory has had but little vitality of its own. We have already referred to the difficulties of this view. It is really indistinguishable from materialism. For, to say that a series of sensations passively received makes up the mind is to say that the mind is a function of the brain. All other philosophers mean by the mind that which thinks, that which has a series of sensations. It is absurd to say that a series of sensations has a series of sensations, either actively or passively. This view can really mean nothing but that the brain is the mind. These writers are thus endeavoring, by using the term mind in a new and strange signification, not equivalent to "that which thinks," to escape the charge of materialism.

Mr. H. Spencer has grafted the associationalist psychology upon the hypothesis of evolution. He recognizes the absurdity of defining mind as a series of sensations. "The feelings called sensations cannot of themselves constitute mind. . . Mind is constituted only when each sensation is assimilated to the faint forms of antecedent like sensations." (Psychology, I, 185.) This means, we suppose, that memory is an essential power of mind. Again;—"The progress of correspondence between the organism and its environment necessitates a gradual reduction of the sensorial changes to a succession, and by so doing evolves a distinct consciousness, a consciousness that becomes higher as the succession becomes more rapid and the correspondence more complete." (I, 403.)

Why successive changes necessitate consciousness Mr. Spencer does not explain; but these and other passages seem to imply that, at a certain stage of progress, there arises a new kind of being, capable of memory and consciousness. Accordingly, he has a chapter on the "Substance of Mind," in which he undertakes to prove that if there be any substance underlying the phenomena it must be unknowable. "If every state of mind is some modification of this substance of mind, there can be no state of mind in which the unmodified substance of mind is present." (I, 146.) Very true! Substance is known only through phenomena, as all philosophers admit. Being, apart from quality, relation, or phenomenon, is equivalent to non-being. Again he says:—"Knowledge implies something known, and something which knows." (II, 307.)

But in many other passages Mr. Spencer speaks of mind very much as do Bain and Mill. He speaks of "the successive changes which constitute intelligence." (I, 403.) He says;—"The proximate components of mind are of two broadly contrasted kinds, feelings and the relations between feelings." (I, 163.) "The multitudinous forms of mind known as different feelings may be composed of simpler units of feeling." (I, 156.)

The origin of mind he describes as follows. "As soon as the organism, feebly sensitive to a jar or vibration propagated through its medium, contracts itself so as to be in less danger from the adjacent source of disturbance, we perceive a nascent form of the life classed as psychical." (I, 392.) But such actions are plainly automatic; mind, then, on this theory, is not that which thinks and feels, but something made up of nervous shocks. Indeed, he uses this very phrase "nervous shocks" in just this way. Professor Fiske, in "Cosmic Philosophy," tendered the amendment, "psychical shocks," which Mr. Spencer accepted as expressing his meaning, showing that in his view nervous shocks and psychical shocks are only different names for the same phenomena.

Mr. Spencer admits, in the following passages, that his theory is inadequate to account for the phenomena commonly known as mental action. "Even could we succeed in proving that mind consists of homogeneous units of feeling of the nature specified, we should be unable to say what the mind is. . . . Let it be granted that all existence distinguished as subjective is resolvable into units of consciousness, similar in kind to those which we know as nervous shocks, each of which is a correlative of a rythmical motion of a material unit or group of such units. Can we then think of the subjective and objective activities as the same? Can the oscillations of a molecule be represented in consciousness side by side with a nervous shock, and the two be recognized as one? No effort enables us to assimilate them. That a unit of feeling has nothing in common with a unit of motion becomes more than ever manifest when we bring the two into juxtaposition." (I, 157, 158.)

All views of this character proceed on the supposition that matter is not the dead, merely space-filling reality of the ordinary view, but a far different thing, "having within it the promise and potency of all terrestrial life," and so of mental phenomena also. "Materialistic views which really have any faith in their own affirmations, proceed from the assumption that 'matter' is something far better than the name denotes, or than it appears from the outside, but has a property of its own, out of which spiritual states are developed, just as out of another property are developed extension, impenetrability, etc." (Lotze, Dictate, Psychologie, §60.)

But to affirm that there is but one substance, a "two-faced

somewhat," with two sets of attributes, physical on one side and mental on the other, is a doctrine not practically distinguishable from pantheism. It matters little whether we call the one substance Matter, or God, and the system pantheism, or materialism, or cosmism, it meets with all the difficulties and objections of pantheism.

The psychological objection to such a scheme is, that it cannot account for the phenomena of the unity of consciousness, and the individuality of minds. (1) Unity of consciousness cannot arise from a congeries of material atoms. The philosophers who hold this theory make much of atoms, molecules, elements, nerve-cells, and the interaction of these elements, whether these things are consistent with their monism or not. A consciousness resulting from a consensus of such atoms or elements should be manifold or fragmentary. All analogies of reasoning require that, in order to produce a unitary consciousness out of such a collection of elements, there should be some dominant entity, perduring throughout the changes of the atoms, and making use of them for higher ends.

"It is impossible," says Lotze, "on this view to conceive that unity of consciousness which is a fact of experience, and which must not be arbitrarily withdrawn because it is mysterious, in order to explain the rest more easily." And he goes on, in a passage too long for quotation, to show that all physical analogies, such as the new force which is the resultant of the composition of forces, are inapplicable and misleading. (Dictate, Psychologie, §61.)

What has to be accounted for is not simply a series of feelings, but a "series aware of itself;" the ineradicable belief in the unity and identity of the thinking principle of each person. (See Drbal, empirische Psychologie, 15.)

(2) The conscious separate individuality of each mind, is inexplicable on such a theory. If matter be a continuous sub-

stance, underlying with its single being all atoms and molecules, and endowed with divine as well as material attributes, this might be conceived to account for a kind of diffused intelligence or omniscience, as in the pantheistic hypothesis, or to account for a consciousness residing in each molecule separately, but it cannot account for an individual consciousness, of limited extent. Mr. Spencer, accordingly, speaks constantly of "mind," the origin and composition and substance of mind, not of "a mind," my mind, or your mind.

"The notion of an indefinite thought-stuff, which admits of integration, implicitly assumes the materiality of thought, and results from the fancy that thoughts may be found among external objects. But thoughts are acts, and not stuff or material. As such they must have a subject. My thoughts demand a subject, and that subject is myself. As such subject or agent, I am a substance, in the only intelligible sense of that word." (Bowne, Metaphysics, 382.)

It is then mere assumption to declare that the brain is capable of producing all the mental phenomena, without any higher principle, by reason of the double set of attributes pertaining to the atoms or molecules of which it is composed. And a multitude of facts about the brain go to show this result correct.

1. Structure and development of brain and mental capacity are not always in proportion, either in man or in the lower animals. The brain of the mollusk is not less developed than that of the insect, but the latter is capable of far higher "psychical action," even higher than fishes and amphibia, though these far more nearly resemble man in nervous structure. The monkey tribe most resemble man, but elephants and dogs are more intelligent. The brain of the dolphin is commonly said to be the most developed of the lower animals, but no great mental gifts accompany it. The brain-structure of the pachyderms, elephants and swine, do not differ much, it is said, but

the difference in intellect is great. The brains of idiots, according to Longet, are sometimes larger and with completer convolutions than those of highly gifted men.

2. Disease or accident has removed parts of the brain without destroying the integrity of thought or memory. Longet relates a case where a young man lost an entire hemisphere of the brain without conspicuous loss of mental power. Volkman describes the case of a man who shot two balls into his head, lost a large quantity of brain, and became blind, but was stronger in intellect than before.

3. Size of brain, either absolute or relative, furnishes no criterion of mental ability. Elephants and whales have larger brains than men. But some animals are said to have larger brains in proportion to their weight than men. If the authority of Cuvier be not sufficient to establish this last proposition, we may yet affirm, on the authority of Huxley, that the differences in cranial capacity among men are far greater than between men and apes. But the mental differences among men, on the contrary, are far smaller than between men and apes.

These considerations seem sufficient to establish the view that the brain is not an adequate cause of mental action. "The uncritical imagination is, of course, much impressed by the excessive fineness of the elements, and by the darkness which surrounds brain-physiology; and this darkness and mystery pass for argument. . . . But the question as to the reality of the soul does not depend on brain-physiology at all. The question turns on the nature of consciousness and on the impossibility of producing the one from the many and the identical from the numerically changing. So long as these ideas are hostile and mutually exclusive, so long will materialism be impossible as a rational theory." (Bowne, Metaphysics, 375.)

The phenomena of the human intellect, then, seem to require as their ground a simple, individual, unitary substance in each person, of a different nature from matter, yet able to be in connection with a material organism.

This supposition does not indeed obviate all difficulties. It would be to be supposed that on such a subject human faculties would be able to trace but a very little way the hidden reality. We make no pretensions to solving all the problems, or answering all the questions which can arise. But, on the other hand, the most candid representatives of evolutionism and empiricism also disclaim all such pretensions. "The latest results," says Mr. Fiske, "of scientific inquiry, whether in the region of objective psychology or molecular physics, leave the gulf between matter and mind quite as wide as it was judged to be in the time of Descartes." (Cosmic Philosophy, II, 445.)

But if we accept the doctrine of the individuality, unity, simplicity, and immateriality of the human soul, there arises an interesting question,—How far do the mental phenomena of the lower animals compel us to the same conclusion with reference to beast-souls? Very little is known on which to base an argument on this point, but the following considerations seem to us of weight.

1. We know so little about the consciousness of the brutes that we cannot confidently say whether it is of such a nature as to require a simple and individual subject in each animal.

2. It is not at all certain that immateriality involves either immortality or moral freedom; so that we may perhaps admit an immaterial substratum of physical life, or of the mental life of the brutes, without in the least derogating from the superior dignity of the human soul and intellect.

3. We have seen reason to believe that man has mental powers higher in kind and not simply in degree than those of the brutes. If this be accepted, we may perhaps even hold that man's physical system and associative mental life are the

product of evolution, but that at a certain time God breathed into man a nobler spirit, endowed him with personality and immortality.

Another solution should be mentioned, as of import e in the history of thought, namely the theory of metempsychosis. Philosophers of a certain turn of mind have been wont in all ages to believe that souls pass through lower stages of existence in various lower animals before entering human bodies, and may return again to the bottom round of the ladder of being, to begin once more their weary ascent, as a punishment for sin. This is poetic imagination, not sober speculation.

Another interesting question is the location of the soul in the body. If it be immaterial we cannot probably properly speak of it as being in any point or points of space. Yet many writers, though accepting the immateriality of the soul, have sought to discover its location in the body. Descartes placed it in a part of the brain called the pineal gland, which however, is not a gland at all, and is now known to be of no more importance to the mental life than any other part of the brain. Others have located it in the whole cerebrum, and some in the whole body.

Lotze, accepting the Herbartian doctrine that the soul is a single element, a monad, yet declares that it may occupy more than one point of space at the same time, in the brain or the body.

More important is the question of the relation of soul and body. That there is such a connection, that each has a wonderful power over the other, has been a commonplace of philosophy for many ages. A vast number of instances, many of them very familiar, might be repeated. How soul and body operate on each other, either in these abnormal ways, or in ordinary perception or volition, cannot be said to be within the range of human investigation. The pantheistic or monistic explanation, that they are both of the same essence, seems at first promising. But on reflection we see that it is just as hard to understand how changes in one set of qualities can produce changes or motions in another set of qualities of the same substance, as it is to understand how two distinct substances can operate on one another. Monism, whether it spiritualizes matter or materializes spirit, can afford no real assistance.

The mystery and difficulty may, however, be divided, if not diminished by the reflection that action and reaction between two atoms of matter are just as inexplicable and mysterious as the mutual influence of soul and body. But here we are looking over the boundary of the field of metaphysics, to enter which the present is not a proper occasion. (See Bowne's Metaphysics, 113.)

The subject of the immortality of the soul belongs to the science of theology.

THE FEELINGS.

PRELIMINARIES.

I. DEFINITIONS.

1. The term "Feeling" has been discussed already at some length (pp. 59-64). Putting aside its popular and colloquial uses, it means, in psychology, the capacity for experiencing pleasure and pain. "A feeling" is thus a particular experience of this kind, or a particular class of such experiences. But these experiences are so complicated with the various processes of the intellect, and so modified by the various relations,—physical, social, and moral,—in which they occur, and the different occasions,—internal, external, simple, and complex,—which excite them, that the term "The Feelings," with the definite Article, is unavoidably used to denote an extensive range of our mental and social life. It is our present task, therefore, to analyze these experiences, and trace in them the elements of Feeling and of Intellect.

A single caution is perhaps necessary. In speaking of Feeling as mental power, we do not imply that the mind is an aggregate of parts or faculties, mechanically adjusted to each other. (See p. 13.) But rather, the different forms of the mind's activity form an organism, as it were, being means and ends for one another. The three forms or methods of mental activity are inseparable. We are obliged to describe them separately, but neither pure Intellect, nor pure Feeling nor pure Will can exist.

2. Throughout these discussions the terms Pleasure and Pain have a wide signification; the former means any agreeable feeling, the latter any disagreeable one. It would be well if usage permitted the term Unpleasure, giving us two correlative words, like the German *Lust* and *Unlust*. In the absence of such a convenience, we are obliged to use the ordinary terms, pleasure and pain.

II. NOMENCLATURE.

We call this power of the mind by the name Feeling, and the various products of its activity we call Feelings; but we do not choose this nomenclature because it is perfect or free from objection, but because it is, on the whole, the most convenient, and is already in somewhat general use.

Other names are used by various writers, but they all seem to us to be still more objectionable. Dr. McCosh and others use the title "The Emotions." We object to this that it is commonly and properly used in a narrower signification, which will be explained later on. It is hence an unusual, if not inaccurate, use of language, to speak of Appetite, Desire, Æsthetic feeling, Moral feeling, etc., as Emotions, for Emotion is properly used to denote a class of feelings, parallel with these. Again Emotion always means a product, and cannot denote the power of experiencing the feeling; an infelicity which is avoided by saying Feelings and Feeling.

Many American writers use the term Sensibility, in the Singular, for the power, and in the Plural for its products. This word, however, is generally used by English writers in a different meaning, including sensation, and not including the higher kinds of feeling. Thus, Calderwood, in the additions to Fleming's Vocabulary, defines Sensibility as "the capacity for receiving impressions, belonging to the extremity of the nerves of sensation." It is, besides, a long and awkward word, and is colloquially used in the meaning of "sensitiveness."

The term "Susceptibility," used by some, besides being still longer and more awkward, has the disadvantage of having a passive signification, and thus seeming to imply that this power of the mind is receptive only.

III. CLASSIFICATION.

Most writers on this subject deem it necessary to frame a complete classification of the feelings. It is impossible, however, to classify them without cross-divisions. For example, Dr. Thomas Brown divides the Feelings according to time into Retrospective, Immediate, and Prospective; an ingenious and suggestive division. But it obliges him to subdivide each class of feelings, according as they have reference to self or to other persons, and again according as they have or have not moral quality. This complication brings together under one head such incongruous feelings as cheerfulness, wonder, the feeling of beauty and that of the ludicrous. Nothing can be gained by adhering to such a scheme.

Several writers divide the Feelings into Physical, Intellectual, and Spiritual; but many of them may run through the whole three phases, recurring in various combinations. The cross-divisions thus required lead either to absurd combinations like those of Brown, or to a superficial treatment of the subject. The popular names, moreover, by which they are generally designated, are so inexact and vacillating that no classification founded on them can have any value. But it is impossible to restrict these names to definite and accurate use, because of their extremely common colloquial use.

Attempts have been made, especially by Mr. Herbert Spencer

and his followers, to overcome this difficulty by providing a fully descriptive name for each class of feelings, indicating their origin and connection. This method has been carried to an extreme, with great ingenuity, by Mercier, in "Mind" for 1884. It leads to such cumbrous titles as,—"Self-conservative Environmentally-initiated" feelings, and to such vague terms as "Antagonistic Feeling." This last, for example, is defined by Mercier as "Feeling which corresponds with the relation to the organism of an Agent in the environment which is cognized as actively noxious." It is also subdivided according as the "noxious agent" is of greater or less power, according as counteraction is or is not elicited, and according to the form of this counteraction when elicited, and its success or lack of success. But these subdivisions have to be reduced, at last, to the common, popular terms, whereupon the division is found to be redundant. Each feeling, fear, for instance, may appear under each particular set of circumstances. Such a classification, however interesting, adds nothing to our real knowledge.

We do not attempt any classification of the feelings, but shall describe them in the order, so far as possible, of their physiological relations. But we shall follow out each class or kind of feeling, when once taken up, through all its forms and implications, so far as seems best. Thus, the discussion of Pleasure and Pain, carried up into the pleasures of the sense of Sight, naturally suggests the theory of Beauty; and the Emotions, or feelings which express themselves in bodily movements, are naturally followed by Laughter, and this by the Idea of the Comic.

IV. FEELING AND SENSATION.

1. It is not easy to draw a distinct line between Sensation and Feeling. The internal or organic sensations (see p. 21), occupy the middle ground between them, and are perhaps the substratum, out of which both are developed. For example, hunger and thirst may be said to be pains, or called sensations which give information of emptiness of the stomach and dryness of the throat.

Physical feeling, again, is usually inseparable from sensation. For example, toothache seems purely a pain; but it is always accompanied with a localizing sensation, more or less accurate, conveying information of its locality, in other words, having an intellectual content. The same is true of nearly all physical feelings.

On the other hand, it is held by many authorities that all sensation is accompanied with feeling, that is, every sensation has an agreeable or disagreeable *tone*. The plain fact that we are not always conscious of this tone, they account for by the theory that our attention is usually fixed on the content of a sensation, owing to the importance of this for our daily life, so that its tone is lost to us. (Lotze, Dictate, Psychologie, § 48.) The fact seems to be that feeling is the primitive form of experience, coming earlier in the individual and also in the scale of terrestrial life, than discriminative sensation.

2. Each class of feelings, as of sensations, has a specific quality of its own, which is incommunicable and indescribable. Pleasure and Pain, as general terms, like "color," do not designate anything actual, but an abstraction from specific pleasant and unpleasant experiences. (Lotze, op. cit., § 48.)

And how certain nerve-changes occasion a state of consciousness known as feeling, is as completely unknown as it is why a certain other state, or change, or motion of a nerve occasions a sensation of light or sound.

3. Consciousness accompanies Feeling, as well as sensation. Without the knowledge of Self, running through all our feelings, like a thread by which they are held together, and without a felt possibility of introspection and analysis by the mind, there is no feeling; just as no sensations or intellectual phenomena are possible without the same accompaniment.

V. FEELING AND INTELLECT.

When we rise into the higher regions of the mind, a parallelism may be noted between Intellect and Feeling.

1. There is a similarity in the resemblances and differences between man and the lower animals. The latter are capable of sensation, perception, memory, and common imagination, but are never known to exercise abstract reasoning, creative imagination, or mathematical deduction. So also they are capable of experiencing pain, hunger, anger, fear, love, hope,—but not sentimental affection, remorse, moral approval, sense of beauty or of the comic. In other words, the lower animals have all those feelings necessarily connected with their limited mental experience, but are incapable of those which depend upon a higher range of intellectual activity.

2. We meet here, too, with the same conflict between opposing schools of psychology. Those writers who derive all the intellectual powers from sensation, and make sensations transform themselves into all the higher intellectual phenomena,—are bound, of course, to treat Feeling in the same way, and make simple feelings of physical pleasure and pain transform themselves into all the most complicated, most elevated, and noblest of this class of human experiences.

On the other hand, those who hold, as we do, that human reason cannot be thus accounted for, must also hold that Feeling is not merely parallel with sensation, but is a function also of the Spirit, entering into its highest manifestations.

PLEASURE AND PAIN.

After these preliminaries we have first to inquire into the nature of Pleasure and Pain themselves, the very basis of all the Feelings. Following our general plan, we shall begin with physical pleasure, and pain or discomfort, and discuss the topics suggested by this, before taking up the special kinds of feeling, such as Emotion, or Desire.

It is not always easy to separate between sensations which have intellectual content, and the feelings with which they are accompanied, constituting what is called their *tone*. If we look at the mid-day sun, the pain of excessive light destroys perception. When we are discriminating two shades of color, we receive no pleasure from either, because the attention is absorbed in the intellectual element of likeness or difference.

Recent investigations have done much, however, to explain the physiological processes which accompany physical pleasure and pain.

PHYSIOLOGY OF PAIN.

All action of a nerve, and hence all sensation, is accompanied by molecular change of the nerve-substance, and so by waste. When the waste becomes excessive, through long-continued or violent stimulation, fatigue, disagreeable feeling, or even pain, results. For example, an extremely loud sound, like a cannon-shot; an excess of light, as when staring at the sun; a biting taste, as of cayenne pepper; a strong smell, as of ammonia; all these are disagreeable, and soon become painful, and deaden the sensibility of the organ involved, showing exhaustion.

Disintegration or disruption of tissue is but a more extreme degree of the same experience. For example, raw mustard on the tongue occasions a disagreeable acrid taste, which soon becomes an acute pain; and on any other part of the skin, it causes, if the contact is continued for some time, acute pain and blistering, which is plainly disintegration of tissue. But pain occurs only in those tissues which are "supplied with cerebrospinal nerves." The substance of the brain itself, for instance, is not sensitive, and no pain is felt when it is injured or cut.

PHYSIOLOGY OF PLEASURE.

The physiology of Pleasure of the senses is not so easily traced. But it seems to be proved that pleasure occurs when the waste of tissue consequent on molecular change in the nerve-endings is repaired almost or quite as rapidly as it occurs, or else stimulation and repair alternate at very short intervals. For example, a mass of bright color gives pleasure; and, since green tints predominate in nature, the eye has become adjusted to green, and can endure stimulation by that color far longer than by any other. Hence green is said to "rest the eye," to be less fatiguing.

But change from one color to another gives still more and higher pleasure. "The amount of pleasure is probably in the direct ratio of the number of nerve-fibres involved, and in the inverse ratio of the natural frequency of excitation." (Grant Allen, Physiological Æsthetics, 25.)

It is important to notice, however, that variety and contrast introduce the intellectual element of discrimination, involving a quite different and higher activity than mere sense-stimulation by a mass of color.

How it is that waste or destruction of nerve-substance appears in consciousness as pain, while alternate waste or repair of nerve-substance appear in consciousness as pleasure, is a mystery on which these investigations throw no light.

PHILOSOPHICAL FORMULA.

But the philosophical content, the real meaning of pleasure and pain, may perhaps be not so absolutely beyond our reach, and attempts have been made to reduce it to a formula.

As to physical pleasure and pain, there seems to be some approach to an agreement among the best authorities upon some form of the following theory;—That pleasure is an accompaniment of those experiences which tend to the preservation or well-being of the sentient organism, and pain a concomitant of those experiences which tend to the destruction or injury of that organism. For obviously the opposite arrangement would tend, on the whole, to the extinction of all sentient life on the earth. Mr. Grant Allen, a disciple of Herbert Spencer, says;—"The human or animal organism may be conveniently regarded as a complicated and delicate machine, specially constructed for self-conservation and the production of like organisms in the future. That it should be so constructed as to correspond with the environment is a condition-precedent of its existence at all. Hence every organism, in proportion to the completeness of its adaptation, energetically resists any act which interferes with its efficiency as a working machine; and such interferences are known subjectively as pains." (Physiological Æsthetics, 17.)

And Mr. Spencer has said, to the same effect;—" Pleasures are the incentives to life-supporting acts, and pains are the deterrents from life destroying acts." (Psychology, I, 284.)

"Pleasure," says President Hopkins, "seems to have been intended as an inducement to the performance of acts which are to have remote consequences of which the agents themselves are often either ignorant or regardless. The pleasure of the child, and of the man too, in eating, and in muscular movement, is the inducement to do that which is necessary for the up-building of the body, but for which they generally have no care." (Lectures on Moral Science, 61.)

But this theory must meet the difficulty that pleasures, if too often repeated, become injurious to the organism before they become painful; while pains, if not excessive, grow less by usage and habit, and cease to give warning of injury,—instance, the violently noxious taste of tobacco. Mr. Allen recognizes the difficulty as follows. "Pleasure and pain are only the reflex of the actual state of the nerves, and do not necessarily yield any indications of their future state. Hence, actions which will ultimately yield painful sensations, may in their earlier stages be pleasurable, and *vice versa.*" (Op. cit. 29.)

Mr. Spencer and his disciple both meet the difficulty by making an exception, and declaring that "in the vast majority of cases . . . . whatever is prejudicial or beneficial to the organism as a whole, is generally painful or pleasurable respectively." But in nature the exceptions seem to reach as wide as the rule. Nearly all animals will injure themselves by over-eating when opportunity is afforded them; the pleasures of combat urge many of them to their destruction; in a drought, many animals, when they at last reach the water, will drink themselves to death, if permitted. Pleasure and pain, then, as motives of the physical life, need to be overruled by circumstances or by reason. What Providence does objectively for the brutes, by means of their "environment," is done for man subjectively, by giving him reason and foresight. The formula must recognize this before it can be made universal.

There is a valuable suggestion in Aristotle's definition, that pleasure is action; it is the normal result of proper activity. Lotze has attained a better formula than Spencer's, by reaching it from this side. "Feeling is the consequence and signal of coincidence or conflict between the excitations produced in us and the conditions of our permanent well-being. Pleasure would then follow every use of our natural powers within the limits of these conditions, and 'unpleasure' every one in conflict with those conditions." (Dictate, Psychologie §47.) Here the necessary limitations are supplied, and this formula has the advantage that it is easily carried up into the higher regions of the intellect, and also into the domain of Ethics, where we learn that the highest good results "from the activity of the highest powers in a right relation to their highest object." (Hopkins, Moral Science, 53.)

Yet we need to notice that the formula is a general one, and that pleasure and pain cannot always be antithetically balanced against each other. Some pains are acute, and some are dull; some pleasures are intense, and others are massive. But there is no necessary opposition or correspondence in their respective origins or natures, answering to this relativeness of terms. Acute pain is always the signal of destruction of tissue. If our intensest pleasures were exactly the opposite of acute pains, those activities of the system which are constructive or reconstructive would be the most delightful, and the circulation of the blood, respiration and digestion, would be our greatest physical pleasures. What they really result in, is that massive kind of pleasure called "feeling well," or "exhilaration," and the like, opposed rather to the pains and discomforts of fatigue, dyspepsia, ennui, depression. The converse is also true, that derangement of these functions, especially digestion, produces, not acute pain, but a general tone of feeling, accompanying all one's experience. Thus biliousness produces despondency, dullness, a massive discomfort, pervading the body and affecting the mind. That eccentric and brilliant Divine, Dr. S. H. Cox, declared that he never had known a triumphant Christian death-bed, in a case where the disease was below the diaphragm.

FEELINGS OF THE DIFFERENT SENSES.

A plain distinction exists between the feelings connected with the more ignoble senses, taste, smell, touch, muscular sensation, and sense of temperature,—and, on the other hand, those connected with the senses of hearing and sight. The difference, however, is no greater here than with regard to the intellectual content of sensations. We found that smell, taste, and hearing give no knowledge of the external world; that smell, taste, muscular sensation and sense of temperature cannot be "inlets to the soul" in the same way as sight, hearing, and touch. They cannot convey abstract thought, or furnish means of communication between minds.

Moreover, since the senses of sight and hearing are those through which the intellect is chiefly exercised, in the use of language, the intellect necessarily enters more quickly and perfectly into connection with their objects than with those of the other senses. Again, the direct pleasures of these senses are less intense and absorbing, more refined, and more dependent on culture and attention than those of the other senses. "Every single fibre of the optic and auditory nerves seems capable of differential stimulation, and yields us a distinct and separate impression. Hence, while stimulation and fatigue usually extend over large tracts of the olfactory and gustatory systems, every single fibre of the optic and auditory apparatus, with its connected center, is probably capable of separate pleasure and separate fatigue." The nerves of sight and hearing are also capable of far more rapid alternations than the others. "There is reason to believe that the optic fibres and terminal organs are repaired, in ordinary cases, seventeen times per second, and those of the auditory nerves thirty-three times per second." (Grant Allen, op. cit., 97–99.)

IMPORTANCE OF SIGHT.

These facts make clear the intellectual pre-eminence of the sense of Sight, show that the intellect pervades and interpenetrates our sensations of sight in a peculiar way. And this serves to confirm the view that the sense of beauty, which is almost exclusively connected with the sense of Sight, is entirely an intellectual perception and pleasure. Even Grant Allen is obliged to admit that "minute intellectual discrimination is one of the marks that differentiate the Æsthetic Feelings from the other pleasures and pains."

There may be particular experiences in which it is difficult to say whether sense-pleasure or intellectual pleasure predominates. But this gives no confirmation to the theory that all our feelings are only combinations or developments of the feelings of sense. The feelings called social, intellectual, sympathetic, æsthetic, spiritual, cannot be thus dissolved away. We speak of the pain caused by hearing of a friend's death, and also of the pain of a cut or burnt finger. But it is plain that, although both experiences can be brought under our general formula, as being both depressing and injurious to life in the large sense, and hence properly called by the same name of *pain*, yet they have nothing in common in their own nature. Their resemblance consists in the fact that one sustains somewhat the same relation to the social and mental life that the other does to the physical life. We speak of the pleasures of eating, of hearing music, of seeing pictures and landscapes, of reading about noble deeds, of doing good, of loving holiness; but the general resemblance among them, by which we class them all as pleasures, is far less characteristic than their specific differences.

The pain of hunger, the pain of a burn, and the pain of neuralgia, have plainly a very close resemblance. The disagreeable feeling of a bad taste or smell, of a discordant sound, of a coarse combination of colors, have an evident resemblance to the positive pains just mentioned. But the feeling one has on witnessing cruelty, or on being cheated, or on learning of a friend's death, or on seeing one's house in flames, all these closely resemble one another, but differ widely from the other classes of feelings, and can never be derived or compounded out of them.

DIGRESSION ON MUSIC.

We have given the pleasures of sight far higher rank than those of hearing. But the art of music, dependent on the sense of hearing, has attained such a wonderful development in recent times that we take brief notice of it here, as a transitional topic between sense-pleasure and Æsthetics.

The feeling of music is by some called an emotion; but it does not come within the definition of emotion proper. Nearly all the peculiar effects of music are due to association. An exile in a foreign land weeps on hearing his national air, though it be the liveliest of tunes. The plaintive wailing of the bag-pipes excites the Scot to martial ardor and courage. "Yankee Doodle," though a British burlesque, arouses no anger, and though an utterly trivial air, excites no contempt, in any American bosom, for long association has made it stirring and patriotic. "America" excites our patriotic ardor now, though originally a Jacobite air, composed to honor the exiled tyrant James. "The Marseillaise" means nothing to us, to the Frenchman it is frenzy. When "program-music" is played, those of the audience who have the "program" exhibit feeling at the right places, the others make mistakes. The fact seems to be,—Music excites the nerves in ways having some general correspondence with its style and rhythm. A lively tune, by its rapid alternations and transitions, causes a kind of tumult of the nerves, which is associated with joy. A slow tune is of course calming in its effects. The piercing note of a fife must of course affect the nerves differently from the low notes of the pipe-organ. But beyond these things the entire effect of music on the feelings is due to association and culture.

The simple pleasure of music, apart from specific feelings excited by it, depends largely on rhythm, which is also important in poetry, dancing, military evolutions, gymnastic exercises, and other sources of pleasure.

Rhythm gives alternation of stimulation, and hence short intervals of rest and repair to the organs involved, and also satisfies expectation on each recurrence. Hence when the movement is once set up, its mere continuance causes pleasure, and its alteration or sudden discontinuance gives a slight shock, like a "false step" in dancing or marching.

There is here also, evidently, an intellectual element, above mere sense-stimulation, not unlike that involved in contrast of colors. The same principle is, moreover, involved in the pleasure given by single musical tones. Such a tone is pleasant because its sound-waves recur with regularity, and is still more pleasant when compounded of several tones or overtones, giving regularly recurring "beats" or interferences of air-waves, as explained by the science of acoustics. But a single tone, however sweet, soon becomes tedious and unpleasant, because so few nerves are involved that all soon become wearied. And the higher intellectual element of contrast, comparison, and unity, is needed to constitute beauty in any true sense of the word.

ÆSTHETICS.

The science of Æsthetics treats of the nature of beauty, the principles of the fine arts, of criticism, and of taste. The word is derived from a Greek word meaning perception, and so would be expected to apply to all perception through the senses. Kant did so use it in his "Critik of Pure Reason," where "Transcendental Æsthetic" means the metaphysics of sensation. The word is hence in some respects an unfortunate one. Some recent writers have undertaken to reduce it to its ancient or its Kantian meaning, as a help toward reducing all feeling to sense-feeling. Thus Mr. Grant Allen, in his work already quoted, treats at full length of pleasure and pain, and endeavors to show "the purely physical origin of the sense of beauty."

We must, then, guard against supposing that the term, though a convenient one, gives in itself any explanation of the feeling or idea of beauty. We are obliged, indeed, after all, to use the phrase Idea of Beauty to denote the metaphysical side of this mental product.

The word Beauty refers usually to Sight alone among the senses. The objects of the other senses are seldom called beautiful, and then generally in a figurative way. Even in music, some of the most descriptive words applied to it as beautiful are borrowed from sight, such as color, light and shade. Comparatively few natural sounds can be called even agreeable, while a vast variety of natural objects and scenes are beautiful to the eye.

BEAUTY NOT SENSE-PLEASURE.

What, then, is the difference between mere sense-pleasure, occasioned by color, for instance, and the feeling of beauty? We hold that the difference lies in the activity of the intellect, and that in proportion as the intellect is active in relation to beauty, the feeling is elevated and pure.

The lower animals can enjoy pleasure of the senses, even of the sense of sight. Bright and varied colors are agreeable to them. But they have no "Idea of Beauty," no Taste, no perception of ugliness, no feeling of beauty.

The intellectual activity connected with beauty may be said to begin very low down in the scale, with the element of attention. Beauty is not obtrusive upon the very senses, does not force itself on our attention, like a cannon shot or a strong odor. We are obliged to look for it; we have to give it our best attention, or we cannot recognize it, and then it does not exist for us.

A higher intellectual element, essential to real perception of beauty, is found in the power of discrimination. "The vulgar are pleased by great masses of color, especially red, orange, and purple, which give their coarse nervous organizations the requisite stimulus: the refined, with nerves of less caliber but greater discriminativeness, require delicate combinations of complementaries, and prefer neutral tints to the glare of primary hues. Children and savages love to dress in all the colors of the rainbow." (Grant Allen.)

The eyes are restless organs; they perpetually adjust themselves in various ways to their objects; they are the constant instrument of intellectual discrimination; they minister constantly to this intellectual function, which affords a peculiar intellectual delight. Mr. Allen himself seems virtually to admit that this is the true explanation, for he says that in the perception of beauty or ugliness, "as the emotional element [sense-feeling], is weak, it [beauty or ugliness] is mainly cognized only as an intellectual discrimination." (39.)

But there are still higher intellectual elements in beauty. Order, proportion, symmetry, fitness, are called beautiful, and enter, indeed, into nearly all beauty; yet they are purely intellectual relations, not to be attained by sensations, unless the mind be present to compare and abstract those sensations. Again, a geometrical demonstration is often, and correctly, called beautiful, and so may be an argument, legal or metaphysical, a scientific experiment, a mechanical invention.

There is also an element which may fairly be called ethical, sometimes described as "disinterestedness." A beautiful object may be enjoyed by many persons; there can be no monopoly of it. Lotze makes this the peculiar mark of æsthetic feeling, that it is "universal," it is not exhausted by one individual. "The objects of Fine Art, and all objects called æsthetic, are exempt from the fatal taint of rivalry and contest attaching to other agreeables; they draw men together in mutual sympathy; and are thus eminently social and humanizing. A picture or a statue can be seen by millions; a great poem reaches all that understand its language; a fine melody may spread pleasure over the habitable globe." (Bain.)

BEAUTY INTELLECTUAL.

But how is beauty explained or accounted for by referring it to the intellect? We are here thrown back upon the ultimate law or formula that pleasure or happiness results from the proper activity of our powers in a right relation to their appropriate objects. It is the natural function and perpetual effort of intellect to discover unity, to reconcile contradictions, to find resemblances, to classify under wider genera, to reduce all things to a few conceptions or to one; such is the boundless task which the intellect sets itself.

Natural science is the classification of things, reducing them to ever fewer and wider classes, and attempting to show their relation to a few forms or to one. Physical science is the attempt to show that all forces are but forms of one force, and all kinds of matter but a few original sorts or one sort. Mathematical science is the attempt to provide an *organon* by which this can be done, or, what is the same thing, to unravel the necessary judgments contained in the universe, and show them related in a system.

Success, or apparent success, in any part of this endless task gives intellectual pleasure. A reconciliation between two apparent opposites, a discovery of unknown resemblances, a new discrimination, which always involves resemblance, is delightful.

When the matters thought of are trifling, as the sound of two similar words, in the pun, we call it a kind of wit, and are excited to a "sudden glory of laughter."

When the objects are of different rank, as, one physical and the other moral, we have figures of speech, similes and metaphors, always accounted beautiful since the dawn of poetry. When Homer compares a warrior to a lion or a torrent, it is the endless striving and passion of the mind for unity which makes the simile beautiful. And if, in our day, these comparisons have come to seem trivial, it is because so many more important and more perfect unifications have been made possible in the progress of knowledge.

Newton's identification of attraction in the solar system with gravity on the earth, is always considered one of the most beautiful of demonstrations, even by those who have no knowledge of it as a mathematical process. The more recent assimilation of the stars and the earth, by means of the spectroscope, will always be deemed one of the most beautiful of all discoveries.

CONFIRMATIONS.

1. It is a strong confirmation of this theory that it explains many difficulties which have excited much discussion. One such point is the similarity of beauty and some kinds of wit, already alluded to, which has been puzzling to some. The theory helps also to explain the beauty of symmetry, the having two or more sides alike; although the pleasure which this gives is partly accounted for, no doubt, by association, since the human body and nearly all the higher animals, many leaves, etc., are symmetrical. It explains, too, why an admirer or critic of beauty seems to feel within him an ideal, a standard, which nevertheless is not a definite pattern, but an idea of perfection in general, which can never be absolutely realized. Imitation, either of a pattern or an ideal, in itself gives us pleasure. If it is trivial we laugh at it; if it is serious and worthy we call it beautiful; if too long continued it is fatiguing. Imitation evidently exercises in a high degree the comparing and reconciling activity of the mind. This theory seems also to explain why æsthetic feeling is felt to be unselfish and universal. When we find in any object, or interpret into it, any congruity, or attempt at or tendency toward such congruity, with this necessary and universal action of the intellect, we receive æsthetic pleasure, and say "here is something beautiful."

2. Another confirmation of this view is, that it not only rises naturally from sense-phenomena to the grandest and widest conceptions, finding beauty everywhere, but it can advance higher still, to conduct, to moral relations. A beautiful character is one which, among opposing temptations, preserves a rational consistency, a unity wrought out of variety. "We experience the sense of beauty in witnessing the conformity of conduct to a high standard of moral excellence, which excites

in our minds a pleasure of the same order as that which we derive from the contemplation of a noble work of Art." (Dr. Carpenter.)

3. A third confirmation of this theory is that it explains the phenomenon called Ugliness. This, though called the opposite of beauty, does not excite a painful feeling, unless it be in abnormally sensitive natures. Ugliness may sometimes be the expression of hateful moral qualities, and to this point we shall return. But to the intellect it is the inharmonious, the asymmetrical, that which cannot be reduced to unity, that which resists the efforts of the mind. It gives the intellect a shock of failure, of inability to accomplish its end, to realize itself,—a feeling of disappointed effort. And, since beauty is so general in nature and art, its absence gives a shock of disappointed expectation. But no such contrast can be traced between beauty and ugliness as between pleasure and pain, for ugliness is only lack of beauty, while pain is a positive experience of destructive action.

4. A fourth remark upon this view is that it takes up into itself many partial views which have proved, each by itself, quite inadequate. Such are the views that beauty consists in unity, in variety, in order, in fitness or adaptation, in usefulness, in harmony, in rhythm, in contrast, in curved lines, in expression, in social convention. Most writers have assumed that there must be some one principle or quality in which beauty consists; that every beautiful object must be beautiful for the same reason. An amazing number of theories have been constructed, in the attempt to discover and prove such a principle. From Plato to Ruskin, the ablest and most ingenious writers have labored with this problem, but hardly any two have agreed. Their views may be found in special treatises; we cannot make room for them here.

If our view be correct, nearly all these theories contained a part of the truth, while each committed a fundamental error in seeking for a single quality as the cause of all beauty. Æsthetic feeling is rather an accompaniment of all felicitous and successful operation of the mental powers. Beauty is therefore in the mind, just as color is; the quality in the object is something which evokes the creative activity of the intellect, from which results æsthetic pleasure. A large number of such qualities may thus awaken the intellect,—order, symmetry, fitness, rhythm, expression, etc.; these qualities may be moral, mental, or conventional; these objects may be abstract relations, mathematical or metaphysical. "Yet even those writers," says Dr. T. Brown "who would be astonished, if we were to regard them as capable of any faith in the universal *a parte rei*, believe in universal beauty *a parte rei*, and inquire what it is which constitutes the beautiful, very much as the scholastic logicians inquired into the real essence of the universal." (II, 60.)

CONCLUSION.

We think it is evident from these higher discussions, without more formal proof, that beauty is something beyond mere sense-feeling, and that no theory of it as a combination of such feelings, can answer the great philosophical questions which arise concerning it. There is to be accounted for, not only a feeling, but also an idea; not merely a correspondence between the physical world and the nervous system, but a correspondence between the principles of the world and those of the intellect.

Yet similar concessions and exceptions remain to be made, with those which we made when speaking of Space and Time. Undoubtedly much of our perception of beauty is due to association of ideas, habit, culture, social convention, individual preference,—out of all which a vast structure of æsthetic Taste is reared. And this accounts for the diversity of taste among different individuals, nations, periods, and stages of civilization. "A landscape which bears a resemblance to the scene of our early youth, cannot fail to be felt as more beautiful by us than by others. . The countenance of one who is dear to us sheds a charm over similar features. An author whose work we have read at an early period with delight, continues forever to exercise no inconsiderable dominion over our general taste." (Dr. T. Brown.)

Our objective knowledge of beauty in nature and art, in thought and character, is of course derived from experience. All our lives we are imbibing knowledge of the beautiful, forming our taste, learning what is considered beautiful and what ugly. But this experience itself could not exist without a peculiar capacity in the mind, beyond mere perception, to cognize objects under such a relation. When discussing Space, we found reason to believe, that although an objective knowledge of space-relations is undoubtedly derived from experience, yet that knowledge could not be accounted for without supposing some necessity of the mind to cognize external objects under those relations. So in this case, the objective knowledge of beauty through experience cannot be accounted for without a similar presupposition. If we call the one the Idea of Space, we may well call the other the Idea of Beauty.

EXPRESSION.

It is held by some that beauty consists largely in the expression of character and moral worth. Kant, especially, made the highest beauty consist in symbolizing moral qualities. But beauty and expression are two different things. Fine qualities of character, disposition, manners, etc., are beautiful in themselves, and so, in a certain sense, the expression of them is beautiful. Moral and spiritual beauty may properly be called higher in degree than physical beauty, but this does not prove that the latter has its existence in symbolizing the former. The following considerations seem to us sufficient to prove the complete separation of the two things.

1. Many of the most beautiful human beings are depraved in character and weak in intellect.

2. Much of this expressiveness is conventional, and founded on association.

3. At best, the observer can only recognize those qualities which he himself possesses, or is capable, through experience, of appreciating. A coarse savage is necessarily incapable of perceiving refined qualities of character, and hence of finding beauty in their expression. Beauty can symbolize the highest moral qualities only to him who has himself some share of the same qualities.

EMOTION.

We now return from the excursion in which we followed out the natural suggestion of the fundamental elements of Pleasure and Pain, and begin the discussion of the specific kinds of feeling. According to our plan, we begin with that kind which has most to do with our physical organism.

The term Emotion is often used in a vague and wide sense, and even applied to all the Feelings. But its proper as well as etymological meaning is restricted to those feelings which presuppose previous sensation or representation, being excited by ideas of pleasure or pain in the mind, and which "manifest their existence and character by some sensible effect upon the body." (Fleming, Vocab. of Phil.) In violent emotion the disturbance or tumult of the nervous system is the most prominent fact, which is well expressed by the old term, "commotion."

The expression of Emotion by bodily movements is due to an excess of nervous excitement, which, unable to be discharged in other ways, overflows upon the motor nerves, and produces involuntary movements.

REFLEX MOVEMENTS.

Indeed, the bodily movements accompanying emotion are a development of that class of activities called automatic or reflex. For example, tickling the sole of the foot of a sleeping person causes the foot to be drawn up, without sensation or volition. In the case of a person whose lower limbs are paralyzed, similar irritation may produce violent convulsions, though the patient cannot move his feet voluntarily, and has no sensation in them. So, a very slight irritation of the end of a nerve, by a sliver of glass or a filing of iron, has been known to cause convulsions out of all proportion with the importance of the cause; "and a trifling injury may in this way end in tetanus or lock-jaw." "Strychnia so affects the nerves that, on the occasion of the slightest stimulus, they react in convulsive activity." (Maudsley.)

In a similar way, when an *idea* is fitted to produce emotion, it may result in bodily movements having no relation to the importance of the idea, but to the peculiar condition of the mind and nervous system, and various mental and physical relations. "To all appearances a violent emotion may act sometimes in the same way as a strong physical shock to the nervous system, for it may produce in some instances convulsions, fainting, loss of sensation, paralysis of movement, deafness; exactly the effects which a strong electric shock may produce." (Maudsley, Physiology of Mind, 350.)

A piece of news which is of no importance to one person,

may give a severe shock to another, and this, in a person of particularly sensitive organization, may find expression in screams, contortions, or even suspension of the action of the heart. A "ticklish" child laughs when the *idea* of tickling is excited by pointing the finger at him. The mere recollection of a funny scene often produces laughter, and the memory of a danger escaped often causes a shudder or a start.

SPENCER AND DARWIN.

The ordinary expression of emotion, however, is by the muscles of the face. Physiologists explain this by a "wave of nervous energy" contracting many muscles at once, a "diffused nervous discharge" which, says Mr. Herbert Spencer, excites, first, "the small muscles attached to the easily moved parts, such as the face, afterwards more numerous and larger muscles moving heavier parts, and eventually the whole body." Mr. Darwin investigated the expression of emotion, both in man and in the lower animals, with his accustomed thoroughness and ability. We cannot make room for an extended view of his theories, and anything briefer could not do them justice.

Emotion is as fatiguing to the system as voluntary exertion. Fear, grief, sorrow, anger, exhaust the vital force, the nervous energy. And, if the expression of emotion is suppressed, it may exert a depressing influence equivalent to the shock of a violent emotion. Those who conceal their griefs and show no outward signs of sorrow, are more likely to "die of a broken heart" than those who express emotion by violent gestures and loud cries.

The physical expression of emotion is by some considered an essential part of it, without which it is called "suppressed emotion." In ordinary language, however, the emotion and its expression are quite different things, the one a feeling, a psychical experience, the other a movement, a physical experience. Consciousness testifies that feelings usually expressed in this way may be entirely suppressed, so far as physical movement goes, and yet the experience, of fear, anger, or other feeling, continues in the mind.

EXPERIMENTS AND THEORIES.

This remarkable distinctness and yet connection between emotion and its expression has led to some curious theories and experiments. It is said to be a common experience of actors, that when they imitate the conventional expression of any emotion, they experience the emotion itself, the feeling in the mind. Edmund Burke said that he had successfully tried the experiment. "I have remarked that on mimicking the looks and gestures of angry, or placid, or frightened, or daring men, I have involuntarily found my mind turned to that passion whose appearance I endeavored to imitate." A theory has hence been formed that the bodily changes come first, and the feeling is a result of them, that emotion *is* "a feeling of the bodily changes as they occur."

"What kind of an emotion of fear would be left," says Professor W. James, "if the feelings neither of quickened heart-beats nor of shallow breathing, neither of trembling lips nor of weakened limbs, neither of goose-flesh nor of visceral stirrings were present, it is quite impossible to think. Can any one fancy the state of rage and picture no ebullition of it in the chest, no flushing of the face, no dilatation of the nostrils, no clenching of the teeth, no impulse to vigorous action, but in their stead limp muscles, calm breathing, and a placid face?" "In rage, it is notorious how we 'work ourselves up' to a climax by repeated outbreaks of expression. Refuse to express a passion, and it dies. Count ten before venting your anger, and its occasion seems ridiculous." ("Mind" for April, 1884.)

However useful the practical suggestions which can be drawn from this view, it is contradicted by observation and by consciousness. "The motor expressions of the emotions are really the movements which would be manifested in greater degree if the emotions were realized in action. . . . . . In the desire for revenge [rather in rage], the gratification of which is to injure the offender, the natural weapons of offence are put in action, animals ejecting their poison, thrusting out their stings, attempting to tear, bite, or kick, and man, clenching his fist, stamping his feet and gnashing his teeth, as he would do if he were actually taking his revenge. In terror, the satisfaction of which is the averting of a great impending danger, the struggles for preservation are seen in the starting back, the shrinking, the sudden standing still, and the open mouth by which a deep inspiration is taken in order to prepare for exertion." (Maudsley, Physiology of Mind, 379.)

Such facts show that the expression of emotion, though nearly always associated with the mental experience, is a consequence, and not, in normal cases, an antecedent of it. And evidently, in any experiment like that of Burke, the idea of the particular emotion which is to be produced must already be in the mind at the beginning of the experiment. It is true that hypnotized persons or somnambulists, when put into the posture of prayer, for example, or of fighting, sometimes display the appropriate feeling in their words and actions. But it is quite possible in such cases that the posture suggests the feeling by association of ideas, instead of causing the emotion directly.

We are often directly conscious that the mental part of an emotion comes first. For example, when a joke is heard we know that we do not experience the feeling of the ludicrous because the joke causes the peculiar muscular convulsions called laughter. Or, if I am afraid of a snarling dog, I know that my fear is not the consequence of running away, but of the idea of a bite, and the conception of pain, associated in my mind with a snarl, and this psychical experience leads to the physical movements.

Emotion varies according to the nature of the exciting idea, and according to the circumstances and character of the person experiencing it. Each such variation might be called a class of Emotions. Obviously, if all the ways in which different ideas can arouse feelings that manifest themselves in expression or gesture should be enumerated, the list would be a long one. We shall discuss only the principal kinds of Emotion, but in doing so we shall find that many others, usually distinguished, can be grouped around these. We begin with Fear because it has the best known and most strongly marked physical effects.

FEAR.

The Emotion of Fear is aroused by the idea of pain as about to affect one. Its typical expression is seen in a cur, which, at sight of a whip in his master's hand, puts his tail between his legs, and crouches whining to the ground. In man its bodily effects are progressive in intensity. Turning pale and trembling are among the first, then weakening at the knees, cold sweat, shortness of breath, goose-flesh, and motions of the viscera, culminating in complete paralysis, so that the victim is unable either to run away or defend himself. In this extreme form the emotion is called Terror, and may be found also in the lower animals, where the "charming" of birds by serpents is an instance of fear-paralysis.

An element of pain obviously runs through the experience called Fear, in all its forms, and this pain is sometimes almost or quite equal to the pain which is dreaded. Yet this pain has a preservative function, as inciting attempts to escape.

What we have thus far said applies to fear of physical injury. Apprehension of social or mental or remotely future ills, is rightly classed under Fear, though the expression in the face is far less strongly marked, and is called Melancholy, or Anxiety. Various other terms are employed to denote different kinds of fear, as modified by circumstances or by combination with other feelings, such as, Anxiety, Terror, Dread, Suspicion, Awe, Distrust, Timidity, Diffidence, etc. Detailed distinctions between them would be aside from our present purpose.

ANGER.

Defensive Emotion, in its most usual form, is called Anger. It is aroused by the smart of actual pain, or by the apprehension of pain as about to be inflicted by some agent. Obviously the same idea of future pain may excite either fear or anger, according as the "noxious agent" is overwhelming in power, or not, and according to the power, character, and feelings of the person experiencing the emotion. The specific difference between fear and anger is, that in the former, attention is fixed upon the pain, in the latter upon the agent that causes the pain. While fear prompts to escape, anger prompts to defense, at first, and afterwards to retaliation. The expression of anger is in general the opposite of that of fear; the latter is depressing in its effect on the organism, the former exciting. Many animals, of various species, erect their hair or feathers and arch their backs or expand their wings, when angry, so as to appear larger and more terrible to their enemies. (See Darwin.)

The signs of anger are a general nervous excitement, a flushed face, labored respiration, trembling, change of voice, etc. If the excitement proceeds without restraint, it usually terminates in violent movements, which relieve the nervous tension. "The gestures of a man in this state," says Darwin, "usually differ from the purposeless writhings and struggles of one suffering from an agony of pain; for they represent more or less plainly the act of striking or fighting with an enemy."

The first shock of anger is painful and exhausting, but the accomplishment of its purpose gives pleasure; the immediate discharge gives a kind of relief; and the averting of danger gives relief from fear, as well as the pleasure of self-assertion; the prevention of future attacks, through destruction of the "noxious agent" or fear excited in him, also yields satisfaction.

The extreme form of anger is called Rage, or Frenzy. When the immediate manifestation is suppressed or unsuccessful, yet the feelings continue excited toward the same object, this lengthened feeling is called Hatred, and its gratification is called Revenge. Here emotion is no longer pure, but purposive actions are planned and performed for the gratification of malevolent feeling. Accordingly, Hatred is usually treated of as an Affection, the opposite of Love. But as love, in its lowest form, is the expression of physical relations, so hatred begins with anger. Many names are given to different kinds and degrees of defensive feeling, in various relations of life, and in various combinations with other feelings, as,—Animosity, Antipathy, Hostility, Hatred, Aversion, Abhorrence, Dislike, Resentment, Malice, Spite, Vindictiveness, etc.

GRIEF AND JOY.

These approach more nearly than any other emotions to pure pleasure and pain. Grief and Joy are feelings excited by important events affecting one's self; when we grieve or rejoice with others, this is called sympathetic emotion. We experience grief for the loss of a friend, a child, a fortune,—not for a stranger or a penny; it usually implies frustrated or disappointed affection for a sentient object. A good illustration of grief is a dog at his master's grave, howling and refusing food. David's lament for Absalom is a remarkable literary expression of grief.

Joy is typically expressed by the dog that wags his tail and licks his master's hand, and gambols about him. The evolutionists have not yet clearly explained why a very similar action of the tail expresses almost contrary emotions in the lion and in the dog. Various degrees of grief, under varying circumstances, are called Melancholy, Regret, Sorrow, Distress, Affliction, Woe, Misery, Tribulation, etc. Many different names are also applied to varieties of joy.

EXPECTATION, WONDER, ETC.

Several other feelings might well be described as Emotions, but are for the most part complicated with other mental experiences, and of little psychological importance. We give an example or two of the way in which they can easily be analyzed.

Expectation has a characteristic bodily expression, well illustrated in a cat watching for a mouse. It is the feeling aroused by some event as about to happen. But evidently it is in itself only an intense attention. The nerve-force is loaded up, as it were, and waiting for a definite perception to pull the trigger and discharge its force in activity. If the expected event is disagreeable, as when the mouse is expecting the cat, apprehension, or fear, is the name usually given to this feeling. When the object is remote and agreeable, and a mental or social rather than a physical event, the feeling is called hope. On Expectant-Attention see page 66.

Wonder is the vague pleasure associated with that which is new and great, extraordinary, and not well understood. A low form of this feeling, common to some of the lower animals, is called curiosity. It also receives other names when complicated with other experiences, as,—Astonishment, Surprise, Admiration, Awe, Amazement, Marveling, etc. The bodily expressions of all these are very much alike,—an erect posture, eyes distended, mouth generally open. Shakespeare says, "I saw a smith stand with open mouth, swallowing a tailor's news." Mr. Darwin accounts for the open mouth by unconscious preparation for great exertion by a full inspiration.

Wonder lies at the basis of natural religious feeling. Primitive man, beginning to reflect on the vast forces and inexplicable phenomena of nature, is at first overwhelmed with wonder, then seeks a cause for these things, and readily turns toward a supernatural cause.

LAUGHTER AND THE LUDICROUS.

Laughter is a peculiar convulsion, affecting chiefly the muscles of respiration, but sometimes spreading to all parts of the body. It may have a purely physical cause, as hysteria, or tickling. According to Mr. Herbert Spencer, laughter is the expression of a general excitement of the nerves. "An overflow of nerve-force, undirected by any motive, will take first the most habitual routes. It is through the organs of speech that feeling passes into movement with the greatest frequency. . . . . Hence certain muscles round the mouth, small and easy to move, are the first to contract under pleasurable emotion." The respiratory muscles are also in constant use, and so emotion next " convulses not only certain of the articulatory and vocal muscles, but also those which expel air from the lungs."

Laughter, it is important to notice, is not necessarily connected with the Ludicrous. It may arise, besides physical irritations, from joy, gladness, any sudden access of mental pleasure. The lower animals cannot laugh, though they seem to be capable, in some cases, of joining in the merriment of their masters. On the other hand, the perception of the ludicrous, may or may not excite laughter.

THE COMIC.

The cause of the Emotion of the Ludicrous, or the Comic, as a mental feeling, has been the subject of much dispute among philosophers, from Aristotle down. As in the case of beauty, it has generally been assumed that there must be some one objective quality belonging to every comic thing or event. Most writers have fixed upon Incongruity as this quality.

In the celebrated theory of Hobbes, "Laughter is a sudden glory, arising from sudden conception of some eminency in ourselves, by comparison with the infirmity of others, or with our own formerly." But this misses the point, and confounds the laugh or chuckle of coarse self-conceit, with perception of the comic.

Bain says the occasion of the Ludicrous is the degradation of some person or interest possessing dignity, and refers the pleasure of degrading things thus to the sentiment of Power and the release from a state of constraint. But this is to deny and explain away the idea of the comic as completely as did Hobbes. Both these explanations depend upon incongruity, but do not attempt to explain its comic quality.

Spencer has proceeded a step further, remarking that the incongruity must be *descending*, because serious thought or perception requires more nerve-force than trivial thought, and a trivial incident, suddenly intervening, sets free a large part of the force which is being expended, so that it finds a way of discharge in laughter. This explains the outward explosion of laughter in a large class of cases, but it goes no further. For a case of descending incongruity may be comic to some persons and tragic to others.

Bain's principal illustration of the ludicrous is the case of a pompous, finely dressed man, who falls into a muddy ditch. Nearly all the spectators of such a scene would laugh, and some of them undoubtedly would laugh with a spice of malice, of triumph, on account of the victim's pomposity, which would seem to them to deserve a fall. Now, suppose that the victim were falling over a precipice a thousand feet high; hardly any one, even his bitterest enemy, would be malicious enough to laugh. Or suppose it is a helpless little child that falls into the mud, however finely dressed it may be, hardly any one would laugh. These incidents would be *tragic*, not comic. Or, in the first example given, the victim's wife and daughter, if they were to see him fall into the mud, would be far from laughter, would rather be filled with sympathy, pity, and helpfulness. Or, the tailor, who had not been paid for the fine clothes thus ruined, may be supposed to be filled with despair and grief. To these persons the incident is tragic, to the others comic.

We are now prepared to see that simple incongruity is not a sufficient explanation of the comic. Different writers place the incongruity at different points, scarcely any two agree, and few seem to be aware that the point needing explanation is how incongruity can give pleasure. It would seem that incongruity should give pain, and we find that in tragic scenes it does do so; and we also found, when discussing Æsthetics, that the solution, the reconciliation, of an incongruity, gives pleasure, as being a successful exercise of high intellectual power.

When we witness the woes of an Œdipus or a Lear, on the stage, the incongruity between their sufferings and their merits gives us pain; we weep *that such things can be;* we abandon ourselves for the moment to the belief that there is no remedy, no alleviation, that the universe is full of suffering. It is an outburst of pessimistic feeling. Shakespeare felt this, and made his Hamlet utter it freely. To him the world seems out of joint. He is the embodiment of the tragic, pessimistic, painful, feeling of incongruity.

The feeling of the Comic, on the contrary, is an outburst of the unconscious optimism of the soul, in view of incongruities which seem trifling, or temporary, or partial,—not eternal, or universal. The comic woes of a Davus or a Sganarelle amuse us, partly because they are deserved, partly because they happen to a degraded person of no importance, and also because they are comparatively trifling. The incongruity is reconciled by the feeling, while in the perception of beauty it is reconciled by the intellect, and in tragedy it is not reconciled at all. If the man who falls into the mud is seriously hurt, the spectators cease laughing and crowd around with apologies and offers of assistance.

The perception of the comic will of course vary with the character and culture of the person experiencing it. A coarse person laughs only at coarse jokes. His merriment is unrestrained, and often mixed with malice, even though the victim of his joke suffers great pain. A gentleman or lady sees nothing comic in such a scene, but laughs at a play upon words or a witticism, which the coarse man would not even understand.

It is important to notice that the comic is usually mixed with other elements, which few writers are at pains to separate. In coarse laughter the element of "glorying" or boasting, the self-feeling, on which Hobbes based his whole theory, is usually prominent, and a spice of malice is often perceptible. In sarcasm, and sneering, and "sardonic grins," there is a dash of hatred, plainly visible, and a good deal of self-conceit. It implies the Carlylean dogma, that nearly all men are fools, except the speaker.

Humor is the purest expression of the comic; it is sheer incongruity, without an after thought as to the serious nature of life. Wit is biting, it lays hold, it has claws; it is on the borders of the tragic on one side and the beautiful on the other; it has a purpose to accomplish; it often brings congruity out of incongruity; it often, in the gayest manner, causes pain.

It is a curious fact that the ancient Greeks, especially Aristophanes and Lucian, exploited almost every kind and combination of the comic, and left very little for the moderns to invent in this kind of literature.

APPETITE.

Returning from the excursion suggested by the emotion of Laughter, and pursuing our usual plan, we begin again with the feeling called Appetite. Those physical cravings which demand what is necessary for the continuance of the organism, are usually called Appetites. They are such as Hunger, Thirst, Craving for air, Longing for exercise, Desire to sleep. It is usual to add Sexual feeling to the list. These cravings, in their primitive, coarse, strictly physical form, belong to the organism alone, are common to man and the lower animals, and are not properly termed feelings.

Some recent writers advocate the view that we desire food, for example, on account of the pleasure we have in eating it, and the satisfaction we feel after having filled ourselves. But we hold that this is true only of the developed, cultivated, or artificial appetites. The desire of sleep, for instance, is obviously a purely physical, involuntary craving. Hunger, too, must be an automatic craving on the first occasion in one's life, before the pleasure of eating has been experienced. Moreover, in the grossest examples of desire of food, as in swine, we find animals eating everything eatable, without distinction, and without apparent pleasure.

Appetite, in its developed, artificial form, becomes worthy the name of Feeling, and important for the social and mental life. Yet in its utmost refinement it is necessarily a self-regarding principle, openly based on physical sensations, and ranks the lowest among springs of action or motives.

Appetite may be defined as Desire of physical pleasure.

"By repeated indulgence the appetites become more frequent and imperious in their demands. Strange and artificial means are employed to gratify them; and, by the growing power of habit, a man may not only become addicted to the gross and frequent indulgence of his implanted appetites, but may raise up within him a host of factitious wants. . . . The effect of Association, too, is strikingly seen in the choice and use of articles which are selected to gratify our appetites. Different kinds of meat and drink are relished, at different periods of life, by different classes of society, and by the inhabitants of different countries. In all this the influence of fashion and custom is powerfully exhibited." (Fleming, Moral Philosophy, 60.)

Each nation has its favorite dishes, its favorite stimulants, and its favorite narcotics. The organism becomes habituated to tobacco, opium, alcohol, and other powerful drugs, which modify the nutrition of the nervous system, and the craving for them becomes a desire for excitement or for relief from depression and uneasiness. Thus the natural appetite called thirst has a monstrous development in the habit of the superfluous and useless or injurious consumption of stimulating liquors, ending in the vice of drunkenness. In this development the appetite becomes quite perverted, and the craving is for the abnormal state of the nervous system, caused by the liquor, not for the liquor itself. Thus also hunger is turned into a vice, called gluttony.

"A life of pleasure" hence means, not merely devotion to sense-pleasure, but to all kinds of excitements, gambling, gay company, and various distractions; a life excluding the highest pleasures, void of the best feeling.

DESIRE.

The term Desire is in universal use in English to denote an appetency or craving one step higher than Appetite. Desire is to the mind what Appetite is to the body. Both are self-regarding feelings, but, while appetite craves pleasure of the senses, desire craves objects which give pleasure, and that, usually, of a higher kind. And, while appetite develops into love of excitement, desire develops into love of abstract things, such as knowledge, power, glory.

The principle of desire is the pleasure of possession. To have a thing for one's own is a pleasure above the gratification of appetite, and which is probably not shared by the lower animals. In the usual division, the specific kinds of desire are feelings having reference to things which can in some sense be possessed, such as, Desire of Property, of Power, of Glory, of Knowledge, etc.

It is obvious that a somewhat long list of the Desires could be made out by subdividing and enumerating the various objects of human longing, such as, desire of continued existence, of Society, of Liberty, of Happiness, etc. But, in our view, the important objects of desire may be classified under a few general heads, and other feelings which receive this name are compounded of a variety of experiences.

Desire of Happiness, for example, should not have a place on the list. Happiness is not something which can be possessed, but a state, the result of possessing objects of desire. Or, if the term, Happiness, be used to denote something which can be possessed and desired, then the desire of happiness must be a generic one, including all the others, and equivalent to desire at large.

Desire of Continued Existence, is a term used by President Hopkins, in the sense of repugnance to death or suicide. But we cannot find here the element of possession, common to other desires. Fear of pain and change, with aversion to the cessation of pleasure, seem sufficient to account for this feeling. For it is notorious that when all the pleasures of life are withdrawn, existence becomes a burden to many, and love of life is not sufficient to deter them from suicide.

Similarly with the desire of Society. Society is the natural state of man, and when thrown out of it by any peculiar circumstances he seriously feels the deprivation. But Society is the condition which renders possible the exercise of all the desires, and which in turn is sustained by their normal activity. Thus, although desire is self-regarding, it becomes the instrument in great degree of moral and social development, and so a link between the Appetites and the Affections.

Without the Desire of Property, for example, in its members, Society could hardly exist, certainly not be progressive. Those Socialists who endeavor to put a stop to acquisition and accumulation by individuals, would, if successful, reduce men to a lazy and impotent herd.

It should be noticed that in connection with the Will, the term Desire has a different and wider meaning.

We shall now describe briefly the most important kinds of Desire.

DESIRE OF PROPERTY AND POWER.

Desire of property is not, as some writers say, a longing for the objects which will gratify our sense-feelings. That would be only Appetite controlled by Intellect. The Desire of Property seeks the gratification of the sense of possession, which is a mental pleasure depending on the Natural Affection of Self-love. This desire is hence quite different from the desire which an animal has to catch game in order to eat it, though some writers confound the two. Specific objects are desired because they give pleasure in this way, by being possessed. To desire them for the sake of sense-pleasure is developed appetite.

The Desire of Property is thus very slightly distinguished from the Desire of Power. The former is power over things, the latter is property in persons, or power over persons. When the desire of property degenerates into the miser's love of gold, it becomes a mere artificial Appetite; the miser gloats over his gold, feels of it, enjoys the sensations it gives, thinks not of what it can purchase, but longs for it as a drunkard does for drink.

When the Desire of Power becomes excessive and unregulated it is called Ambition, a term which is used, however, in other meanings. But in ambition, in this sense, Self-love has a part, especially in the form of Self-esteem. A great ruler comes to think himself worthy of the service and adoration of whole nations, and finds his chief joy in making millions do his bidding.

Again, we may desire property on account of the indirect power which it gives us over persons, or we may desire power on account of the facility it will give us in acquiring property.

DESIRE OF KNOWLEDGE.

This Feeling might well be divided between the desire of property and that of power. We desire knowledge either to have it as our own, for the pleasure of possession, or to use it in getting power over others in order to procure other possessions. Knowledge must, indeed, be considered as, in itself, a higher good than property or power, since it pertains more completely to the intellectual life, less to the social life. The desire of knowledge is universally recognized as pure and praiseworthy. Yet it is perhaps equally capable with the others of mixture with self-love, and is, like them, a self-regarding feeling.

Desire of Knowledge may be perverted, artificial, and abnormal. When turned toward trifling objects, especially if they do not really concern us, it is called inquisitiveness. When it attaches an exaggerated importance to forms, it is called pedantry. There are men who spend their lives in mousing out unimportant facts of history, and rejoice when they have found one, like a miser over hidden treasure. This love of knowledge corresponds to avarice. It loves facts for themselves, or for the pleasure of novelty, or for the vanity of discovery,—not for usefulness to mankind.

Yet it is difficult to say what knowledge is worthless. The most apparently useless of items, especially in the sciences, may prove the key to unexplained and difficult problems.

THE AFFECTIONS.

We have found that the Appetites have reference to pleasure of the senses and excitement of the nerves; that the Desires have reference to the pleasure of possession, and its derivatives; that both are self-regarding, are easily complicated with self-love, and easily degraded into vicious, unworthy, or abnormal feelings. We have now to notice a class of feelings higher in every respect than these. They have reference, not to things, but to persons; they are not entirely self-regarding; they are connected with the highest pleasures of the social, moral, and religious life; their mere exercise affords the intensest pleasure, or, when they are perverted, the acutest pain. They are usually divided into Natural Affections and Moral Affections.

"They are that part of the constitution of man by which he is so put in relation with his fellows that society becomes possible." (Hopkins, Moral Science, 130.)

The simplest and most primitive of the Affections are the direct accompaniment of physical relations. The higher, more developed, and more complicated Affections arise out of family and social relations, and are developed in scope, breadth, and purity, by and with the general social, intellectual, and religious progress of the race. We begin with the class nearest allied to the physical organism, as in our usual plan.

NATURAL AFFECTIONS.

These are usually divided into Benevolent and Malevolent. But it is in dispute whether there be any natural feeling which can properly be called malevolent. We prefer the terms Defensive and Punitive Feelings, and hold that any feeling truly malevolent is a perversion, or artificial or abnormal development, of a necessary defensive endowment. We have already described defensive feeling in the form of Anger, and shown how it may change into Hatred, which is usually called an Affection. The terms benevolent and malevolent imply Will, while the Natural Affections do not. "Where an animal, as the parent bird, does good to another, it is from no rational estimate of the good as a motive lying before it, and so as good willing, but from a beneficent, spontaneous, constitutional impulse, prompting from behind. . . . It is equally true of the beast of prey that he has no malevolence towards his victim. He does not hate him, he simply wishes to eat him. . . . There is no natural affection, either in animals or in man, that has for its object the production of evil for evil's sake." (Hopkins, Outline Study of Man, 217.)

Whether the defensive and punitive feelings be Natural Affections or prolonged, half-suppressed, and complicated Emotions, may be a question of some difficulty, but does not seem important. Their perversion into hatred, cruelty, malice, and all strictly malevolent affections, is the work of Sin, and its discussion belongs to moral philosophy and theology. The Will must be investigated before this point can be understood.

The beneficent natural affections are thus reduced to Love, Sympathy, and Self-love, which we shall briefly describe.

LOVE.

One difficulty in using the term Love is the ambiguity and wide range of the word. From the grossest physical appetites, through a vast range of different feelings of various kinds, up to the purest and loftiest feeling of adoration toward the Deity, Love is applied to all. Men are said to love any savory dish or any favorite drink, to love pleasure, to love excitement, to love their mothers, to love their friends, to love themselves, to love their country, to love all men, to love God. Love is thus found among the Appetites, Emotions, Desires, and Affections.

In describing Love as a natural affection, we of course do not use the word in any such vague sense, but confine it to love for sentient beings, and to disinterested love.

Some writers have denied the possibility of disinterested affection, and declared that all human feelings are really egoistic, that we love others because they give us pleasure, or because it gives us pleasure to love them. But a love which is not altruistic is not worthy of the name of love. (The term Altruism was invented by Comte, as a correlative to Egoism, and has been widely used by Herbert Spencer and his disciples.) Egoistic love of others is a contradiction in terms. "A desire for our own happiness cannot be an element of affection, and when, for the sake of that, we pursue toward others such a course as affection would prompt, the whole source and character of our happiness, if we gain any, is gone." (Hopkins, Moral Science, 131.)

Simulated love may gain lower ends, satisfaction of desire or appetite, but it cannot bring the pleasure which is the reaction of pure altruistic affection; and this fact is quite generally recognized. Thus Mr. Herbert Spencer says,—"Pure egoism is, even in its immediate results, less successfully egoistic than is the egoism duly qualified by altruism, which, besides achieving additional pleasures, achieves also, through raised vitality, a greater capacity for pleasures in general." He also says that even among the lower animals "parental sacrifice is not accompanied by the consciousness of sacrifice, but is made from a direct desire to make it." And he adds,—"If we trace these relations up through the grades of mankind, and observe how largely love rather than obligation prompts the care of children, we see that achievement of parental happiness coincides with securing the happiness of offspring." (Data of Ethics § 79 and 92.)

The best type of altruistic Natural Affection is the love of a mother for her child. This is the direct result of the physical relation between them. In the lower animals it subsists only as long as the young need the mother's care to sustain life. In the human race this care is needed for several years, and maternal love changes its character, though losing, generally, nothing of its strength with time.

In the progress of civilization or intellectual and spiritual culture, the mutual love of parent and child becomes refined, until it is the highest expression for purity, and is used as the type of the relation between God and the human race.

As the exercise of parental love gives the highest pleasure, well deserving the higher name of happiness, so its disappointment gives the deepest pain. The loss of a child causes the deepest grief, the ingratitude of a child, "sharper than a serpent's tooth," causes the heaviest sorrow.

When love extends to strangers or to the whole race, as in the case of a missionary or an apostle, it belongs rather among the Moral Affections, involves the action of the Will, and deserves the name of a Benevolent Affection.

The lower animals are capable of a good deal of natural affection for one another and for human beings, springing out of relations of constant companionship and complete dependence.

SYMPATHY.

This term, as its etymology denotes, means "with-feeling," pain or pleasure excited by the knowledge of the pain or pleasure of others. We call it a Natural Affection because it is spontaneous, and not under the control of the will, and because it has beginnings in the physical organism.

Thus, if we see a person rowing, or swimming, or balancing on a tight-rope, we sway our bodies in unison with him, if we are deeply interested. If one person yawns in a company, the others are impelled to yawn. "Unpractised assistants at surgical operations often faint; a boy has been known to die on witnessing an execution. We have all experienced the uncomfortable feeling of shame produced in us by the blunders and confusion of a nervous speaker. We find ourselves unable to avoid joining in the merriment of our friends, whilst unaware of its cause; and children, much to their annoyance, are often forced to laugh in the midst of their tears, by witnessing the laughter of those around them." (Herbert Spencer, Social Statics, 115.)

The fullest treatment of Sympathy has been by Adam

Smith, who has founded a complete system of Ethics on this one principle, drawing out the facts in a similar way, and with a like industry to that employed in his "Wealth of Nations." He has noticed, what is quite obvious, that Sympathy depends largely on the Imagination. We put ourselves in the place of another, and imagine how we should feel in the same circumstances. Edmund Burke also says, "sympathy must be considered as a sort of substitution, by which we are put into the place of another man, and affected in many respects as he is affected."

This operation of the imagination is shown in several ways, mentioned by Adam Smith. "We sometimes feel for another a passion of which he seems to be altogether incapable. We blush for the impudence and rudeness of another, though he himself appears to have no sense of the impropriety of his own behavior. . . What are the pangs of a mother, when she hears the moanings of her infant? In her idea of what it suffers, she joins, to its real helplessness, her own consciousness of that helplessness, and her own terrors for the unknown consequences of its disorder. The infant, however, feels only the uneasiness of the present instant, which can never be great. . . . We sympathize even with the dead, and overlooking what is of real importance in their situation, that awful futurity which awaits them, we are chiefly affected by circumstances which strike our senses, but can have no influence upon their happiness." (Theory of the Moral Sentiments 6–8.)

Even a fictitious recital in a play or romance, brings sympathetic tears to the eyes of the sensitive. This kind of Sympathy has many degrees. "Those sensitive hearts," said Goethe, "any bungler can move them;" meaning that much sympathy is superficial. He himself, in his Sorrows of Werther, described the disappointment and suicide of his young friend so vividly, that the book is said to have caused scores of suicides.

It is a curious fact that sympathetic grief is often pleasurable. The phrase "luxury of grief" has some truth in it. We enjoy sympathizing with the griefs of another, and he enjoys rehearsing the occasion of his pain and suffering it again in our company.

Sympathy, in the true meaning of the word, is neither egoistic nor altruistic. We do not sympathize with another because it gives us pleasure to do so, nor because our sympathy gives him pleasure, but because we have a natural impulse to do so.

The term is often used, however, though not, we believe, by accurate writers, in the sense of general benevolent or altruistic feeling. In this meaning it would come among the Moral Affections.

SELF-LOVE AND SELFISHNESS.

The term Self-love is a valuable one, as denoting a proper and rational Egoism, in distinction from Selfishness, which is an excessive and irrational Egoism. The term "Self-regarding" is also in general use now; as, Self-regarding Virtues, contrasted with Altruistic Virtues. It is not easy to draw a theoretical line between a proper and an excessive Self-love, between a proper self-respect and a foolish self-conceit. But it is agreed by most recent ethical writers that there is such a line, and that self-love may be laudable or even necessary, and that self-conservation is a duty.

Mr. Herbert Spencer has argued at great length that self-love is necessary even to the existence of altruism; that altruism, as a sole principle of action, would defeat itself, equally with egoism. This argument, one of the ablest and most striking in Mr. Spencer's works, is found in the latter chapters of the Data of Ethics. He cites the evils of indiscriminate charity in society, and of excessive self-sacrifice in the family. "Every one can remember circles in which the daily surrender of benefits by the generous to the greedy has caused increase of greediness, until there has been produced an unscrupulous greediness intolerable to all around." He points out that unthinking altruism would often lead to the death of those so disposed, and so to the injury of society; and that those who profess to be guided by pure altruism generally show in their actions a good mixture of egoism. After many other, more abstract arguments, which we cannot summarize, he concludes thus:—

"It is admitted that self-happiness is, in a measure, to be obtained by furthering the happiness of others. May it not be true that, conversely, general happiness is to be obtained by furthering self-happiness? If the well-being of each unit is to be reached partly through his care for the well-being of the aggregate, is not the well-being of the aggregate to be reached partly through the care of each unit for himself? Clearly, general happiness is to be achieved mainly through the adequate pursuit of their own happiness by individuals, while, reciprocally, the happiness of individuals is to be achieved in part by their pursuit of the general happiness." (§ 91.)

Our main objection to this argument is,—it seems to assume that there is really some danger of excessive altruism becoming the rule in society. On the contrary, the machinery of criminal law is employed to a vast extent in repressing excessive selfishness, while thousands of preachers and other moral teachers, employed in cultivating a very moderate type of altruism, do not have an alarming amount of success. The number of those who need to be urged to moderate their altruism and cultivate egoism is still comparatively very small.

The fact is, men act from mixed motives, some selfish and some unselfish, and are often egoistic in some relations of life and altruistic in others. Indiscriminate alms-giving, for example, is no proof of altruistic feeling; it is usually done to save trouble and annoyance, or from superstitious motives. Again, a man may be kind and liberal to his family, but harsh and extortionate to his employes.

The opposites, subjectively speaking, of Self-love, are self-reproach, self-abasement, and the like. Modesty and humility are rather opposites of self-conceit and self-complacency, and are not entirely incompatible with self-respect or self-love.

A refined and rational selfishness in intelligent persons, would evidently require a proper subordination of the lower powers and feelings, because the higher give more exquisite and long-continued pleasure. It would also require that selfishness itself should not be too obtrusive, becoming self-conceit, arrogance, self-esteem, since these repel our fellow-men, and so make life less pleasant.

Many terms are in common use, expressing different degrees and combinations of Natural Affection, such as, Passion, Gratitude, Kindness, Trust, Faith, Vanity, Conceit, Self-complacency, Modesty, Friendship, Sociability, Courtesy, Resentment, Wrath, Indignation, Humanity, Philanthropy, Patriotism, Pity, Compassion, etc. To discriminate these is no part of our present purpose.

MORAL AFFECTIONS.

Some writers confuse the Natural with the Moral Affections, but, on the plan we have adopted, the distinction is plain, and, at least in theory, easily preserved. The Natural Affections spring out of natural relations, that is, physical or social relations, not moral relations. Under the first we love our relatives, because we are born into intimate relations with them; not to love them is called unnatural. We love those who do us favors; not to do so is called ingratitude. We love, in a less intimate way, and are ready to benefit, our neighbors and friends, because of our social relations with them; not to do so is called base and churlish.

But Moral Affection is love and approval toward all who display moral excellence, self-sacrifice for worthy objects, purity, truthfulness, whether exerted toward ourselves or not. Or it is indignation and disapproval against those who display moral wrong, cruelty, injustice, etc., whether against ourselves or not. It has a still higher reach, too, in love for those who are morally base and wrong, and self-sacrificing efforts to make them better morally. This has the highest reward, and gives the highest happiness. "If ye love them which love you, what thank have ye?"

We may find aid in understanding moral feeling if we expand an illustration of President Hopkins. Suppose a perfectly good being to meet a perfectly bad one. What would be the feelings of the former? He could not love the latter, in the same way that he would love a being like himself. He would certainly feel repugnance, dislike, abhorrence, though he would strongly desire that being's moral good. But suppose the evil being to perform some wanton act of injury against the good being. There would then be condemnation, a holy resentment, a desire that the guilty being should be stopped in his career of evil, that justice should be done him, as a restraint and warning.

This moral feeling of opposition is by some called malevolent, as the opposite of benevolent. But to understand malevolence, in any proper sense of the term, we must imagine the feelings of the evil being while doing a wanton injury. He hates the good being, and wills to do him wrong; or he takes pleasure in the sufferings of others.

It is evident, then, that Moral Affections involve the will, are either benevolent or malevolent. But we hold that the latter, as exhibited in man, are not a part of his original nature, but are exhibitions of an evil will, a nature perverted by sin.

The discussion of the moral qualities of actions, of the

nature of good, of the nature and obligation of benevolent feeling and action, belong to the science of Ethics or Moral Philosophy. It requires previous study of the Will, and we do not deem it best to discuss Moral Affection more fully here.

THE RELIGIOUS FEELINGS.

These are the Emotions, Desires, and Affections, as related to and modified by the objects of religious contemplation. As the objects with which religion has to do are the most sublime of all objects, so the Emotions and Affections they excite are the purest and grandest of which the mind is capable. The Universe, the Eternal Creator, the happiness of the entire world, the Fatherhood of God, the immortality of man,—such subjects, when truly contemplated, necessarily arouse wonder, awe, reverence, godly fear, gratitude, and love.

Many variations and combinations of the Moral Feelings receive distinct names, such as,—Mercy, Forgiveness, Thankfulness, Justice, Esteem, Self-denial, Self-control, Benevolence, Piety, Holiness, with their opposites.

THE WILL.

DEFINITIONS AND DISTINCTIONS.

I. WILL.

As Intellect is the mind perceiving, judging, and reasoning, and as Feeling is the mind experiencing pleasure and pain, so Will is the mind exercising Volition.

It is incorrect to speak of the Will as the power of action. There is much action properly called spontaneous or involuntary or automatic, in nature, in the physical organism, and in the mind. The word "action" is ambiguous, and may either mean physical operation in the series of causation, or purposeful and moral activity of a free agent. (German Wirken and Handeln.)

Many of the activities of nature curiously simulate the purposeful activities of volition. The roots of a plant select from the soil just those elements which are necessary for its peculiar development, and, in general, reject all others. Animal tissue absorbs from the circulating blood those molecules which it needs, and, in general, rejects all others. When it fails in this discrimination, the result is abnormal growth or poisoning. The tendrils of plants curl themselves around their support with every appearance of volition.

In the animal organism we find still higher involuntary activities. The spinal cord is the seat of a power of reflex movement, some of whose phenomena we have already referred to. The cerebellum is supposed to be the seat of that co-ordination of actions which renders possible all mechanical skill. A vast amount of activity in the organism is either beyond the sphere of volition, like the beating of the heart; or partly and occasionally under voluntary control, like respiration or winking; or, originally voluntary, ceases to be entirely so through long practice, like the specific muscular efforts in walking.

A considerable portion of the activity of the mind, too, may be called spontaneous. Man "finds a succession of thoughts bubbling up, like waters from a fountain, of which he knows not the source, and the flow of which he can no more stop than he can the flow of a river. . . . Man also feels desires springing up. These he may or may not gratify, but there they are, a part of his nature. The natural affections, too, put forth their tendrils like a vine, and quite as independently of any will of man." (Hopkins, Moral Science, 81.)

II. VOLITION.

The term Volition is generally used to denote the whole function of the Will. Yet a completed act of volition involves two distinct elements, Executive or External Volition, and Moral Volition or Choice. These, indeed, are sometimes called two distinct kinds of volition, while, on the other hand, some writers confound the two elements, and fail to make any distinction between them. "These elements of Will, choice and volition, have not been distinguished as they should have been, and, in consequence, the discussions respecting the Will have been perplexed." (Hopkins, Outline Study, 225.)

The two elements differ in several ways. The result of an executive volition is an external act or mental process; the result of a choice is a state of the will, which may be called a state of choice or of determination, and which results in external volitions, or a series of them, whenever the proper conditions are supplied. They differ in their nature; the former is mechanical, the latter spiritual and free. They differ in the matter with which they are concerned; the former has to do with the activities of physical and social life; the latter with rational and moral decisions and purposes. The former is shared by the lower animals, the latter belongs to man alone of earthly beings, and is what constitutes him a person. "Thus does the Will imply and involve the two great elements of Intellect and Force. Intellect, it implies, in connection with choice, for the purpose of comprehension and rationality; and Force in connection with volition, for the purpose of execution. We see, then, at this point, the two elements of which Will is composed, the power of choice, and the power of volition, each of which is essential to the being and the expression of personality, in which, in order to constitute Will, the two must unite." (Hopkins, Outline Study, 224.)

It would be well if the term Volition could be restricted to the meaning of executive volition, and the higher function of moral volition could be called by some other name, such as Choice, as is done by Dr. Hopkins. But if the term Choice be used, we need to remember that it does not include deliberation, as it often does in popular usage. The term Volition is so often used, however, in the wide sense, that the student needs, in any event, to be familiar with it in both meanings, and we can hardly escape all such use of it.

Many recent writers, especially evolutionists, use the term Volition in the external sense only, and even stoutly deny that there is any other kind of volition. Bain, for example, describes at great length the supposed origin, growth, cultivation, and perfection of voluntary movement of the different muscles of the body; he then describes the voluntary command of the feelings and thoughts, which he attributes to Attention and

Association. This is the highest function he permits to Will. Choice he degrades to decision between different objects of desire. "When a person purchases an article out of several submitted to view, the recommendations of that one are said to be greater than of the rest, and nothing more needs be said. It may happen for a moment the opposing attractions are exactly balanced, and decision suspended thereby, . . . but when the decision is actually come to, the fact and the meaning are that some consideration has arisen to the mind, giving a superior energy of motive to the side that has preponderated. . . . The designation, liberty of choice, has no real meaning, except as denying extraneous interference." (The Emotions and the Will.)

But such a decision as Dr. Bain here describes is wholly an act of judgment, applying some previous volition, determining to select and buy that one of a certain set of articles which should fulfill certain conditions. As Dr. Bascom has said, "Bain gives the theory of brute life, we are striving to give that of rational life." Choice, or moral volition, is not simply the act of an ass between two bundles of hay, as we shall attempt to show later on.

I. EXECUTIVE VOLITION.

Executive Volition is not the origin of physical force. Modern science has triumphantly established that all the physical force exerted by the organism is furnished by the transformation of molecular energy. Volition pulls the trigger, or lights the fuse, so to speak, which sets free the mechanical force stored up in the body. If nutrition is insufficient, or the force has been exhausted, or the nerves are paralyzed, volition cannot be executed. "Mental causation, in regard to physical matters, bears a direct ratio to the amount of force contained in the food taken into the system, or otherwise received from the external world; at least it can never go beyond this. Thus it would appear that force is directed, not generated, by the soul." (Everett, Science of Thought, 50.)

Force is the material with which volition is occupied, the element, the atmosphere on which it depends. "Volition," says President Hopkins, "presupposes force, or rather is nugatory except in a being endowed with force."

How it is that the mind can direct force, can occasion the discharge of force, is unknown. That it actually does so is clearly seen in the phenomena, already mentioned, of reflex movements and the expression of emotion. An idea, a perception, a representation, a piece of news, may occasion violent movements of laughter, or involuntary screams and convulsions. The idea in the mind has of course no mechanical force, and cannot even "pull the trigger" which discharges nerve-force. But when the idea, in some unknown way, has become recorded in the brain, it may affect the whole physical organism in various ways.

"The soul does not in any case produce motions of the body by its own immediate operation. But it produces a certain inner state, of desire or will, in itself. From this arises a physical movement, by a process unknown to consciousness and independent of the will.

"Man can only will. That a realization follows does not at all depend on him, but on the circumstance that, in the order of nature, a certain change of state of the motor nerves is joined to a definite state of the soul. Where this connection is broken, will remains a mere desire without any consequences." (Lotze, Dictate, Psychologie, § 53, 58.)

Indeed, it is held by recent writers, including Lotze, that all power of directing the energies of the body is acquired; that the soul only finds out that the body is movable through experience of its involuntary movements. It is at least certain

DEFINITIONS AND DISTINCTIONS.

that facility and accuracy of movement are acquired, and that when a movement is perfected by practice, it tends to become involuntary or automatic.

A knowledge of these facts, together with a misapprehension of the true location of freedom, seems to have been the source of a number of erroneous definitions of volition.

Spinoza said that the will and the intellect are one and the same. Hobbes said that the will is the last desire in deliberating. (Leviathan, 28.) Dr. T. Brown said that volition is a "feeling which the body immediately obeys." Mr. Austin said, "by volitions we mean desires which consummate themselves." Bain says, "our voluntary actions consist in putting forth muscular power."

These writers have seen that volition is not a muscular movement, but apparently have not seen the truth, that volition is the act of the mind which occasions or commands that movement. But volition seldom orders a single disconnected movement, but usually an action, or series of actions, and the specific movements follow according to habit and association. This introduces our next distinction.

2. GENERIC AND SPECIFIC VOLITIONS.

Another necessary distinction is that between specific, subordinate or secondary, and generic or primary volitions or choices. The latter are those which involve and necessitate subordinate volitions under them. Obviously, the lowest rank of subordinate volitions will always be executive volitions.

For example, if I determine to take a certain journey, that is a generic volition; for it requires me to take all necessary measures to carry it out, such as providing funds, securing my ticket, packing my trunk, taking leave of my friends,—all those acts which my habits and condition determine for me in such a case. But each of these may have under it, in turn, subordinate volitions,—walking to a certain house or office, putting certain articles in my trunk, and the like. These acts in their turn involve many specific muscular movements, some of which are automatic, some co-ordinated, some habitual, and some definitely willed. But the whole series is a necessary consequence of my generic volition; and when I come to decide, in each specific case, which of two or more actions is best adapted to further my generic volition, the decision is an act of judgment, not of will, and the carrying out of my decision is an executive volition.

But again, this generic volition may be subordinate to others above it in rank. My journey may be part of a plan to engage in business, to get an education, to enter a profession; and since such a plan involves a whole life, generic choices or volitions can seldom be higher in rank than these. The highest possible generic choice is easily seen to be the determination to be always governed, in every relation of life, by the best motives, rules, and maxims,—to act in accordance with the law of God as known and understood.

Another example,—" I have a strong desire to drink of some grateful beverage, or to eat of some tempting food; but I find or fear that to do so might be injurious to my health. I pause, and hesitate; but at length decline the dangerous gratification. According to Dr. Brown [and Prof. Bain], there is nothing in this case but the desire of eating or drinking being overcome by the desire of health,—that is, a weaker desire by a stronger." According to the older advocates of free-will, whenever the tempting dish is presented, I balance anew the motives on each side, and reach a free decision. According to more recent advocates of free-will, I have previously decided to avoid whatever I know to be injurious to my health, and when the gratification is offered me, I have only to decide, by an act of judgment, whether it comes under the class of things injurious to my health, and if so it is at once rejected. This implies, it will be noticed, that the generic volition is imperious and unchangeable; this may be the case, but in fact generic volitions are subject to change or suspension. I may forget it, under strong excitement; I may give it up when appetite or desire is strong. But, in such a case, I have afterwards a feeling of shame for my inconsistency or sin. A truly rational being does not lightly change a generic choice or volition, when once made in the full light of reason.

Some terms, used to denote generic rational choice, and the state of determination which it produces, may perhaps require explanation.

1. Immanent Preference. This denotes the state of the Will when a choice has been reached, but no opportunity of completing it by executive volitions has been afforded. Here the generic volition is constantly in force. "A continual state of choice," says Dr. Hopkins, "is as much a condition of our lives, at least in our waking hours, as continual thought." The value of right preferences of this kind can hardly be overestimated. "The immanent preference of objects and ends," says Dr. Hickok, "must widely affect the entire personal character, though the action towards the object externally be always restrained. The whole inner experience of the man is modified by it, and all his habits of meditation and silent reflection become tinged with the color of his secret preferences." The Bible attributes moral quality to these preferences. "Thou shalt not covet." "Whoso hateth his brother is a murderer." "It was in thine heart to build an house to my name, thou didst well that it was in thine heart."

2. Governing Purpose means a generic choice manifesting itself in subordinate volitions, prompting and guiding them. "The action, as will, has not terminated in the choosing; it flows on in a perpetuated current toward its object, and the spirit

may be said to be in a permanent state of will." The act of choice, by which the mind entered upon this state of will, may have passed out of memory, or may have never been very clearly in consciousness. A man may have almost unconsciously formed the governing purpose to amass riches, may have "set his heart on getting rich," as his friends say of him, "and the purpose itself may have strengthened so insidiously, that the man has no conception what a very miser he has become; but there needs only to be suddenly interposed some threatened danger to his wealth, or some obstacle to any further gains, and at once the perturbed spirit manifests the intensity of its avarice." (Dr. Hickok.)

3. Disposition, Character, Heart, and other terms, are often used in a way which implies the conception of generic choices.

III. MOTIVES.

The term Motive is used in several distinct senses, the more important of which must be carefully distinguished.

1. OBJECTIVE MOTIVES.

In popular speech the term Motive is applied to the outward object through apprehension of which by the Intellect, Feeling becomes excited, and so the Will set in action. But here there is generally a conscious or half-conscious ellipsis. When we say, "money was the motive of his actions," we mean the love of money, the desire of property. It is incorrect to speak of the external object as directly moving the will. All are agreed that intellect must first apprehend the object, and feeling must be aroused to activity by this apprehension.

Some writers use the term Motive in a way which at first sight seems to refer to the external object, but it will usually be found that this is not their meaning. Thus Jonathan Edwards says,—"By motive I mean the whole of that which moves, excites, or invites the mind to volition, whether that be one thing singly, or many things conjunctly." But he also says,—"Whatever is a motive, must be something that is extant in the view or apprehension of the understanding or perceiving faculty." Here the motive is, not simply the external object, but the object as viewed or apprehended by the mind. But even this is not in accordance with the best recent philosophical usage.

President Day, again, uses similar expressions. "An object which is in view of the mind, has a tendency to move the will." But he adds, "that which immediately excites the volition is an affection of the mind, an emotion, an internal motive." This, we believe, is always really understood. An external object cannot be a motive, in any proper sense of the word. All motives are subjective.

2. SUBJECTIVE MOTIVES.

All motives are, properly speaking, subjective. The distinction between objective and subjective motives is then a cautionary one, having no real value in the discussion of the Will.

But the term subjective is often applied to motives in another and peculiar way, implying that the same object or event may be the occasion of more or less urgent desires or emotions, when apprehended by one person than by another, or by the same person in different circumstances, and hence of different volitions. "A man of slow, narrow intellect is unable to perceive the value of an object, or the advantage of a course of conduct, so clearly or so quickly as a man of large and vigorous intellect.

" The consequence will be, that with the same motives (objectively considered) presented to them, the one may remain indifferent to the advantage held out, while the other will at once apprehend and pursue it. A man of cold and dull affections will contemplate a spectacle of pain or want, without feeling any desire or making any exertion to relieve it; while he whose sensibilities are more acute and lively will instantly be moved to the most active and generous efforts. An injury done to one man will rouse him at once to a frenzy of indignation, which will prompt him to the most extravagant measures of retaliation; while, in another man, it will only give rise to a moderate feeling of resentment." (Fleming, Moral Philosophy, 177.)

This important variation in the power of motives should rather be called relativity than subjectivity of motives. It evidently has no relation to the Will, but only to the Intellect and Feeling.

3. MOTIVE AS CAUSE.

The term Motive is most widely used to denote that state of Feeling which precedes and determines an act of the Will, "the terminating state or affection of the mind which immediately precedes the volition." But this does not, of course, imply that the motive is the sole cause. "Motives do not produce volitions without a mind. They are not the agent They do not love and hate, resolve and choose. But if a motive has any influence on the determination of the will, it is *one* of the antecedents on which the volition depends. The agent does not will without motives, nor do motives will without an agent." (President Day, Inquiry, 59.)

The definition of Edwards includes this meaning of Motive also. But it should be noted that, in his time, Desire was considered a part of the will, and not classed among the feelings.

Popular language also makes use of this sense of the word Motive. Thus we say, "his motive in running away was fear," "my motive in asking was mere curiosity." Moreover, we always expect some such motive and search for it. We say, "what motive could he have had for so strange an action?" And we are satisfied with the answer that it was revenge, or avarice, or remorse.

Of course, if the Motive is the cause, or part of the cause, of volition, questions will arise as to the connection between the state of the Feeling and the Will. This has indeed been the subject of various theories and of much controversy. Those who deny freedom easily settle the point by saying that the connection is a causative one, the state of the Desire being the cause of the state of the Will. Believers in freedom are bound to show where freedom resides.

It is generally admitted that freedom does not reside in the intellect or in the feelings. When an external object is presented to the sense-organs (proper conditions being implied), the mind cannot help perceiving it, and perceiving under the categories of Space, Number, and Identity; cannot choose but classify it, and experience associations connected with it. No more can it escape the feelings aroused by this perception, with its accompanying associations. The question is, whether these feelings irresistibly cause, or only afford opportunity for the volition that follows.

Perhaps the best and at the present time most usual answer, on the part of those who believe in freedom, is that the mind has a power of rational choice by which it can select the highest and noblest motives, and act according to them. On this theory, motives are the material with which the Will works, the medium in which it operates, the atmosphere that sustains it, rather than the cause of its activity. The full answer to the question must be postponed until we have made further preparations.

4. MOTIVE AS END.

Another use of the term Motive is to denote the End (object, purpose, final cause) of an action, that for which it is done. Here is obviously introduced a quite different and higher conception. We have now the idea of a rational being, purposely adapting his activities to a pre-conceived and previously chosen end; formerly we had the idea of a being capable of feeling, acted upon by external objects or events, and aroused to activity in response. The difference is that between volition and choice.

Under this view, motives are expressed by the phrase, "in order to be or to do something." For example, we may eat in order to be strong, and this is a different thing from eating because the appetite of hunger impels us to satisfy a natural want, though the resulting action be the same. Or, again, a better example, I may take exercise in order to grow strong; and this is a different thing from exercising, like a child or a colt, because of an overflow of nervous energy. The one may evidently be called a rational action, the other not. Again, a man may pursue a dangerous and disagreeable course of action in order to rescue an acquaintance from vice or crime. Such an end would be in the highest degree rational.

This introduces the further truth, that ends, as well as volitions, are of different ranks, rising one above the other. The motive of a subordinate volition is a subordinate end; the motive of a generic volition is an ultimate end; the motive of a supreme choice is a supreme end. A supreme choice and end control all inferior choices and ends.

5. STRENGTH OF MOTIVES.

The comparative strength of Motives has been the subject of a good deal of discussion, especially with reference to the question whether the Will is always determined by the strongest motive.

If by strength of motives is meant the strength which they ought to have, as guiding the will to the best actions, and the whole man to the highest ends of his being,—even thus, it might be very difficult, often, in the complication of human life, to decide which subordinate volitions are best in harmony with the supreme choice, and thus a wide field would be left open for discussion with regard to the strength of motives.

But the facts in relation to the relativity or subjectivity of motives, explained above, render all calculations of the strength of motives quite beyond human power. There can be no way of measuring their efficacy except by the result. There seems no way out of the difficulty but to admit that the will is always as the strongest subjective motive; yet men often obey motives which seem to others strangely inadequate.

6. CONFLICT OF MOTIVES.

This conflict may be of various kinds. (1) It may be a conflict between several Desires or Appetites which cannot all be gratified. For example, I may wish to eat my cake and keep it too; here the conflict is between the present and the future. Some minds depict to themselves the future more vividly than others, and are inclined to postpone all present enjoyment to a good time coming.

(2) The conflict may be between taking what we can get, or striving for the impossible. Half a loaf is better than no bread, though we strongly desire and greatly need a whole loaf. We may be obliged to choose between education and wealth, or honor and power, with their varied gratifications. Here again different temperaments of mind will be displayed, some striving frantically for the unattainable, others wisely limiting the range of their desires.

(3) The conflict may be between lower and higher ends. Physical necessities are usually more pressing than intellectual wants, more imperious than spiritual needs. To subordinate the lower propensities, the habits of life, the customs and fashions of society, to a rational end, is always considered a triumph.

A supreme choice of a rational end is sometimes made with sufficient strength to carry with it all intermediate or subordinate volitions, and bear down all opposing motives. But this is seldom the case. Temptations are still felt to have power, even by the best of men, and the conflict of motives is unceasing. Often strength of impulse, or habit, or desire, overcome the perception and judgment of the intellect, and make a certain subordinate end seem to be in harmony with the supreme choice, though it is really in conflict, and is afterwards seen to be so.

IV. DESIRE.

The term Desire, when used in connection with the Will, usually denotes the last state of the Feeling before volition, whatever its specific nature. Thus it may include all the appetencies of human nature,—Appetite, Desire in its limited sense, and a large element of Affection. Desire, in this usage, being the last preliminary before volition and the "terminating state" of feeling is often, not inappropriately, called "incipient volition." It is easy to see, therefore, why Desire was so long considered as an act of the Will.

Sometimes, however, Desire is said to be the opposite of volition. Thus Bain says that we only desire what we cannot get. "Desire is the state of mind where there is a motive to act without the ability, . . . a transformation of the Will proper, undergone in circumstances where the act does not immediately follow the motive." We submit that a transformation of volition into non-volition needs some other explanation.

This contradiction is reconciled by the distinction between Volition and Choice. If volition is merely executive, only resulting in external actions, then Desire may properly be the name of the preceding state, inseparable from volition. I desire to move my hand, and the motion immediately follows. Volitions would then be properly called "desires which consummate themselves." But if volition is a rational or moral choice, then several desires may be presented to the mind, the gratification of which is the end of action or motive, and among them the mind will select that one which, all things considered, seems to it the most desirable. Desire, on this theory, is a necessary pre-requisite of volition, not as a cause, but as furnishing the objects of choice. Thus Dr. Brown and Dr. Bain have attempted to join the first meaning of volition with the second meaning of desire, and the result is confusion.

The broad meaning of the term Desire in connection with the will, suggests that mentioned under Feeling, as generic desire, the sum of all the desires, the desire of happiness, or of "good." The full definition of Good belongs to the science of ethics. But the term Happiness may properly be used as including all possible good, whether of the agent or any other sentient being, and so be the sum of all rational ends. The only rational supreme choice, then, is a determination to seek the happiness, in the highest sense, of all sentient beings. Now, this does not mean what Herbert Spencer calls "pure altruism," that is, excessive, irrational, and useless self-sacrifice. Mr. Spencer has most ingeniously shown, from the objective side, what indeed is generally admitted, that such self-effacement is positively immoral. A rational choice must of course be rationally carried out. Popular language recognizes this truth. For when a man devotes himself unselfishly to trifling ends, and spends his life for what is intended for the good of others but is important only in his own eyes, we call him a fanatic or a lunatic. Yet popular language also recognizes the other side of the truth; for when a man acts for self alone, with no altruistic ends, we call him selfish, worldly, mean, misanthropical, criminal, according to the degree of outwardness with which he acts out his principle of life. But when a man adopts the sublime end of the highest good of his race or nation, and pursues it amid the seductions of pleasure and the threats of power, we call him a hero, a saint, a martyr,—even though he make mistakes and failures.

Now, is such a rational choice possible? We affirm that it is. Yet we admit that vast numbers of human beings never make this choice, but live a life of habit and association and mere volition in accordance with desire, or even a life of positive selfishness and injustice. Indeed, if the Will be nothing but executive volition, they *must* live thus, and all higher endeavors are an illusion. We admit, moreover, that many who think they have chosen this highest end, nevertheless do not consistently perform all the subordinate volitions which logically belong to their choice. The urgency of desire misleads the intellect, and they make mistakes; or overwhelms the determination and they suspend the supreme choice. But that man can rationally choose an end beyond his own individual happiness, the satisfaction of his own desires, may be shown by various considerations. We mention three of the most important.

1. Consciousness. We directly know that we can take for our end, in any definite course of action, or in the conduct of life, the good of others or of the universe. This is denied by some, and of course we cannot disprove their denial concerning their own consciousness. But there is another argument from consciousness.

2. We are conscious of the obligation to act unselfishly, hence such action must be possible. This is the celebrated argument

of Kant, which he applies to free-will. We are not concerned here with the nature or reality of obligation, subjects which belong to ethics. But certainly the consciousness of obligation is a great fact in human nature, which cannot be explained away.

3. Experience of human life exhibits many actions performed without hope of reward, or even under the certainty of death, through adherence to a lofty Ideal, and pursuit of ends outside of self. For example, a foreign missionary can hardly have any selfish motives for going abroad. Yet the heathen, for whose benefit he goes, have great difficulty in believing that his motive is altruistic, and are only slowly convinced that such a thing is possible. For, in their state of moral degradation, they have little experience of such actions. A Christian civilization, however, should afford many such instances.

FREEDOM OF THE WILL.

The time-honored phrase, "Freedom of the Will," should be avoided as much as possible, though it has been used by so many writers that the student must become familiar with it. Some of the objections to it are:—

1. It seems to imply that a will may be enslaved or not free. But in fact Will means freedom. A mere necessary sequence of events from perception to desire and from desire to executive volition is not Will. The phrase Free-will is thus a pleonasm. This confusion arises from using the term Will in the sense of physical execution, as well as of volition in the true sense.

2. It seems to imply that man's will may be free, and the

rest of his nature not free, though what is really meant is that the Will is the ruling power of the mind, and if that is free the man is free. It is better to speak of human freedom, or the freedom of man. The real question is,—Is man capable of a rational choice, and, if so, how? Our previous discussions have led the way up to this question, so that we have only to unfold the true doctrine on this subject from the definitions and distinctions already given. We shall first examine the application of the more important of these distinctions to some errors, objections, and questions.

I. FREEDOM AND CAUSATION.

The most important recent objections to the doctrine of Freedom spring from the modern scientific views concerning causation. Science declares that every event must have a cause; but in seeking a cause for a physical change it really seeks a force which will account for that change, and, by the grand truth of the correlation of forces, it is often enabled to trace causal force in ways until recently unknown and incredible. This correlation has been traced in the muscular movements of animals. If it be asked, what causes the movement of my arm, the answer must be, that the force is supplied by the transformation of stored-up chemical energy in my food into mechanical energy in my arm. Volition does not supply this force, and to a certain extent the force would discharge itself spontaneously, as in the play of young animals. But in an ordinary movement the signal for the discharge of muscular force is given by an impulse along the motor nerves. This impulse originates in a state of one part or another of the brain, or spinal cord, or the ganglia. For example, if a gun be unexpectedly discharged near me, I start or "jump," without volition. A part of the nerve-impulse received is diverted to the spinal cord and causes a reflex movement, while another part reaches the cerebrum and occasions a sensation of sound. But in an ordinary movement the impulse originates in a state of the brain, and this state may have an immediate cause, in sensation, or may be the result of an idea, a state of the mind.

The term volition ought to be restricted to this part of the process, namely, the state of the mind. For how this state of the mind occasions a state of the brain is unknown and inscrutable, as in the reverse cases of sensation and feeling. And the lower part of the process is wholly mechanical. But we cannot hope to so restrict the term, for it is much used with reference to muscular movements, especially by materialistic writers. Thus, Ribot has diligently collected a large number of very interesting cases of what he calls diseases of volition. But they are nearly all cases of partial or total paralysis of certain motor nerves, often complicated with disease of the brain.

Now many writers carry this idea of physical causation over into the mind, and declare that a state of the mind is an event which requires a cause just as a state of brain or muscle does. Lotze meets this objection by a simple denial that the reign of causation is universal. He gives the first coming into being of atoms of matter, and their original atomic vibration, as instances of events which cannot be caused. Physical science takes these for granted, and only attempts to account for the changes which now occur. "The objection that freedom is an exception to the causal nexus which rules elsewhere throughout the entire universe, rests on the groundless assumption that complete uniformity must necessarily reign in the dependence of the whole universe. Investigation of the moral world seems to lead just as necessarily to the conception of freedom, as investigation of nature leads to the conception of causal nexus. If we begin with causal nexus we of course shall find no place for freedom. But if we begin with a persuasion that free activities do really have place in the world, we are obliged to assume also the causal nexus. For Will cannot bring about its purpose unless it can rely upon fixed and definite circumstances with which its operations can be carried on." (Dictate, practische Philosophie, § 21.)

This is made still clearer, we think, by the distinction between executive and generic volitions. Freedom belongs to rational choice, executive volitions are necessitated. "What we need to know is the point of freedom. That is in choice, and in that only. Choice being once fully made, volition follows of course. It may not follow at once; the choice may abide alone, but when the volition comes it is born of choice. . . . . The one is the essential element of freedom manifesting itself in the spiritual realm, and is the immediate object of the divine government; the other simply instrumental and executive, and is that of which human governments chiefly take cognizance. And in connection with these two elements, of Will, the one free and the other necessitated, we may see the harmony there is between freedom and necessity, and the need of necessity in order to freedom. If the freedom is to result in responsibility, or is to avail anything with respect to conduct, there must be in connection with it a system of necessity. A man stands by a stream of water. He has the power to turn it in this direction for the purpose of irrigation, or in that for the purpose of destruction, and this power he has, with the attendant responsibility, simply because the stream is subject to invariable and necessary law. If he could not control it by such a law, he could not know what the consequences would be, and would not be responsible for them. Hence the region of freedom is wholly conditioned on the regions of necessity, physical, vital, and intellectual." (Hopkins, Outline Study of Man, 225.)

The modern advocates of necessity strengthen their position

by reference to the admitted uniformity of human action. "The prediction of human conduct," says Bain, "is not less sure than the prediction of physical phenomena." Mr. Buckle, that eloquent and dashing writer, made much of this line of argument, relying upon the statistics of crime, suicide, etc. So far as this argument refers to rational action, it rests upon the pre-supposition that conduct which is not necessitated must be capricious and unreasonable. But in fact, the exact opposite is plainly true. Rational action is the least capricious of all action, and in proportion as action is rational will it be certainly the same in the same circumstances. If we can predict what a man will do in certain circumstances, it is because we know his dominant or supreme choice, his governing purpose, his *character*. If he has an established truthful character we say "he *cannot* lie," and this is called moral inability, and much discussion has been expended upon it. If we know that a man's dominant choice is to have no rational volition, but to be guided by the solicitations of appetite, we predict his actions as we would those of a horse or a dog, with no less certainty, and no more, for he is on the same level, and leads the same kind of life. And of course there will be a good deal of uniformity in his actions. Or, if we know that his supreme choice is to obey the law of God, we may yet inquire into the operations of his intellect, how he understands that law, before we feel like predicting his conduct.

The necessarian says, "you cannot act otherwise than you do; your conduct is the result of motives which arouse your feeling and thus determine your will." The older advocates of freedom replied, "yes I can act otherwise than I do; I am free in every action, in each executive volition; I have power of contrary choice in them all." But most of the recent advocates of freedom would reply, "I know that my executive volitions are in large measure dependent on my character, and habits, and previous volitions, and circumstances, and the influence of motives. But this character, and these habits, and the subjective value of these motives, are greatly modified by my previous rational and moral choices, and above all by my supreme choice, and this I know was freely made." Thus the distinction of executive, intermediate, and supreme volitions, a distinction chiefly elaborated by the New England theologians, has thrown more light on the doctrine of the Will than any other modern discovery.

II. FREEDOM AND THE SOUL.

Most of the arguments against Freedom rest on the assumption that the mind or soul is a thing, subject to ordinary causation, having material qualities, inert in itself, and only aroused into action by the causative force of motives. This view would in consistency require the denial of moral responsibility. Many of these writers are not willing to purchase consistency at such a price; but Dr. Bain goes all lengths, and says, "The term responsibility is a figurative expression of the kind called 'metonomy' where a thing is named by some of its causes, effects, or adjuncts, as when the crown is put for royalty, or the mitre for episcopacy." (The Emotions and The Will.)

We have already argued (pp. 198–207), that the mind is not a material *thing*. The mind is, in truth, a self-active entity, a person. But when it acts it must act in some particular way, must do what is within its power, must act under the limitations of its nature and of its situation in a world of matter, and a world of other beings like itself. It may pursue rational ends, and this is freedom; it may select suitable means to attain them, and this is wisdom; it may select unfit means or intermediate volitions, and this we call foolishness. Or, it may choose not to pursue rational ends at all, but select only among the inferior ends of pleasure, and the animal life, and the social state; and this is to abdicate freedom, to give one's self up to the "slavery of the will." The majority of human beings seem to live thus.

The reason why the mind acts is unknowable; it is its nature to do so. Volition or choice is the activity of such a spirit in view of certain ends, among which it can choose. It does not decide blindly; such a decision would not be a responsible one. It does not decide groundlessly; such a decision would not be rational. It decides in view of the Good; but, "if the motive, even of Good," says Lotze, "had a mechanically operating power to produce a decision, this decision would be a natural product, devoid of responsibility or moral judgment." (Op. cit. § 22.) Will, then, has its existence among motives as a bird floats on the air, or a fish in the water. They are the conditions of its being, for Will is this department of the activity of the soul, namely, as related to ends or motives.

Even Edwards seems to have thought of the soul as a thing, under the dominion of motives in a causal nexus. His illustrations, when arguing from necessity, are drawn from external actions and physical causation. His very definition of freedom seems to imply this. He says a man is free when he is at liberty to act as he pleases, under no external restraint. Such freedom should rather be called physical, or social, or political freedom, not rational. An act of rational choice may have no relation whatever to external restraint. If a man choose to worship God in his heart, force cannot alter his choice. Threats of torture or actual pain may cause him to conceal his choice or deny it, they cannot affect the choice itself. Only rational motives can do that.

It should be remembered, however, in quoting or reading Edwards on the Will, that it is not a complete theory. Its title is, "An Inquiry into the Modern Prevailing Notions of that Freedom of the Will which is supposed to be essential to moral agency, virtue and vice, reward and punishment, praise and blame." It was an attack on the Arminian doctrine of the "Liberty of Indifference." In the specific task which he had set himself he was successful; but many of his arguments are exceedingly abstract, and some of them are now seen to be mere logical puzzles. Liberty of Indifference is usually understood to mean, "a power to determine in opposition to all motives, or in absence of any motive." The usual argument now used against it is to show that it is not rational. "A being with this kind of liberty would not be a reasonable being; and an action done without a motive is an action done without an end in view, that is, without intention or design, and, in that respect, could not be called a moral action." (Fleming, Moral Philosophy, 191.)

The truth that the soul has original activity of its own may be so stated as to lead to a curious complication. Thus, if we say that it originates one of its own states by our act of will, then it may be replied that this act of will must be caused by a previous state of will, and so on in an infinite series. Or, as Edwards expressed it, "If the will determines itself, it must be by an antecedent volition, that volition again must be determined by another going before it, and so on in an infinite series." The best escape from this puzzle seems to be to drop the phrase "act of will" and substitute "act of mind." The mind acts as Will when it acts in the sphere of motives, and in so acting it determines its state, we may say, to be a state of choice. But this determination is not its purpose, any more than, in perceiving, the mind as intellect determines itself to a state of perceiving. When we say the Will determines itself, that is only a roundabout way of saying that the mind acts, as Will, among motives, that is, acts rationally.

III. FREEDOM AND GOD'S FOREKNOWLEDGE.

Those who believe that God foresees all events have experienced great difficulty in reconciling this truth with the doctrine of human freedom. The argument for necessity drawn from the divine foreknowledge was strongly pressed by Edwards. His argument is contained in three divisions.

1. After proving from the Bible that God already knows all future events, Edwards says that this foreknowledge, being already fixed and certain, is necessary; and hence all events indissolubly connected with it are necessary; but the volitions of moral agents being certainly foreknown, are thus connected with this foreknowledge, and hence are necessary.

Reply has been made to this argument on the ground that certainty and necessity are quite different things. This was well stated by Dr. T. Reid. "I know no rule of reasoning by which it can be inferred that because an event certainly shall be, therefore its production must be necessary. The manner of its production, whether free or necessary, cannot be concluded from the time of its production, whether it be past, present, or future. That it shall be, no more implies that it shall be necessarily, than that it shall be freely produced; for neither past, present, nor future have any more connection with necessity than with freedom. I grant, therefore, that from events being foreseen, it may justly be concluded they are certainly future, but from their being certainly future, it does not follow that they are necessary." (Active Powers, Essay IV.)

President Day detected in the argument a double meaning of the term Necessity. "As some have made the liberty of the will to consist in a freedom from the determining influence of motives; so to be subject to such motives, they have called necessity. But if a man can be determined, by motives, to will in a particular way, this does not imply that he is induced to will against his will. The use of a term in so different and in some respects, opposite senses, is the occasion of numberless misapprehensions. According to some philosophers, the dependence of our volitions upon anything preceding is necessity; whereas, in common language, the want of dependence of our actions upon our volitions, is what is called necessity. Why should necessity, in the one case, signify dependence, and in the other, the opposite of dependence. Liberty and necessity are generally understood to be inconsistent with each other. But if very diverse meanings are given to both these terms, it is not certain that every kind of liberty is inconsistent with everything which any one may choose to call necessity." '(Day on the Will, 89.)

President Tappan compared this argument of Edwards to a logical puzzle, and illustrated it as follows: "A man in a given place must necessarily either stay in that place or go away from that place; therefore, whether he stays or goes away, he acts necessarily. Now, it is necessary, in the nature of things, that a man should be in some place; but then it does not follow from this that his determination, whether to stay or go, is a necessary determination. His necessary condition as a body is entirely distinct from the question respecting the necessity or contingency of his volitions. And so also in respect of the divine foreknowledge; all human volitions are subject to the necessary condition of being foreknown by that Being 'who inhabiteth eternity;' but this necessary condition of their existence neither proves nor disproves the necessity or the contingency of their particular causation." (Review of Edwards' Inquiry, 255.)

2. But Edwards proceeds, in the second division of his argument, to affirm that the method of the divine foreknowledge must necessarily be, like all other knowledge, through evi-

dence. "For a thing to be certainly known to any understanding, is for it to be evident to that understanding; and for a thing to be evident to any understanding, is the same as for that understanding to see evidence of it; but no understanding, created or uncreated, can see evidence where there is none. And therefore, if there be any truth which is absolutely without evidence, that truth is absolutely unknowable, insomuch that it implies a contradiction to suppose that it is known. But if there be any future event, whose existence is contingent, without all necessity, the future existence of the event is absolutely without evidence." (Inquiry, Part II, ch. 12.)

On this theory, God foresees that a man will perform certain actions, because He knows the constitution of that man's mind and the motives which will be brought to bear upon it; in other words, He has the same kind of knowledge of future events that men have, and no other. It may be doubted whether this kind of foreknowledge is inconsistent with freedom. But the usual reply to the argument is that it assumes too much information on our part as to the methods of God's knowledge.

How can God know all that is going on in the world at any given moment? It is impossible for us to conceive the method of it, or to know anything about such a matter. Nay, —we cannot even conceive how a man knows a single event, going on before him. All knowledge is inexplicable to us. The method of the divine foreknowledge may be, for aught we know, a direct intuition for which time does not exist, no more involving necessity in the event foreknown, than our knowledge of any event at the present moment makes that event necessary.

3. Edwards argues in the third place that to suppose that God foreknows contingent events, is to make his knowledge inconsistent with itself. For if he infallibly knows that a thing

will be, which yet may not be (for this is implied in contingency), then he knows it to be both necessary and contingent at the same time. As this argument is made up out of the other two, so the replies to those are equally good here. God has endowed man with liberty; man will therefore certainly will, and will freely; but God may yet foreknow his volitions, without thereby taking away his freedom.

Many able men have been content to accept both these doctrines, though apparently contradictory, each on its own evidence, and seek for no reconciliation. Thus John Locke said in one of his letters,—"I cannot make freedom in man consistent with omnipotence and omniscience in God, though I am as fully persuaded of both as of any truths I most fully assent to."

DIRECT ARGUMENTS FOR FREEDOM.

The usual direct arguments in favor of Freedom are drawn from consciousness, and may be either direct or indirect.

1. DIRECT TESTIMONY OF CONSCIOUSNESS.

It is usually said that we are directly conscious of freedom. Some writers make this a first truth, a condition of all thought. Descartes said,—"It is so manifest that we possess a free will, capable of giving or withholding its assent, that this truth must be reckoned among the first and most common notions which are born with us." Bishop Butler said,—"It may justly be concluded, that since the whole process of action, through every step of it, suspense, deliberation, inclining one way, determining, and at last doing as we determine, is as if we were free,—therefore we are so." And Kant said,—"Whatever individual cannot, from the constitution of his nature, but act under the idea of freedom, is, on that very account, in a practical relation free."

Dr. McCosh says,—" I claim for the mind a power to choose, and, when it chooses, a consciousness that it might choose otherwise. This truth is revealed to us by immediate consciousness, and is not to be set aside by any other truth whatever. It is a first truth, equal to the highest, to none of which will it ever yield. Whatever other proposition is true, this is true also, that man's will is free." But on this use of the term Consciousness, see page 80.

The belief in freedom is just as much a necessary and original principle of the mind as the belief in the uniformity of causation. Hence it is useless to argue against the former on the basis of the latter. This is arraying two necessary beliefs against one another. Kant has worked out this opposition in one of his antinomies of the reason, and leaves it as insoluble, though elsewhere he argues in favor of human freedom.

Most necessitarians admit the belief in freedom to be universal, but declare it to be an illusion. Spinoza said that a stone flying through the air, by an impulse from without, would, if it had consciousness, believe itself to be flying of its own free will. And Schopenhauer adds that the stone would be right! Leibnitz said that for man to declare himself free is as though the magnetic needle were to exult in pointing to the pole. Many similar opinions might be quoted from more recent writers. It may be admitted that when I am conscious of power to the contrary in my external conduct, this does not prove that I could act differently under *all* the circumstances; for the most important of these circumstances is my previous generic volition. But I know that there was a point where I made a free choice between certain rational ends, and could have chosen differently. "Let a man be required to choose between property and integrity, and he knows by necessity, and with a conviction which nothing can strengthen and which nothing can shake, that he is free to choose either. The discussions about the freedom of the will have been endless, but nothing has ever shaken the conviction of the race in regard to the elementary idea of freedom as involved in choice." (Hopkins, Outline Study, 231.)

2. INDIRECT TESTIMONY OF CONSCIOUSNESS.

The great argument for human freedom is the conviction of obligation and responsibility. We have an irresistible native conviction that we are morally responsible for our actions; but we cannot be responsible for our actions unless we are free. The associationalists tell us in vain that the sense of responsibility and the feeling of remorse are illusions, due to the conventions of society, the instructions of infancy, the restraints of public opinion; they remain ineradicable. Doubtless much has by some writers been attributed to moral judgment which was really due to convention, education, and habit. But a distinction may usually be clearly drawn between the two classes of feelings. Some persons may feel more pain when detected in misspelling a word than when caught in a falsehood, but that does not prove that the two pains are of the same origin. We believe that consciousness makes a clear distinction between, for example, the disappointment one feels at not attaining some desired end, the indignation that arises on being cheated, the humiliation of having forgotten the rules of good manners, the shame of being found out in a crime,— and, on the other hand, remorse within one's own soul for wrong choices known only to the soul and its Maker. The conventional character of the former is usually dimly recognized, while the profound personal nature of the latter, its position at the very center of being, is seldom unrecognized.

"The conceptions of praise and blame, of merit and guilt," says Lotze, "completely lose their characteristic meaning, if we apply them to things which are necessary. If these conceptions are not pure hallucinations, they imply freedom to choose between two possible but not necessary decisions."

Dr. Fleming says, "The fact that a power has been given to us by which we distinguish between right and wrong implies that we have liberty to use it. The same thing is implied in the sense of obligation which accompanies the perception of the distinction between right and wrong. The feelings of approbation and disapprobation which we experience in our minds, the sentiments of praise and blame with which we contemplate the character and conduct of our fellow-men, and the ideas of merit and demerit, reward and punishment, which we cannot help entertaining in reference to ourselves and others, all proceed upon the fact that man has been endowed with some measure of active power, and freedom in the use of it." And, we would add, irrespective of the origin of these feelings, sentiments, and ideas; even if they were the result of association, the power of forming them would imply, it seems to us, the power of making use of them.

We append some other arguments for human freedom.

3. UNIFORMITY OF HUMAN ACTION.

It is argued that all law, government, society, and business proceed on the supposition of human freedom; that it would be absurd to command or forbid certain actions, if man were not free to do or forbear; that in society and business we always expect men to decide rationally and freely in favor of that course of action which seems best to them.

But this argument has been adopted by recent writers on the other side, who say that all society, law, and government depend on the efficacy of motives; that the law affixes a penalty to certain actions as a proper and certain means of preventing such actions, and not as an appeal to human freedom. "All human institutions, as well as human conduct, are practically founded on a recognition, implicit or explicit, of the reign of law in the province of mind; education, the penal code, social regulations, legislative enactments, rest upon this basis, and emancipation from their sanctions is treated as crime or insanity. The plain design of these enactments is to constrain people to act in a certain way, by supplying the motives which shall determine the will." (Maudsley, Physiology of Mind, 411.)

It may be replied to this, that those who enact these laws and regulations, and undertake to enforce them, are at least free in adopting such a plan. But a more complete answer has been suggested already in the remark of Dr. Hopkins, that executive volitions are the object of human government, while supreme choices are the object of divine law. The latter demands that the heart be right, and expects the actions to be right in consequence. The former cannot reach the heart, but addresses itself only to the external volitions. "There will be a radical difference between the idea of freedom as consisting in the power of choice, and in the power to carry out our choices. The one is absolute, and so belongs to us that to be deprived of it we must be destroyed. The other is contingent, and we can be deprived of it by accident or disease, or by the will of others." (Hopkins.)

The common herd of men are too apt to abandon the privilege of rational choice, and permit themselves to be guided by the solicitations of immediate desire. Law and penalty are intended for such. Those who have made a rational supreme choice and continue in it do not come into conflict with any reasonable enactment. It is thus that we understand Christ's declaration, that he came not to call the righteous but sinners to repentance. And also the Apostle Paul's declaration, "ye are not under the law, but under grace." "But now we are delivered from the law, that being dead wherein we were held;

that we should serve in newness of spirit, and not in the oldness of the letter." We believe also that the great Apostle recognized the two kinds of volition. "I delight in the law of God after the inward man; but I see another law in my members, warring against the law of my mind, and bringing me into captivity to the law of sin which is in my members." "Israel, which followed after the law of righteousness, hath not attained to the law of righteousness. Wherefore? Because they sought it not by faith, but as it were by the works of the law." There is a deeper obedience and morality than of the outward conduct; it is that of the heart.

4. POWER OF RATIONAL CONDUCT.

It is urged that man is free because he has the power to form and carry out a plan or system of conduct. Dr. Fleming says,—"The thousands who have wisely formed and steadily kept their aim through life are so many witnesses to prove that man is not the passive subject of some dark and invincible necessity, but that his happiness and misery are in his own hand, and that he has not only understanding to discern between good and evil, but liberty to choose, and power to adhere to that choice, till it be carried out to its final and happy accomplishment." Rational volition or choice implies freedom; but it does not follow, as often asserted, that because it is free it is therefore capricious, arbitrary, and unreasonable. On the contrary, as we have already shown, rational action is necessarily the most uniform, reliable, and uncapricious of all action. All rational beings, if they use their privilege and act rationally, would act precisely alike in the same circumstances, provided they all had intellects just alike, with which to perceive motives or ends of action, and feelings just alike, to be aroused by them.

IV. LIMITATIONS OF FREEDOM.

The limitations of Freedom of the Will which are usually mentioned are not properly limitations of choice, but rather restrictions of physical or social action. Free agency cannot be complete in this sense, while one is yet under the rule of his parents, or when he is in the power of a tyrannical government, or when disease or accident has prostrated the body or impaired the brain. Such limitations might be called objective.

The real limitations of choice may be called subjective. One cannot will things impossible, choose between ends not presented to the intellect, or will contradictions. One who has abdicated the privilege of rational choice and lived long without it, has strong habits and associations to overcome before he can enter upon a new rational and moral life.

A curious limitation of freedom is laid down, in connection with a remarkable and important admission, by Mr. Malcolm Guthrie, who, though he has written three volumes against Herbert Spencer, is himself a decided evolutionist.

"The great practical question is this;—Has man the power of choice amongst motives? Has he the vaunted power of self-rule, and can he cultivate it? We can only reply that, as a matter of fact, some have it and some have it not; that some have it in some respects and not in others. As a matter of possibility, most men may attain in a considerable degree to the power of self-rule by judicious self-culture. . . . Some feeble minds and flighty or impassioned natures, as well as idiots, may not be able to reach it, and some fools may lose it after they have got it; but as a general rule, a high degree of self-rule may by most people be attained, and the possession of it is for the most part happiness."

A New and Complete

INDEX.

Absolute, the Monistic, 109.
Abstraction 174.
Æsthetics 223 to 231.
Affections, the, 250, 251, 257.
ALLEN, (Grant,) on pleasure 215, 219, æsthetics 224.
Altruism 251.
Anger 237.
Animals, the Lower, 191; their sensations 18, 34, judgment of distance 45, consciousness 78, knowledge of space 91, of time 95, of identity-similarity 114; their reasoning 179, stupidity 195; nature of their minds 205.
Antinomies, Kant's, 145, 289.
Appetite 244.
A Priori Concepts 85, 117.
ARISTOTLE 129; on qualities of matter 69, association 155, the syllogism 181, 183, pleasure 217; his theory of the Comic adopted and defended 240.
Association 154; of sensations 15, 22, 47, 54, 56, 58; does not account for Cause 103, nor perception 125, nor induction 190; in brutes and in men 193.
Associational philosophy 140.
Attention 64.
Axiom of the syllogism 181, of induction 187.
BACON on design in nature 110.
BAIN (Dr. A.) 142; on perception of distance 44, 47, of form 39, 40; on binocular vision 49, touch 51, feeling 60, causation 101, Uniformity 102, 187, identity-similarity 115, 118, perception 143, realism and nominalism 176, the syllogism 183, induction 185, the Ludicrous 241, volition 263-5, desire 274, responsibility 282.
BASCOM (Pres. John) on consciousness in the lower animals 78, their knowledge of space 91, of time 95, language 192, instinct 195; volition 263.
BEAUTY 223—231.
BERKELEY 138, on vision 24, 47, theory of matter 73, 139.
BOWEN (Prof. Francis), Kant's theory of space 89; Descartes 131, Malebranche 135.
BOWNE (Prof. B. P.) on Kant's thing-in-itself 74, monism 109, sensationalism 120, concepts 175, brain and mind 204.
BROWN (Dr. T.) 141; on perception 41, causation 101-4, associaton 155, 230, the feelings 210, volition 265.
BURKE, on emotion 234, sympathy 254.
BUTLER, on freedom 288.
CALDERWOOD, on sensation 17, attention 65, identity 116, intuition 122, imagination 164, induction 175.

CARPENTER (Dr. W. B.), on sensation 17, solidity 46, localization 55, attention 66, the feeling of moral beauty 227.
Causation 97—110.
Choice or volition 261—267.
Cœnæsthesis or vital sense 130.
Colloid state of bodies 27.
Color, sensations of, 35-6.
Comic, the Idea of, 240.
COMTE, on consciousness 77.
Concept, a mental product 174.
Conceptualism 179.
Consciousness 74, authority of 80, uses of the word 83.
Criteria of first principles 123.
DARWIN on emotion 233, 237.
DAY (Pres. Jeremiah) on motives 269, 270, freedom 285.
Deduction and Induction 180.
DESCARTES 131, on qualities of matter 69, consciousness 81, freedom of the will 288.
Design or teleology 110.
Desire as feeling 246, desire as motive 274.
DRBAL on vision 48, localization 57, feeling 61, attention 64, nature of the mind 202.
Dreams 91, explained, 159.
EDWARDS (Jonathan) on motive 268, necessity 283-5.
Emotion 231—243.
Empirical philosophy 118, 140.
EUKEN on teleology 111, necessary ideas 120.
EVERETT (Prof. C. C.) on executive volition 263.
Expectation 88, 239.
External world, how known, 39, 52. See also under each sense.

Fear 236.
Feeling, uses of the term, 59, feeling and feelings 208—213.
FERRIER (Prof. James) 75.
FISKE (John) on causality 102, similarity 117, Cosmic Philosophy 144, induction 186, matter and mind 205.
FLEMING's Vocabulary of Philosophy on feeling 60, space 88, emotion 231, appetite 245, motive 270, freedom 284, 291-3.
Form, how perceived, 38.
FOWLER on induction 185.
Freedom of the will 276—295.
GUTHRIE (Malcolm) 294.
Hallucinations 59, 162.
HAMILTON (Sir Wm.) 145, on feeling 62, qualities of matter 71, consciousness 83, space 85, 89, causation 101, 106, relativity 113, perception 128, association 155, imagination 163, the syllogism 181.
Happiness, desire of, 246.
Hearing, the sense of, 30.
HEGEL 139, his theory of beauty adopted 225.
HELMHOLTZ on sound 31.
HERBART 134, on sensation 61, space 88, perception 134.
HICKOK on the will 267-8.
HOBBES on laughter 241, definition of the will 265.
HOPKINS (Pres. Mark) on perception 41, 52, causation 103, induction 189, pleasure 216, the affections 250, volition 261, 262,-4-7, freedom 280, 290-2.
HUME 139, on substance 73, causation 101, association 155.

HUXLEY on sensation 15; his pseudo-idealism 140.
Hypnotism 162.
Idealism as to perception 128.
Identity and similarity 112.
Illusions and hallucinations 58.
Imagination 163.
Induction 185; not the same as associative expectation 190.
Instinct automatic 193.
Intuitive ideas 117.
JAMES (Prof. W.), emotion 234.
JEVONS on the concept 175.
Judgment as a mental power 172
KANT 139, on substance 73, space 88, time 93, the Judgment 171, æsthetic 223, freewill 288.
Knowledge, desire of, 248.
Laughter 240.
LE CONTE (Prof. Joseph) on sight 34, primary colors, 36, binocular vision 46-8.
LEIBNITZ 133, on space 88, his monadology 107, theodicy 134, necessity and freedoom 289.
LEWES on causation 105, intuitions 119, induction 189, mind of the brutes 192.
Localization of sensations 54.
LOCKE 136, on qualities of matter 70, consciousness 76, space 85, identity 116, intuitions 117, perception 137, reasoning 171.
LOTZE 135, on philosophy 9, sensation 16, 19, perception 22, taste 28, vision 43, muscular sensation 53, feeling 61, impenetrability 72, qualities of matter 74, space 88, 90, time 93, causation 98, monism 109, identity 112, concepts 174, universals 177, materalism 201, the soul 206, feeling 212, pleasure 217, volition 264, freedom 279, rational choice 283.
MAHAFFY on Descartes 131.
MAINE de Biran on cause 105.
MALEBRANCHE, notice of, 135.
MAUDSLEY on emotion 232-5, freedom 292.
Mathematical reasoning 184.
Matter, qualities of 67, nature of 71, 134, 140, 202; Mill's view 142, materialist view 201.
McCOSH (Pres. James) on causation 103, relativity 113, conceptualism 179, universals 180, freedom of the will 289.
Memory 95, 147.
MILL (John Stuart) 141, on substance 73, causation 102, uniformity 103, relativity 113, intuitions 119, association 120, definition of matter 142, syllogism 181, induction 185.
Mind, sensational theory of 80, 199, its unity etc., 202-3.
MORRIS (Prof. G. S.) 119.
Motives and volition 268.
Muscular sensation 52.
NEWTON on space and time 96, gravitation 168, induction 185,
Nominalism 177-8.
OCCAM's razor 107.
Odyle, Reichenbach's 67.
Pantheism 202-7.
Parcimony, see Occam's razor.
Perception 14, 22, and under each special sense; of direction 43, distance 44, solidity 46, 55; errors in 58, 66, ratio with feeling 62; of matter 73; unconscious 81; necessary elements

84, under relations of space 87, causation 98, identity 113; theories of 125-6.
PLATO 129.
Pleasure and pain 214.
PORTER (Pres. Noah) 145, on perception, 33, 127, 146, localization 57, feeling 60, attention 65, substance 74, consciousness 77, 80, 83, space, etc., 92, 95, causation 100, necessary principles 121-4, imagination 164, induction 188.
Pre-established harmony 109.
Psychology defined 10.
Qualities of matter 67, 73.
Realism 128, 176.
Reasoning power, the 171, 130.
REID 144, on perception 22, time 95, freedom 285.
Relativity of knowledge 113.
Religious feeling 259.
RIBOT on the will 279.
RUSKIN on sight-perception 47.
SCHOPENHAUER on space and time 95, the will 289.
Self 79, self-love 255.
Sensation 15—24, feeling in 59.
Sensational philosophy 140.
Sensations classified 20; association of, 24, projection of, 54, rhythm of, 54; unconscious 82.
Sensibility or feeling 209.
SHAKESPEARE on memory 158, imagination 165, feeling 242.
SIDGWICK on predication 182.
Sight 33, in æsthetics 220.
Smell, sense of, 25.
Solidity, perception of, 46.
SMITH (Adam), sympathy, 254.
Somnambulism 91, 152, 161.
Space 84—92.
SPENCER (Herbert), 143, on sensation 16—19, vision 42, touch 49, feeling, 64, attention 66, qualities of matter 72, consciousness 77, 83, space 88, necessary principles 119, the unknowable 144, memory 158, syllogism 182, pleasure 216, emotion 233, laughter 240, love 252, sympathy 253, self-love 255, altruism 275.
SPINOZA 136, on volition 265, freedom 289.
Substance and attribute 73.
Syllogism 180-2.
Sympathy 253.
TAINE (H. A.) on vision 41, on perception 57.
TAPPAN on necessity 286.
Taste, the sense of, 27.
Thing-in-itself of Kant 74.
Time 92, time and space 96.
Touch, the sense of, 49.
UEBERWEG, the syllogism, 183.
Ventriloquism 32.
Vision 33, in the lower animals 34, 42, 45, binocular 46, 48.
Volition 260—265.
WEBER on touch 50.
Will, the, 260—295.

www.ingramcontent.com/pod-product-compliance
Lightning Source LLC
Chambersburg PA
CBHW022109230426
43672CB00008B/1324